GCSE ENGLISH IN A YEAR

Peter Turner

GW00546671

Hodder & Stoughton

A MEMBER OF THE HODDER HEADLINE GROUP

Author acknowledgements

I would like to thank my friends and colleagues at Bournemouth and Poole College of Further Education for their advice and assistance in the preparation of this book, in particular Angela Braga, Mary Brightwell, Barbara Britton, Martin Edwards, Maureen Griffin, Nell Leyshon, Sara Southerden and Linda Turner. I would also like to acknowledge the help and encouragement of my friends Kate Edwards and Helen Rawles. A considerable debt of gratitude is owed to past and present students of Bournemouth and Poole College of Further Education who have allowed their work to appear in this book: Melanie Gerrey for her artwork, and Val Clarke-Allen, Louise Guppy, Hannah Hawkins, Kathleen Moore, Jeremy Thorp, Spencer Wakeling and Jason West for their writing. For their role as guinea-pigs in testing some of the units in the book I would like to thank my Access English GCSE class of 1996–97. For her patient assistance in the final preparation of the manuscript I would like to thank Anne-Marie Gilbert. Finally, more than just thanks goes to Lyn Gerrey, for her constant support and encouragement while I was writing the book.

The author and publishers would like to thank the following for:

Photographs and visual material:

p185© Archive Photos™; p102 (middle) © BBC Worldwide Publishing; p202 © The British Library London, supplied by The Bridgeman Art Library; pp162, 188 © Corbis-Bettmann; p30 © Corbis-Bettman/Hulton; pp281, 299 © Corbis-Bettman/UPI; p116 © Hulton Deutsch Collection Ltd; p172 (right) © Library of Congress, USA; p166 © Lavazza/Roose & Partners and J. Lyons/Duckworth, Finn, Grubb & Waters; p5 © Mary Evans Picture Library; p63 © National Film Archive, London; pp35,57,235 © Popperfoto; pp 173, 172 (left), 240 © Popperfoto/Reuters; pp128, 247 © Rex Features Ltd; pp98, 102 (top and bottom), p255 © The Ronald Grant Archive; p 174 © Henri Winterman; p268 © RSC Barbican.

Copyright text:

Unit 1 *The Afterlife: An Investigation into the Mysteries of Life After Death*, Judy Piatkus (Publishers) Limited, 1993; **Unit 3** 'My Oedipus Complex' by Frank O'Connor by kind permission of Peters Fraser & Dunlop Group Ltd on behalf of the estate of Frank O'Connor; *Lake Wobegon Days* by Garrison Keillor, Faber and Faber Ltd,1993; **Unit 4** *I Know Why the Caged Bird Sings* by Maya Angelou, Virago Press, 1994; *The Wild Swans* by Jung Chang, Flamingo, 1993; **Unit 6** 'The Pearl' by John Steinbeck in *Short Novels*, Minerva; 'Death' by Norman Mailer from *The Presidential Papers*, Penguin, 1968; 'The Birds' by Daphne du Maurier reproduced by kind permission of Curtis Brown Group Ltd on behalf of the Chichester Partnership © Daphne du Maurier; **Unit 8** 'Soap Opera' by Andy Medhurst © The Observer; **Unit 9** 'Translating the English, 1989' is taken from *The Other Country* by Carol Ann Duffy published by Anvil Press Poetry in 1990, *Notes from a Small Island* © Bill Bryson 1995, published by Black Swan, a division of Transworld Publishers Ltd. All rights reserved. **Unit 11** 'On the Western Circuit' by Thomas Hardy from *The Collected Short Stories*, Papermac; **Unit 16** 'England their England' by Hanif Kureishi © New Statesman, *Go Tell it On the Mountain* © James Baldwin 1953, reproduced with permission from Laurence Pollinger Literary Agents; **Unit 17** 'A Hanging' by George Orwell © Mark Hamilton as literary executor of the estate of the late Sonia Brownell Orwell and Martin Secker and Warburg Ltd; **Unit 21** 'The Tube ...' by Terry Jones © *The Guardian*, 'Curse of the ...' by Jonathan Glancey © the *Independent*; **Unit 25:** 'The Blue Bouquet' by Octavio Paz from *Eagle or Sun*, 1990, Peter Owen Ltd, London, 'The Flowers' by Alice Walker from *In Love and Trouble*, Women's Press, 1984

Every effort has been made to trace copyright holders of material reproduced in this book. Any rights not acknowledged here will be acknowledged in subsequent printings if notice is given to the publisher.

CONTENTS

PREFACE

The SCAA Standing Orders, out of which the GCSE English syllabuses for 1998 and beyond have emerged, were not written with one-year courses in mind. To cover all the requirements of the syllabus in a year is a daunting task. The objective of this book is to simplify the task for teachers, and to provide a course which is all-inclusive for all the syllabuses, and which can be covered in two terms of an academic year, leaving the third term for examination practice.

The book is designed in 25 units, each intended to cover a week's work. In practice, of course, it is impossible to provide the right amount of material for a week's study, as a week can mean anything from two hours (or even less) to five hours. It is inevitable, therefore, that pruning and selection will take place if the allowance of time for English is small; the units are conceived with this in mind. It is not essential, of course, to use the entire book. It is, however, designed as a progressive course, so that a knowledge of the aspects of English study covered in one unit is helpful with subsequent units.

There is nothing in the book that is not directly related to the coursework and examination requirements of the syllabuses from 1998 onwards, and each unit ends with an explanation of the specific relevance of the material to each of the syllabuses. The first twelve units, intended for the first term, all contain explanations and rules relating to sentence-structure, punctuation and/or spelling. Overall, therefore, *GCSE English in a Year* is a complete course for those wishing to study for GCSE English in a year.

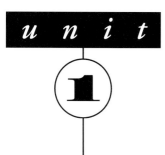

STRANGE . . . BUT TRUE?

This first unit involves a lot of talking. There are two reasons for this. Firstly, finding out a bit about the other members of the class is obviously valuable in itself, and this is the main objective of the first activity. Secondly, talking (or 'speaking and listening' as it is called as an assessment activity) is a major aspect of the English GCSE course. It counts for 20 per cent of the assessment.

After the introductory conversation session, most of this unit is concerned with group discussion of a topic: the paranormal. This may be used as a first speaking and listening assessment. An introductory writing exercise is also suggested, as a follow-up to the discussion.

Conversation and report back

One of the speaking and listening assessed activities will involve paired orals. As initial practice for this, and as a way of finding out about one another, the class should break up into pairs. For the next few minutes, talk to your partner about his or her life – family background, career history and/or aspirations, spare-time activities, likes and dislikes, feelings about school/college, and so on.

Each of you will be asked to report back to the rest of the class for one minute on what you have found out about the person you have been talking to. You might choose to arrange the oral session as an interview, with the interviewer taking notes, or you might take a minute at the end of the conversation to jot down the main things you intend to say about your partner, from memory. At the end of the session, everyone should know at least something about everyone else.

Discussion: the paranormal

Group discussion will be the main form of oral activity, and speaking and listening coursework assessment can take place at any time when you are engaged in class discussion. It might, in fact, begin with your contributions to the discussion session on the paranormal.

The paranormal is defined in the *Oxford English Dictionary* as: 'phenomena or powers . . . whose operation is outside the scope of the known laws of nature.' Obviously this is an enormous topic, covering all kinds of phenomena for which there is no accepted or satisfactory explanation. Examples would include:

- communicating with 'the other side' through mediums or ouija boards

- ghosts and haunted houses

- people who claim to have had previous lives or near death experiences

- poltergeists

- astral projection and levitation

- zombies

- werewolves

- black and white magic.

You can tackle the topic of the paranormal through a free-ranging discussion with no particular structure, or you can deal separately with different phenomena.

As a possible stimulus to discussion, three or more common manifestations of the paranormal are explored through extracts from books and articles, after a general overview of the whole topic in a magazine article by Susan Blackmore.

The lure of the paranormal

Why do so many people believe in the paranormal? The answer to this question, and the recent research exploring it, tell us little about the paranormal itself but much about the way our minds work.

There have been many surveys in the paranormal. The proportion of people claiming belief varies with the sample and the question asked but is usually well over half. More interesting is the main reason given: that people have had psychic experiences themselves.

There are three obvious explanations for this. First, they might really have experienced the paranormal. If this is true, we need to re-write much of science, and soon. Secondly, they might be making it up. For anyone who has had these experiences, this does not seem a plausible explanation. Thirdly, they might be misinterpreting perfectly normal events – suffering from what we might call a 'paranormal illusion'.

Susan Blackmore, New Scientist, 22 September 1990

● Which of the three explanations of the paranormal offered above do you tend to support?

Ghosts

Belief in ghosts goes back to the dawn of human history, and is common to all civilisations. In the following extract from a book called *The World of Ghosts and the Supernatural*, Richard Cavendish describes a recent lawsuit involving ghosts.

Resident ghosts

An unusual case reached the Manhattan Supreme Court in 1990. A Wall Street bond-trader had put down a deposit on an 18-room Victorian house in Nyack, New York, a suburb of New York City. He subsequently found out that the house was haunted by three ghosts, all from the pre-Revolutionary War era. They were a young naval officer, a young woman and an elderly man. At this he demanded his money back, but the vendor refused to return his deposit.

The vendor, a Mrs Helen Ackley, said there was nothing wrong with the ghosts, which were 'gracious, thoughtful, only occasionally frightening, and thoroughly entertaining', and she only wished she could take them with her when she moved. 'I feel they are very good friends,' she said. 'It's very comforting to have then around when you are by yourself.' When her children had been young, the ghosts had thoughtfully brought them presents and would also wake them up of a morning by shaking their beds.

The court held for the vendor, but on a subsequent appeal the Supreme Court of New York State ruled the other way, stating that the house was clearly haunted and the buyer should have been informed of this material (or immaterial) fact. The judges clearly enjoyed the case, and one of the grounds for their decision was that the vendor could not deliver vacant possession of the house because the ghosts counted as residents.

Richard Cavendish, The World of Ghosts and the Supernatural

● Does anyone in the class think that they, or anyone they know, has seen a ghost?

PHOTOGRAPH OF COBERMERE LIBRARY TAKEN AT THE TIME OF LORD COBERMERE'S FUNERAL IN 1891. THE SHADOWY FIGURE ON THE LEFT RESEMBLES LORD COBERMERE.

● How do you explain stories of ghostly apparitions? If they are real, *what* are they?

Mediums and spiritualism

Spiritualism (communicating with the dead through mediums) is probably just about as old as religion. In a sense, it is a religion.

In these extracts from a book called *The Afterlife: An Investigation into the Mysteries of Life After Death*, the authors, Jenny Randles and Peter Hough, discuss mediums as a phenomenon, then describe a particular medium.

What mediums do

Mediums see themselves as radio receivers tuned into a particular frequency which carries information from the afterlife. They generally split into two types – 'mental' and 'physical' mediums.

Mental mediums utilise extra sensory perception (ESP) which enables spirit communications to take place. They receive mental impressions from deceased persons which they then try to interpret for the living. These impressions can be received 'clairaudiently' – spirit voices are paranormally 'heard', or 'clairvoyantly' – sensed or seen. Sometimes these communications take the form of automatic writing or drawing.

Mental mediums are much more prevalent than their 'physical' colleagues.

Contact with the dead can take place during normal waking, or in a state of altered consciousness. This latter state can be achieved by staring at an object such as a glass of water or a crystal ball. Sometimes the services of a hypnotist are used. Mediums in the depth of trance often appear to have been temporarily possessed by a spirit. The entity vocalises using the medium's larynx; voice, facial expression and gestures emulate those of the deceased in possession of the medium's body.

Physical mediumship was very prevalent up until the middle of the twentieth century, but has since declined. Here, the medium acts as a channel for psychokinetic (PK) effects initiated by the deceased. These can take the form of levitation of objects and persons, the playing of musical instruments and the sound of discarnate voices. The deceased themselves can occasionally manifest by shaping a substance called 'ectoplasm' which extrudes from the medium's body.

Jenny Randles and Peter Hough, *The Afterlife: An Investigation into the Mysteries of Life After Death*

- Has any member of the class visited a medium, or known someone who has? How impressive was the medium's performance?
- How do you explain the apparent ability of some mediums to give precise information about clients' past and future lives?
- How do mediums explain where they get their information from?

Near death experiences

There seems to be a surprising amount of agreement about 'out of body experiences' among people who have come very close to death or who have actually been pronounced clinically dead and have 'come back to life'.

In a book called *Life After Life*, Dr Raymond Moody constructed a model of 'near death experiences' from people he interviewed who claimed to have had them. This is his model.

Common elements of NDA

You hear yourself pronounced dead by a doctor.
→ You have an unpleasant buzzing or ringing sound in your head.
→ You feel yourself moving through a long tunnel.
→ Emotionally upset, you see your body from a distance, and watch the doctor and nurses attempt to revive you.

→ You begin to notice that you still have a body, but of a different nature from the physical one.

→ Others come to meet you – relatives and friends who have already died.

→ A loving entity, a 'being of light', appears before you.

→ This being, without speaking, communicates to you the idea that you must now evaluate your life.

→ You see an instantaneous but highly detailed playback of your life.

→ You approach a barrier which seems to represent the dividing line between your previous life and the next one.

→ You feel you must go back to your previous life, even though you are intensely enjoying this 'after-life' experience and would like to continue it.

→ You find yourself back in your physical body.

→ You try to tell people afterwards about your experience, but find it hard to put into words.

→ The experience has changed your life, especially your attitude towards death.

Dr Raymond Moody, *Life After Life*

A great many people claim to have had uplifting experiences of 'death', and to have experienced at least some elements of this model, but some report negative experiences. The following is a typical story.

International clairvoyant Peter Lee attracted a list of celebrity clients over the years, but it is his own personal experiences that stick most vividly in his mind.

'I was in Germany, and up the side of a mountain with some people. Suddenly I fell and was conscious of hundreds of little stones rolling beneath my body. I became aware of a clump of grass, or outcropping of some kind, and realised if I didn't grab it I was finished. Reaching out, I caught it firmly. I was relieved. Then it gave way . . .

'As I fell, all the events of my life flashed before me like a roll of film unwinding. Then I was aware of a tunnel of light stretching before me. Instinctively, I *knew* this was a tunnel of *life*, not death. As I drifted along there were people I recognised who had passed away. Suddenly I was snapped back out of the tunnel, and I remember thinking; 'This doesn't feel much like Heaven . . . there's pains in my head . . . my legs hurt . . . I realised I was still alive and on the mountainside. When they picked me up I expected my body to jangle, but by some miracle, no bones were broken.'

Jenny Randles and Peter Hough, *The Afterlife: An Investigation into the Mysteries of Life After Death*

- Is there anyone in the class who knows someone who has 'died' and come back to life? What was their experience?
- Do you think there is a scientific explanation of the kind of tunnel journey towards a 'being of light' which many people report? Do you think it is evidence of an afterlife?

Other paranormal phenomena

You could now go on to discuss some of the other manifestations of the paranormal listed on page 2, such as experiences of seances, astral projection, poltergeists, and so on.

Writing

As an initial writing exercise you could attempt one of the following topics.

- Write about a personal experience or an account of someone else's experience of the paranormal, and comment on the significance of the experience.
- Give your views on the reality or otherwise of one or more of the paranormal phenomena discussed, and their significance.

Working on spelling

One of the criteria for a grade C in GCSE English is accurate spelling. This is something you can work on frequently for brief periods of time, on your own. English spelling is not the most logical and consistent system of spelling in the world, but there *are* rules which you can learn and apply, and these are explained in later units. However, by far the best way to improve your spelling is to keep a systematic record of words you have spelt wrongly in your written work and to check over the correct spelling regularly.

If you spell a word wrongly, the chances are that you have been spelling it wrongly for most of your life. You most probably have the wrong spelling imprinted in your consciousness. Only a conscious and determined effort to re-imprint the correct spelling will put it right.

Try the following suggestion. Buy a pocket-size book with blank pages and each time you make a spelling mistake, write the correct spelling of the word in the book. If your spelling is shaky, you'll soon have a substantial collection of corrected spellings. Get into the habit of looking at the words in your book when you have a few spare moments and maybe get someone to test you on the words you've written in the book from time to time. Eventually the corrected spelling should become imprinted on your visual memory.

The fifteen words which follow are very commonly misspelt. They are all spelt wrongly here. Correct them.

embarassed   lonliness

definateley   completley

arguement   nuisence

sincerley   buisness

excitment   occasionly

therfore   seperate

untill   marrige

begining

SYLLABUS REQUIREMENTS COVERED

All three major speaking and listening activities (explain, describe, narrate; explore, analyse, imagine; discuss, argue, persuade) are covered by the discussion of the paranormal.

THE BASICS OF WRITTEN ENGLISH

To achieve a good grade in GCSE English you need to have a clear understanding of how written English works. As well as being able to spell with a fair degree of accuracy, you need to be confident in your use of punctuation and you need to be able to write grammatically accurate sentences. You therefore need to know the ground rules of sentence-structure and punctuation.

Detailed knowledge of the structure of the English language is not necessary for success in GCSE. However, in order to appreciate what you are doing wrong, when you make mistakes in grammar and punctuation, it is necessary to understand the classification of words into different types. These types of words are called **parts of speech**. There are seven of them: nouns, pronouns, verbs, adjectives, adverbs, prepositions and conjunctions. This is where we shall begin.

Parts of speech

Nouns

These are commonly referred to as 'naming words'. They are words which *name* things, or people, or places, or abstract qualities. They can be subdivided into four main types: common nouns, proper nouns, collective nouns and abstract nouns.

Common nouns are words for things which you can identify with your senses (things which you can see, touch, smell, etc.). Examples include: desk, music, girls, shower, television, pig, wheels, gravy, tongue.

Proper nouns name *particular* people, places, months, etc. They always begin with a capital letter, for instance: Prince Charles, Hannah, River Thames, Buckingham Palace, September.

Collective nouns are the names given to *groups* of people, animals or things, such as: flock (of sheep), board (of directors), fleet (of taxis).

Abstract nouns are words for things which you cannot see, touch, etc., such as emotions, qualities, states of being. Examples include: beauty, hatred, death, deception, anger.

● Name ten more nouns in each category.

Pronouns

These are words which stand for nouns (people, places, animals or things). The basic pronouns are I, you, he, she, it, we, they, him, her, us, them, this, that.

For example, instead of using the noun the *man,* especially if you have used it already in a previous statement, you might use the pronoun *he* or *him;* instead of using the noun the *dogs,* you might use the pronoun *they* or *them.*

● Identify the nouns and pronouns in the following sentences:

The man called to the dogs.

They ran to him and he gave them some biscuits.

John sent Diana a birthday card. She threw it in the bin.

Verbs

These are often referred to as 'doing words', words which indicate actions. The basic form of a verb is the **infinitive** (for example, *to* see, *to* eat, *to* write). The infinitive is the form in which verbs appear in the dictionary.

From this basic form of the verb, *tenses* can be created. The tense of the verb tells you *when* something happens – in the past, present, or future. Examples of verbs with tenses (also known as **finite** verbs) include: he *eats,* he *is eating* (present); he *ate,* he *was eating* (past); he *will eat,* he *will be eating* (future). Thus:

She *is* my girl-friend (present tense of the verb 'to be').

I *ran* round the park (past tense of the verb 'to run').

My aunt *will come* to stay this weekend (future tense of the verb 'to come').

- Name ten verbs in the infinitive. Give a past, present and future form of each.

Adjectives

These are often known as 'describing words'. They are words which *describe* a *noun*. Examples include: a *beautiful* woman, a *tall* building, the *youngest* son, a *red* rose, a *frozen* chicken, *a terrifying* experience, a *vicious* storm.

The words written in italics in the following sentence are adjectives: The *lonely, frightened* child was crying; an *old* man, wearing a *dirty, brown, crumpled* jacket, was comforting him.

- Name the part of speech of each of the other words in the above example. (NB: the word 'the' is known as the **definite article**, and the word 'a' is known as the **indefinite article**.)

- Name 20 more adjectives.

Adverbs

These are words which describe (or modify) any part of speech *other than* a noun. Most adverbs end in '-ly' and describe verbs (they are *ad*ded to a *verb*). They generally tell us *how* an action is done; they also tell us *when* or *where* an action is done.

Here are some examples:

She walked *gracefully* (describing the verb 'walked'; telling us *how* she walked).

He spoke *well* (describing the verb 'spoke': telling us *how* he spoke).

We met *yesterday* (adding to the verb 'met': telling us *when* we met).

I went *there* (adding to the verb 'went': telling us *where* I went).

Examples of adverbs modifying parts of speech *other than verbs* are as follows:

It is a *completely* stupid idea (modifying the adjective 'stupid'; telling us *how* stupid the idea was).

He rose *very* suddenly (modifying the adverb 'suddenly'; telling us *how* suddenly he rose).

- Name ten more adverbs.

Prepositions

These are words which show the relation *between a noun or pronoun* and *some other word* in a sentence. They generally come between a *verb* and a noun or pronoun. Here are some examples:

The cow jumped *over* the moon.

I went *into* the supermarket.

He talked *to* me.

The word preposition literally means 'positioned before'. Most prepositions show the *position* of one person, or thing, in relation to another. Examples of prepositions which indicate *where* one person or thing is in relation to another include:

under	on	below
over	across	above
by	around	beneath
in	between	near
through	among	beyond

Other common prepositions are:

after	of	except
before	like	off
during	with	to
at	for	against

● Identify the prepositions in the following sentences:

I went to the pub with my friends.

The old man got off the bus and walked into the park.

The wicket-keeper whipped off the bails and appealed against the batsman.

What are you doing under the table?

Conjunctions

These are often referred to as 'joining words'. They show a *junction*, or link, between words, phrases or statements. The commonest conjunction is 'and', the next commonest is 'but'. Other conjunctions include:

because	or	whether
although	as	then
unless	so	than

Here are some examples of the use of conjunctions:

The match was abandoned, *because* the pitch was waterlogged. (Joining two statements.)

naughty *but* nice (joining two words).

violent gusts of wind *and* squalls of icy rain (joining two phrases).

- Identify the prepositions and conjunctions in the following sentences:

Although he was terrified, the young soldier went over the top and raced across no man's land into the enemy trenches.

You will go to church whether you like it or not.

Basic sentence-structure

Of all the errors that you can make in written English, the most serious is the writing of improperly constructed sentences. Two types of sentence-structure error are particularly common:

1 Running sentences together (with just a comma, or no punctuation mark at all, between them). Here is an example: 'My brother has broken his leg, it will be in plaster for the next two months.'
2 Writing incomplete statements, for example: 'Hundreds of people rushing round in a state of blind panic.'

The first type is the commonest of all: the second is particularly common in descriptive writing.

In order to be sure of avoiding this kind of error, it is necessary to understand what a sentence actually *is*. How do you define a sentence?

Most people could come up with a definition like this: 'A sentence is group of words that makes sense on its own'. This is true, but it doesn't get us very far. 'The Chinese restaurant' is a group of words that makes sense ... but it isn't a sentence. It is, in fact, a **phrase**. Before we go any further with the attempt to define a sentence, perhaps we should define a phrase. A phrase is a group of words which makes sense, but it does not make complete sense. In other words, it does not make a *completed statement*. Here are some other examples of phrases: 'across the sea'; 'going to see my friends'; 'the silver earrings'.

A better definition of a sentence might therefore be: 'A sentence is a group of words which makes a complete statement'. There is a problem with this definition also, however. How can you be sure that you've made 'a complete statement'?

We need a more precise definition of a sentence than either of these. The following definition ought to be adequately precise, as long as you understand basic parts of speech:

A sentence is a complete statement, or a series of linked statements, containing a subject (a noun, noun phrase or pronoun) and a finite verb (a verb with a past, present or future tense).

A sentence can be any length, from two words to a virtually indefinite number of words. Many people make the mistake of thinking that a sentence has to be longer than just two or three words. It doesn't. As long as a group of words has a **subject** and a verb with a tense, it must be a sentence.

Most sentences contain an **object** of the action, as well as a subject doing the action, but many do not.

Look at the following statements:

1 My brother was snoring.
2 My brother was snoring noisily in the armchair.
3 My bother was snoring noisily in the armchair, he was disturbing my concentration. I punched him to wake him up.
4 The ghost of my father appeared at the top of the stairs.

Number 1 is a simple statement, containing a subject, 'My brother', and a finite (past tense) verb 'was snoring'.

Number 2 is slightly fuller: an explanation is added about how and where the action took place.

What about number 3? How many separate statements does it contain?

There are actually three distinct parts to number 3, the first telling us *what* my brother was doing, the second telling us *the effect* of what he was doing, and the third telling us what '*I*' did as a consequence. It therefore contains *three separate statements*. Many people make the mistake of thinking that if a series of statements is made about the *same person or thing* they should merely be separated by commas, and that only when the *subject changes* should a new sentence be started. This is quite wrong. A single sentence *can* contain several statements, but only if a *link* is established between the statements.

There are two ways of establishing a link between complete statements. The more common way is by using a conjunction, or a linking phrase, like this:

My brother was snoring noisily in the armchair, *and* he was disturbing my concentration. Or:

My brother was snoring noisily in the armchair, *so that* he was disturbing my concentration.

The alternative is to use a **semi-colon** (a punctuation mark whose principal purpose is to **show** that two statements are closely linked), like this:

My brother was snoring noisily in the armchair; he was disturbing my concentration.

If you do not indicate the link between the two statements in one of these two ways, then they have to be written as two separate sentences.

Number 4 contains a longer subject ('The ghost of my father'). This is an example of a **noun phrase** forming the subject of a sentence.

Exercise

Decide which of the following are incorrectly written. Make additions or alterations to those which are not proper sentences, so that they become grammatically correct.

The long and winding road.

I left.

Fluffy white clouds floating across a blue sky.

The walls are very thin.

She was feeling ill, she asked if she could go home.

My mum wants me to get a job, because she thinks it's a waste of time for a girl to go to university when she'll get married and have kids by the time she's twenty-five.

Descriptive writing

As was pointed out earlier, descriptive writing is particularly prone to errors of sentence structure. Partly as a test of your understanding of the basics of sentence-structure, here is a descriptive writing exercise to attempt in class.

- Write a description of either a beach scene or a street scene in either summer or winter. Your description should be about ten to fifteen lines long, and be as detailed and expressive as you can make it. When you have finished, you could swap your description with a friend's, and check one another's sentence-structure. If you are not sure whether a particular sentence is accurate, you could check with your teacher.
- As a companion exercise, which you might do at home after the first description has been checked, you could take the same scene in the opposite season, and try to capture a sense of how it has changed.

Preparation for paired speaking and listening

One of the suggested activities in Unit 5 is assessed paired orals. The suggestions are either to conduct a mock interview for a job, with one student acting as interviewer and the other as interviewee, and then reversing roles, or else for students in pairs to hold less formal discussions about their career plans and hopes for the future. Preparation for this assessment activity can begin now. You can decide who you are going to work with and which of the activities you are going to opt for, so that you will be ready when the time comes for the assessment to take place.

Spelling: homophones

A **homophone** is a word which is pronounced in the same way as another word but which is different in spelling and meaning. Homophones are almost designed to cause spelling problems!

Here are some of the commonest sources of confusion.

● As a test, write down each of the following in a sentence to indicate its meaning:

to/too/two	affect/effect
there/their/they're	accept/except
whether/weather	piece/peace
practice/practise	not/knot
principle/principal	your/you're

SYLLABUS REQUIREMENTS COVERED

Accuracy of written English is now of paramount importance in GCSE. This unit is therefore of relevance to all the writing and reading requirements of both coursework and examinations.

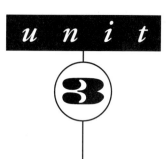

CHILDHOOD EXPERIENCES

Talking and writing about childhood takes up most of this unit. After reading and discussing some brief extracts from works by twentieth-century writers, which deal with childhood, you will be invited to talk about your own childhood memories and then to choose an episode from your childhood to write about.

The first published extract is from a short story about a very young child. The story is called 'My Oedipus Complex' and it was written by the Irish writer Frank O'Connor. The story is set at the time of the First World War (1914–18).

In this extract the child narrator's life has just been disrupted by the return of his father from the war. The child had prayed for his father's safe return, but his father is now a stranger to him and, what is worse, he has usurped the child's place in his mother's big bed. The child has been made to promise that he will not come into the big bedroom and disturb his father's sleep early in the morning. Next morning, the boy wakes up very early as usual and plays with his toys for ages. Then he starts getting very bored and cold.

My Oedipus Complex

At last I could stand it no longer. I went into the next room. As there was still no room at Mother's side I climbed over her and she woke with a start.

'Larry,' she whispered, gripping my arm very tightly, 'what did you promise?'

'But I did, Mummy,' I wailed, caught in the very act. 'I was quiet for ever so long.'

'Oh, dear, and you're perished!' she said sadly, feeling me all over. 'Now if I let you stay will you promise not to talk?'

'But I want to talk, Mummy,' I wailed.

'That has nothing to do with it,' she said with a firmness that was new to me. 'Daddy wants to sleep. Now, do you understand that?'

I understood it only too well. I wanted to talk, he wanted to sleep – whose house was it, anyway?

'Mummy,' I said with equal firmness, 'I think it would be healthier for Daddy to sleep in his own bed.'

That seemed to stagger her, because she said nothing for a while.

'Now, once for all,' she went on, 'you're to be perfectly quiet or go back to your own bed. Which is it to be?'

The injustice of it got me down. I had convicted her out of her own mouth of inconsistency and unreasonableness, and she hadn't even attempted to reply. Full of spite, I gave Father a kick, which she didn't notice but made him grunt and open his eyes in alarm.

'What time is it?' he asked in a panic-stricken voice, not looking at Mother but at the door, as if he saw someone there.

'It's early yet,' she replied soothingly. 'It's only the child. Go to sleep again. . . . Now, Larry,' she added, getting out of bed, 'you've wakened Daddy and you must go back.'

This time, for all her quiet air, I knew she meant it, and knew that my principal rights and privileges were as good as lost unless I asserted them at once. As she lifted me, I gave a screech, enough to wake the dead, not to mind Father. He groaned.

'That damn child! Doesn't he ever sleep?'

'It's only a habit, dear,' she said quietly, though I could see she was vexed.

'Well, it's time he got out of it,' shouted Father, beginning to heave in the bed. He suddenly gathered all the bedclothes about him, turned to the wall, and then looked back over his shoulder with nothing showing only two small, spiteful, dark eyes. The man looked very wicked.

To open the bedroom door, Mother had to let me down, and I broke free and dashed for the farthest corner, screeching. Father sat bolt upright in bed.

'Shut up, you little puppy!' he said in a choking voice.

I was so astonished that I stopped screeching. Never, never had anyone spoken to me in that tone before. I looked at him incredulously and saw his face convulsed with rage. It was only then that I fully realized how God had codded me, listening to my prayers for the safe return of this monster.

'Shut up, you!' I bawled, beside myself.

'What's that you said?' shouted Father, making a wild leap out of bed.

'Mick, Mick!' cried Mother. 'Don't you see the child isn't used to you?'

'I see he's better fed than taught,' snarled Father, waving his arms wildly. 'He wants his bottom smacked.'

All his previous shouting was as nothing to these obscene words referring to my person. They really made my blood boil.

'Smack your own!' I screamed hysterically. 'Smack your own! Shut up! Shut up!'

At this he lost his patience and let fly at me. He did it with the lack of conviction you'd expect of a man under Mother's horrified eyes, and it ended up as a mere tap, but the sheer indignity of being struck at all by a stranger, a total stranger who had cajoled his way back from the war into our big bed as a result of my innocent intercession, made me completely dotty. I shrieked and shrieked, and danced in my bare feet, and Father, looking awkward and hairy in nothing but a short grey army shirt, glared down at me like a mountain out for murder. I think it must have been then that I realized he was jealous too. And there stood Mother in her nightdress, looking as if her heart was broken between us. I hoped she felt as she looked. It seemed to me that she deserved it all.

Frank O'Connor, 'My Oedipus Complex'

- The story explores a child's feelings and experiences in adult language. Pick out two or three details which capture particularly well the authentic feeling of childhood.
- Do you think the child's tantrum is convincingly portrayed? What causes it? What makes it funny?
- Can you remember any temper tantrums that you had as a young child? What were they about? What happened?
- Can you remember feeling resentful about the arrival of a new member of your family, either adult or baby? How did you react to the new person?

Now read the following from a fictionalised autobiography, *Cider with Rosie*, by the Gloucestershire writer Laurie Lee. This extract describes a little boy's first day at school.

The morning came, without any warning, when my sisters surrounded me, wrapped me in scarves, tied up my boot-laces, thrust a cap on my head, and stuffed a baked potato in my pocket.

'What's this?' I said.

'You're starting school today.'

'I ain't. I'm stopping 'ome.'

'Now, come on, Loll. You're a big boy now.'

'I ain't.'

'Boo-hoo.'

They picked me up bodily, kicking and bawling, and carried me up to the road.

'Boys who don't go to school get put into boxes, and turn into rabbits, and get chopped up Sundays.'

I felt this was overdoing it rather, but I said no more after that. I arrived at the school just three feet tall and fatly wrapped in my scarves. The playground roared like a rodeo, and the potato burned through my thigh. Old boots, ragged stockings, torn trousers and skirts, went skating and skidding around me. The rabble closed in; I was encircled; grit flew in my face like shrapnel. Tall girls with frizzled hair, and huge boys with sharp elbows, began to prod me with hideous interest. They plucked at my scarves, spun me round like a top, screwed my nose, and stole my potato.

I was rescued at last by a gracious lady – the sixteen-year-old junior-teacher – who boxed a few ears and dried my face and led me off to The Infants. I spent that first day picking holes in paper, then went home in a smouldering temper.

'What's the matter, Loll? Didn't he like it at school, then?'

'They never gave me the present!'

'Present? What present?'

'They said they'd give me a present.'

'Well, now, I'm sure they didn't.'

'They did! They said: "You're Laurie Lee, ain't you? Well, just you sit for the present." I sat there all day but I never got it. I ain't going back there again!'

But after a week I felt like a veteran and grew as ruthless as anyone else. Somebody had stolen my baked potato, so I swiped somebody else's apple.

Laurie Lee, *Cider with Rosie*

- How does the child feel about the prospect of going to school? What is it like when he gets there? Pick out two or three phrases/sentences which capture the experience particularly well.
- What makes this passage funny?
- Can you remember any particularly funny or frightening things that happened to you at your first school?
- Do you remember your early days at junior, middle or secondary school? How much of a change was it? How soon did you adapt?
- Which period of your school life did you like best, and least? Why?

The next extract is from a semi-autobiographical novel by an American writer called Garrison Keillor. It is set in a small farming town in Minnesota, given the fictional name of Lake Wobegon.

The episode is set on the family farm, where the narrator and his brother and sister, Rudy and Phyllis, are supposed to be picking tomatoes.

Lake Wobegon Days

On this morning in August when I am thirteen, it's hot by ten o'clock. I poked along over the Post Toasties as long as I could, then my mother sent me out to pick tomatoes. Rudy and Phyllis were already out there. I picked one and threw it at a crab apple tree. It made a good *splat*. The tree was full of little crab apples we'd have to deal with eventually, and a few of them fell. My brother and sister stood up and looked: what did you *do*? we're gonna tell.

I picked the biggest tomato I saw and took out a few more crab apples. Then I threw a tomato at my brother. He whipped one back at me. We ducked down by the vines, heaving tomatoes at each other. My sister, who was a good person, said, "You're going to get it." She bent over and kept on picking.

What a target! She was seventeen, a girl with big hips, and bending over, she looked like the side of a barn.

I picked up a tomato so big it sat on the ground. It looked like it had sat there for a week. The underside was brown. Small white worms lived in it. It was very juicy. I had to handle it carefully to keep from spilling it on myself. I stood up and took aim, and went in to the wind-up, when my mother at the kitchen window called my name in a sharp voice. I had to decide quickly. I decided.

A rotten Big Boy hitting the target is a memorable sound. Like a fat man doing a bellyflop, and followed by a whoop and a yell from the tomatoee. She came after me faster than I knew she could run, and I took off for the house, but she grabbed my shirt and was about to brain me when Mother yelled "Phyllis!" and my sister, who was a good person, obeyed and let go and burst into tears. I guess that she knew that the pleasure of obedience is pretty thin compared to the pleasure of hearing a rotten tomato hit someone in the rear end.

Garrison Keillor, *Lake Wobegon Days*

- How is the boy's delight in throwing the tomato and hitting his sister conveyed? Pick out two or three phrases/sentences which capture his delight in his own devilment.
- Can you remember an occasion when you did something to make your brother or sister or any other member of your family cry? What was it? How did you feel about it afterwards?

- What was the worst thing you did when you were a child? How do you feel about it now?

The final piece was written by a sixteen-year-old college student re-sitting GCSE English, named Kathleen Moore.

Escape

I was at Swanage Youth Club with my friend Tracey. She was staying at my house for the night, but we had to get home early because we had the school sponsored walk the next day. Tracey and I began to walk home. It was after nine, but it was late June so the sky wasn't yet too dark. Then I realised that I had left my key inside. I turned to face Tracey. She looked at my face, then asked, 'Have you got any cards?' When I was locked out we used to break in by using about five cards to push the lock down. We both fumbled through our wallets, taking out all the plastic cards. Mostly they were 'phone cards. Eventually we wedged the cards just in the right position, then 'bang', the door flew open.

'I'm starving. Can we make something to eat now?' Tracey begged.

'Let's get ready for bed in case Mum comes back. Then we'll make some rock buns,' I said.

We jumped into our pyjamas and then ventured to the kitchen. Tracey knocked up the mixture while I made the tea and put on the oven.

Footsteps were banging up the stairs, and then the door burst open. In walked Geoff with my Mum traipsing behind. They were both obviously drunk for a change. Geoff walked straight into the kitchen where Tracey was and said, 'Hello, fatty. Eating again?'

I felt my face burning. I was so ashamed of him, and embarrassed for Tracey. I confronted Mum. 'How can you let him talk to my friend like that? I'm not surprised no one comes round any more.'

'Oh, shut up,' Mum sighed.

Geoff heard that and thought that I was starting an argument. He was drunk and lost his temper. He was mumbling, and he threw the cakes all over the kitchen. I could see how enraged he was becoming so I followed Tracey into my bedroom. We weren't in there for more than two minutes when the door was shoved open. I was pushed onto my bed. My throat was being crushed by his clenched fist. I felt so claustrophobic, but I couldn't show any emotion, or speak at all. I think this is what enraged him even more, and made him do what he did next.

I felt him lift me, and then he spoke for the first time throughout the attack. 'I'm going to f---ing kill you, you little bitch!'

He lifted me towards my bedroom window. Although I was trying to withstand his strength he swung me towards the window, but I was kicking and punching too hard for him to keep me in the air, and in his drunken stupor I was dropped at Tracey's feet. She was sobbing uncontrollably. 'I thought he was going to kill you, so I stood in the way of the window.'

I was still in shock as I threw my clothes into a rucksack and pulled Tracey out of the front door. Tracey tripped down the stairs and she was really crying now, so I started to panic. Geoff had only gone to the bathroom, I think, because I had scratched his face, but I knew if he came out and caught us he would be even more angry, then go berserk. I dragged Tracey to her feet and we ran to a 'phone box. She 'phoned up her stepfather to come and get us, but he thought Tracey was acting like a drama queen and wouldn't come and get us. We went to a friend's house and sat up, telling her mum the story, until late. We were so tired that we missed the sponsored walk.

I couldn't go home, so I moved into my aunty's house. At thirteen, this was my first time of many of moving out of home.

Kathleen Moore, 'Escape'

Personal writing

As a follow-up to the group/individual oral work on childhood memories, you could write an account of an experience from your childhood which stood out in some way. You should aim to write between one and two sides, and try to capture the experience as precisely and imaginatively as you can, perhaps using the extracts in this unit as a guide. This might become the first draft of a coursework writing piece.

Individual oral presentation

You could continue the group discussion of childhood memories, or you could return to the topic, in the next lesson, with a series of individual oral presentations.

If you decide on the latter, you should choose an incident from your childhood which stands out because it was funny, frightening, exciting, painful, or unusual in some other way, and jot down some notes about it. In the next lesson, you should be prepared to be called on to give an individual oral presentation lasting about three minutes, which can be assessed for speaking and listening in the 'explain, describe, narrate' category.

Punctuation: the comma

The ability to punctuate accurately is an absolutely central aspect of effective writing. For this reason it is a central aspect of GCSE assessment. The most problematic and complicated of all the punctuation marks is the comma, and to be confident of using commas accurately requires careful study.

Perhaps the best way to study commas is to learn the rules governing their use, and to try and make sure that you apply them in your own writing.

The uses of the comma

1 To separate words or phrases in a list:

> **e.g.** She had eggs, bacon, sausage, tomatoes and fried bread for breakfast.
> His face was thin, pale and drawn.
> We went across several fields, over a stream, past a dairy and along a dirt track to get to the farmhouse.

N.B: There is no need for a comma before 'and' in a list, unless the list is unusually long or complicated.

2 To mark off a person addressed (by their name, a title or some other description) in direct speech:

> **e.g.** 'You can go, Wendy, when you've apologised.'
> 'I think so, sir.'
> 'Get out of my sight, you disgusting creature.'

3 To mark off a **parenthesis** or an aside which interrupts the main statement of a sentence. (A parenthesis is a phrase which adds information or explanation about the subject.)

> **e.g.** Thomas Hardy, a great novelist, lived in Dorset.
> Guy Fawkes, who tried to blow up the Houses of Parliament, was hanged.
> I took my dog, a labrador, to the vet.
> Cats are, I should think, more intelligent than dogs.

4 To mark off a word or phrase which shows a direct connection between a complete statement and the one which precedes it. (The main ones are: 'however', 'moreover', 'therefore', 'nevertheless', 'for instance', 'for example', 'in fact', 'on the other hand'.) The word or phrase is followed by a comma if it precedes a

statement, and it is surrounded by commas if it interrupts a statement.

> **e.g.** I wanted to go to the disco. However, my boyfriend wanted to go home.
>
> I wanted to go to the disco. My boyfriend, however, wanted to go home.
>
> She was afraid of the dark, and she asked me, therefore, if I would walk home with her.

5 To mark off clauses beginning with a word ending in '-ing' from the main statement:

> **e.g.** Arriving early, she found she had time to make herself a coffee.
>
> Having eaten a huge breakfast, he had no appetite for lunch.

6 To separate a clause beginning with 'when', 'as', 'if', 'though', 'although', 'unless' or 'because' from the clause to which it is linked:

> **e.g.** Although he was very poor, he always gave money to beggars.
>
> When you've had enough, let me know.

7 Between two statements joined together with a conjunction:

> **e.g.** The play was very long, and I fell asleep in the second act.
>
> She was deeply upset by his rudeness, but she tried not to show it.

8 To separate spoken words from the verb of saying (she said, he shouted, etc.) in a sentence of direct speech:

> **e.g.** 'I can't come to the concert,' she said, 'because I can't get a babysitter.'
>
> 'For God's sake put your head down,' he yelled, 'or you'll get it blown off!'

9 To mark off interjections, like 'yes', 'no', 'please', 'thank you', 'well', 'to tell you the truth':

> **e.g.** 'Well, yes, er, I'd like one, please.'
>
> 'I think he's, sort of, given up, if you know what I mean.'

10 To separate phrases such as 'don't you?', 'aren't they?', 'isn't it?' which are tagged on at the end of a statement or question:

> **e.g.** 'You like me, don't you?'
>
> 'They'd like to come to the party, wouldn't they?'

Exercises in the uses of the comma

Fill in the commas in the following sentences. Before each sentence write down the number of the rule which applies to it. (**N.B.** not all of them necessarily need a comma at all.)

 1 Los Angeles is I believe the most polluted city in America.

 2 She felt very ill yet she went to work.

 3 If you don't like peanut butter don't eat it.

 4 Although he's very clever he often makes silly mistakes.

 5 I like playing squash but my girlfriend prefers to play tennis.

 6 You can talk to your uncle can't you?

 7 Taking a short cut he quickly found that he was lost.

 8 I would like to know however what you intend to do about your mother.

 9 'Yes he was kind of spaced out and in a you know world of his own.'

10 The palace which was built in the fourteenth century is slowly falling down.

11 Unless you work a lot harder you will fail your exams.

12 'I believe madam that you wish to send your son to my school.'

13 The cats and dogs were all making a terrible noise.

14 Nearly everyone whatever age they were enjoyed the film.

15 'When you leave the building' she said 'please lock all the doors.'

16 I like reading watching television listening to records and chatting in the evenings.

17 There are millions of people who cannot read or write.

18 I went to the theatre and my friends joined me later.

19 He would never for instance go to the cinema on his own.

20 'Let me know Peter if you can join us this evening.'

Spelling: the 'i' before 'e' rule

As was suggested in Unit 1, the best way to improve your spelling is to keep a systematic record of the correct spellings of all the words you spell incorrectly in your written work, and test yourself on them regularly.

However, there are *some* spelling rules which are worth remembering, if you are uncertain of the spelling of words to which the rules apply.

The rule that most people know is the rule that goes 'i before e except after c'. Unfortunately, apart from the fact that there are some exceptions to the rule, the actual rule itself is more complicated than just 'i before e except after c', making it probably the most difficult rule of all to apply.

This *is* the rule:

1 'I' before 'e', except after 'c', *when the 'ie' or 'ei' sound is 'ee'.*

2 When the 'ei' or 'ie' sound is the short 'e' (as in 'leisure'), 'a' (as in 'weight') or 'i' (as in 'height') the reverse is the case. Thus:

'brief' is spelt 'ie' because the sound is 'ee' but it does *not* come after 'c';

'ceiling' is spelt 'ei' because the sound is 'ee' but it *does* come after 'c';

'neighbour' is spelt 'ei' because the sound is not 'ee'.

3 The exceptions to the rule are: seize, weir, weird, protein, caffeine.

● As a test of whether the rule is worth trying to apply, fill in 'ie' or 'ei' in the following words:

dec--t	ch--f	fr--ght
c--ling	for--gn	forf--t
gr--f	shr--k	bel--ve

SYLLABUS REQUIREMENTS COVERED

Two of the core aspects of speaking and listening coursework ('explain, describe, narrate' and 'explore, analyse, imagine') are covered by the oral work in this unit.

The written work, if eventually submitted as original writing coursework, could fit the categories 'explore, imagine, entertain' and 'inform, explain, describe'.

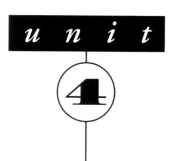

AUTOBIOGRAPHY AND OTHER CULTURES AND TRADITIONS

Two of the requirements of the GCSE English syllabus are the study of 'texts from other cultures and traditions' and the study of 'non-fiction texts' such as autobiographies. This unit addresses both of these requirements.

The main focus of the unit is autobiographies by non-British writers. One of these autobiographies is recommended for the reading scheme for the year: *I Know Why the Caged Bird Sings* by Maya Angelou.

I Know Why the Caged Bird Sings is the first of five volumes of autobiography by the black American writer, poet and academic, Maya Angelou. It deals with her life up to the age of 16.

Maya Angelou was born in 1928 in St Louis, Missouri, in the American 'Deep South', at a time when racial prejudice in the southern states of America was institutionalised: black people were segregated from whites and routinely referred to as 'niggers', good only for menial labouring in the cotton fields and plantations owned by whites. The whole society was organised around the idea of the superiority of the white race; exploitation and mistreatment of black Americans by whites was backed up by all the apparatus of the state.

This episode takes place in the community store owned and run by Maya's grandmother and her Uncle Willy. Almost the entire community is gathered in the store to listen to a radio broadcast of the big fight between the black World Heavyweight Champion, Joe Louis, and the white challenger, Primo Carnera.

I Know Why the Caged Bird Sings

The last inch of space was filled, yet people continued to wedge them-selves along the walls of the Store. Uncle Willie had turned the radio up to its last notch so that youngsters on the porch wouldn't miss a word. Women sat on kitchen chairs, dining-room chairs, stools and upturned wooden boxes. Small children and babies perched on every lap available and men leaned on the shelves or on each other.

The apprehensive mood was shot through with shafts of gaiety, as a black sky is streaked with lightning.

"I ain't worried 'bout this fight. Joe's gonna whip that cracker like it's open season."

"He gone whip him till that white boy call him Momma."

At last the talking was finished and the string-along songs about razor blades were over and the fight began.

"A quick jab to the head." In the Store the crowd grunted. "A left to the head and a right and another left." One of the listeners cackled like a hen and was quieted.

"They're in a clench, Louis is trying to fight his way out."

Some bitter comedian on the porch said, "That white man don't mind hugging that niggah now, I betcha."

"The referee is moving in to break them up, but Louis finally pushed the contender away and it's an uppercut to the chin. The contender is hanging on, now he's backing away. Louis catches him with a short left to the jaw."

A tide of murmuring assent poured out the doors and into the yard.

"Another left and another left. Louis is saving that mighty right ..." The mutter in the Store had grown into a baby roar and it was pierced by the clang of a bell and the announcer's "That's the bell for round three, ladies and gentlemen."

As I pushed my way into the Store I wondered if the announcer gave any thought to the fact that he was addressing as "ladies and gentlemen" all the Negroes around the world who sat sweating and praying, glued to their "master's voice."

There were only a few calls for R. C. Colas, Dr. Peppers, and Hire's root beer. The real festivities would begin after the fight. Then even the old Christian ladies who taught their children and tried themselves to practice turning the other cheek would buy soft drinks, and if the Brown Bomber's victory was a particularly bloody one they would order peanut patties and Baby Ruths also.

Bailey and I lay the coins on top of the cash register. Uncle Willie didn't allow us to ring up sales during a fight. It was too noisy and might shake up the atmosphere. When the gong rang for the next round we pushed through the near-sacred quiet to the herd of children outside.

"He's got Louis against the ropes and now it's a left to the body and a right to the ribs. Another right to the body, it looks like it was low ... Yes, ladies and gentlemen, the referee is signalling but the contender keeps raining the blows on Louis. It's another to the body, and it looks like Louis is going down."

My race groaned. It was our people falling. It was another lynching, yet another Black man hanging on a tree. One more woman ambushed and raped. A Black boy whipped and maimed. It was hounds on the trail of a man running through slimy swamps. It was a white woman slapping her maid for being forgetful.

The men in the Store stood away from the walls and at attention. Women greedily clutched the babes on their laps while on the porch the shufflings and smiles, flirtings and pinching of a few minutes before were gone. This might be the end of the world. If Joe lost we were back in slavery and beyond help. It would all be true, the accusations that we were lower types of human beings. Only a little higher than the apes. True that we were stupid and ugly and lazy and dirty and unlucky and worst of all, that God Himself hated us and ordained us to be hewers of wood and drawers of water, forever and ever, world without end.

We didn't breathe. We didn't hope. We waited.

"He's off the ropes, ladies and gentlemen. He's moving towards the center of the ring." There was no time to be relieved. The worst might still happen.

"And now it looks like Joe is mad. He's caught Carnera with a left hook to the head and a right to the head. It's a left jab to the body and another left to the head. There's a left cross and a right to the head. The contender's right eye is bleeding and he can't seem to keep his block up. Louis is penetrating every block. The referee is moving in, but Louis sends a left to the body and it's the upper-cut to the chin and the contender is dropping. He's on the canvas, ladies and gentlemen."

Babies slid to the floor as women stood up and men leaned toward the radio.

"Here's the referee. He's counting. One, two, three, four, five, six, seven . . . Is the contender trying to get up again?"

All the men in the store shouted, "NO."

"– eight, nine, ten." There were a few sounds from the audience, but they seemed to be holding themselves in against tremendous pressure.

"The fight is all over, ladies and gentlemen. Let's get the microphone over to the referee . . . Here he is. He's got the Brown Bomber's hand, he's holding it up . . . Here he is . . ."

Then the voice, husky and familiar, came to wash over us – "The winnah, and still heavyweight champeen of the world . . . Joe Louis."

Champion of the world. A Black boy. Some Black mother's son. He was the strongest man in the world. People drank Coca-Colas like ambrosia and ate candy bars like Christmas. Some of the men went behind the Store and poured white lightning in their soft-drink bottles, and a few of the bigger boys followed them. Those who were not chased away came back blowing their breath in front of themselves like proud smokers.

It would take an hour or more before the people would leave the Store and head for home. Those who lived too far had made arrangements to stay in town. It wouldn't do for a Black man and his family to be caught on a lonely country road on a night when Joe Louis had proved that we were the strongest people in the world.

Maya Angelou, *I Know Why the Caged Bird Sings*

- How does Angelou create the sense of what it was like to be in the Store as the fight begins?
- How does she create a sense of the increasing excitement of the listeners in the Store as Louis gets on top in the fight?
- How does she convey a sense of the reactions of the listeners when the commentator says, "It looks like Louis is going down"?
- What do the two paragraphs beginning 'My race groaned' and ending 'world without end' reveal about the society in which these people are living?

- What is unusual about the next paragraph (beginning 'We didn't breathe')? Why do you think Angelou has written it like this?
- How does she create a sense of drama as the fight comes to an end?
- What is Angelou revealing about the society in the final paragraph?

The Wild Swans: Three Daughters of China is the autobiography of Jung Chang. It deals with the life of three generations of her family in China, spanning the first eight decades of the twentieth century.

Jung Chang was born in Yibin, in the Sichuan province of China, in 1952. In *The Wild Swans* she chronicles the enormous changes and upheavals which have occurred in the world's most populous country in the twentieth century: from rule by Chinese warlords to rule by the conquering Japanese, to nationalist and then communist rule under the dictatorship of Mao Zedong.

Jung Chang left China in 1978 and is now a university lecturer living in London. This extract is taken from the account of the life of her maternal grandmother, and focuses on the ancient Chinese practice of foot-binding.

The Wild Swans

My grandmother was a beauty. She had an oval face, with rosy cheeks and lustrous skin. Her long, shiny black hair was woven into a thick plait reaching down to her waist. She could be demure when the occasion demanded, which was most of the time, but underneath her composed exterior she was bursting with suppressed energy. She was petite, about five feet three inches, with a slender figure and sloping shoulders, which were considered the ideal.

But her greatest assets were her bound feet, called in Chinese 'three-inch golden lilies') (*san-tsun-gin-lian*). This meant she walked 'like a tender young willow shoot in a spring breeze,' as Chinese connoisseurs of women traditionally put it. The sight of a woman teetering on bound feet was supposed to have an erotic effect on men, partly because her vulnerability induced a feeling of protectiveness in the onlooker.

My grandmother's feet had been bound when she was two years old. Her mother, who herself had bound feet, first wound a piece of white cloth about twenty feet long round her feet, bending all the toes except the big toe inward and under the sole. Then she placed a large stone on top to crush the arch. My grandmother screamed in agony and begged her to stop. Her mother had to stick a cloth into her mouth to gag her. My grandmother passed out repeatedly from the pain.

The process lasted several years. Even after the bones had been broken, the feet had to be bound day and night in thick cloth because the moment they were released they would try to recover. For years my grandmother lived in relentless, excruciating pain. When she pleaded with her mother to untie the bindings, her mother would weep and tell her that unbound feet would ruin her entire life, and that she was doing it for her own future happiness.

In those days, when a woman was married, the first thing the bridegroom's family did was to examine her feet. Large feet, meaning normal feet, were considered to bring shame on the husband's household. The mother-in-law would lift the hem of the bride's long skirt, and if the feet were more than about four inches long, she would throw down the skirt in a demonstrative gesture of contempt and stalk off, leaving the bride to the critical gaze of the wedding guests, who would stare at her feet and insultingly mutter their disdain. Sometimes a mother would take pity on her daughter and remove the binding cloth; but when the child grew up and had to endure the contempt of her husband's family and the disapproval of society, she would blame her mother for having been too weak.

The practice of binding feet was originally introduced about a thousand years ago, allegedly by a concubine of the emperor. Not only was the sight of women hobbling on tiny feet considered erotic, men would also get excited playing with bound feet, which were always hidden in embroidered silk shoes. Women could not remove the binding cloths even when they were adults, as their feet would start growing again. The binding could only be loosened temporarily at night in bed, when they would put on soft-soled shoes. Men rarely saw naked bound feet, which were usually covered in rotting flesh and stank when the bindings were removed. As a child, I can remember my grandmother being in constant pain. When we came home from shopping, the first thing she would do was soak her feet in a bowl of hot water, sighing with relief as she did so. The she would set about cutting off pieces of dead skin. The pain came not only from the broken bones, but also from her toenails, which grew into the balls of her feet.

In fact, my grandmother's feet were bound just at the moment when foot-binding was disappearing for good. By the time her sister was born in 1917, the practice had virtually been abandoned, so she escaped the torment.

However, when my grandmother was growing up, the prevailing attitude in a small town like Yixian was still that bound feet were essential for a good marriage – but they were only a start. Her father's plans were for her to be trained as either a perfect lady or a high-class courtesan. Scorning the received wisdom of that time – that it was virtuous for a lower class woman to be illiterate – he sent her to a girl's school that had been set up in the town in 1905. She also learned to play Chinese chess, mah-jongg, and *go*. She studied drawing and embroidery. Her favorite design was mandarin ducks (which symbolize love, because they always swim in pairs), and she used to embroider them onto the tiny shoes she made for herself. To crown her list of accomplishments, a tutor was hired to teach her to play the *qin*, a musical instrument like a zither.

My grandmother was considered the belle of the town. The locals said she stood out 'like a crane among chickens'. In 1924 she was fifteen, and her father was growing worried that time might be running out on his only real asset – and his only chance for a life of ease. In that year General Xue Zhi-heng, the inspector general of the Metropolitan Police of the warlord government in Peking, came to pay a visit.

Jung Chang, *The Wild Swans*

TODAY, IN A FEW PARTS OF CHINA, YOU CAN STILL SEE ELDERLY WOMEN WITH BOUND FEET

- How did you react to this extract?
- Which details affected you particularly strongly?
- What impressions did you get of the reasons *why* women accepted this particular form of torture?
- Why do you think the tradition eventually died out?
- What impressions of Chinese society in the early years of this century are created in the last two paragraphs?

Wider reading programme

As part of the wider reading programme, it is suggested that you read *I Know Why the Caged Bird Sings*.

Coursework suggestions

- Write a revised draft of the personal writing exercise (a childhood experience), suggested in Unit 3. You might take into account some of the features of writing style discussed in this unit, to produce an improved version of your first draft.
- Choose one or two episodes from *I Know Why the Caged Bird Sings* (e.g. the rape, the religious revival meeting, the Mexican adventure). Write about the episodes. You could include the following:
  - What the episode(s) reveal(s) about Maya herself.
  - What features of the culture in which Maya was brought up are revealed in the episode(s).
  - The way in which Maya Angelou has created comedy, pathos, realism, sympathy, or whatever, through her uses of language.
  - The impact of the episode(s) on you personally.

A period of four weeks is suggested as reading time for this task.

Preparation for writing a magazine article

In the next unit you will be offered the option of writing a magazine article as a coursework assignment to be done in class. It will be necessary for you to do two things in preparation for this task:

- Choose a magazine to write your article for, and bring a copy of the magazine, or an article from it, along to the class, so that you can imitate the 'house style' and presentation of the article.
- Do some research on the subject that you choose for your article, and bring your notes to the class.

Spelling: the '-ful' rule

This is a simple rule to remember and apply. When a word is turned into an adjective by adding the suffix '-ful', there is *always* only one 'l' on '-ful.' Thus:

care + ful — careful

pocket + ful — pocketful

wonder + ful — wonderful

spoon + ful — spoonful

beauty + ful — beau<u>ti</u>ful

skill + ful — sk<u>il</u>ful

mouth + ful — mouthful

Punctuation: the apostrophe

If used at all, apostrophes are often used inaccurately. There are some fairly simple rules for their use, and you should learn them.

The possessive apostrophe

The main use of the apostrophe is to indicate *possession*, to show that somebody or something *owns* something else. If you are referring to 'the cat belonging to Priscilla', you would normally say 'Priscilla's cat'. 'The pyjamas of my husband' would normally be referred to as 'my husband's pyjamas'. These are examples of the possessive use of the apostrophe. An apostrophe is placed before the 's' in 'Priscilla's' to show that you are talking about something belonging to Priscilla, and likewise with 'husband's'.

A small difficulty arises when an article(s) is possessed by more than one person or thing, as in 'the students' phone numbers'. There is a simple rule covering this. If the possessor is *singular*, the apostrophe goes *before* the 's':

e.g. the cat's litter tray
my cousin's house

If the possessor is *plural*, the apostrophe goes *after* the 's':

e.g. the cats' litter trays
my cousins' houses

In some cases the use of the apostrophe is essential for the meaning to be clear. Here is one example. In the following sentence how many students are being referred to?

The students essays were brilliant.

You can't tell whether one student has written the essays or several unless you put an apostrophe before or after the 's' in 'students'.

If you're not in the habit of using apostrophes, there is a danger of *over-using* them at first, to write things like 'the student's essay's were brilliant'. You often see this outside shops, on signs like: 'We sell potatoe's.' You must think *why* you are using an apostrophe.

There is one further minor difficulty in the use of the possessive apostrophe. A few words in English form the plural not by simply adding an 's' but by changing the ending. Examples include: 'woman', 'man', 'child', 'person'. As the plural of 'woman' is 'women' rather than 'womans', there is no need for a possessive apostrophe after the 's' to show that it is more than one woman doing the possessing. So the possessive form of these irregular plurals goes like this:

women's clothes

men's problems

children's toys

people's expectations

Apostrophes are also needed in phrases like the following:

two weeks' holiday

tomorrow's football match

twelve hours' time

However, the following never have apostrophes:

yours	his
ours	hers
theirs	its (unless it is short for 'it is')

The apostrophe for contraction

The other use of the apostrophe is in words which have been contracted:

e.g. it's (for 'it is')   I'd (for 'I would')
      shan't (for 'shall not')   wouldn't (for 'would not')
      they're (for 'they are')   who's (for 'who is')

The rule for placing the apostrophe is that it goes where the letters are missing.

Exercise

Put the missing apostrophes in the following sentences:

My dog has hurt its paw and its limping badly.

Wendys coat isnt in the hall where she left it.

Builders labourers are needed on site tomorrow.

Elephants are killed for their tusks.

The strikers goals saved United in Wednesdays match.

The cars horns were making a dreadful din.

I bought several childrens games for the Christmas party.

SYLLABUS REQUIREMENTS COVERED

The study of writing from 'diverse cultures and traditions' and of 'non-fiction texts', such as autobiographies, is now a general requirement for GCSE English, and this unit is thus of relevance to all the syllabuses.

Analysis of prose extracts is a feature of the examinations of the London, MEG and SEG boards. Analysis of autobiographical writing is likely to feature in the London examination, and analysis of passages from 'diverse cultures and traditions' is an aspect of the MEG and SEG examinations.

The coursework suggestions are relevant to the coursework requirements of the syllabuses as follows:

Suggestion 1:

London: Personal and imaginative writing

MEG: Unit 1

NEAB: Original writing

SEG: Personal writing

WJEC: Best writing

Suggestion 2:

London: Work reflecting diverse cultures and traditions

WJEC: Further reading

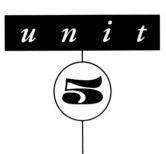

LETTERS, MAGAZINE ARTICLES AND INTERVIEWS

L etter writing is a declining skill in these days of interactive electronic information systems. There are, nevertheless, still times in almost everyone's life when it is necessary to write a letter. We shall begin this unit by covering the basics of letter writing, and follow this up with the most essential letter writing activity of all, a job application. If the letter is written in class, this will allow time to begin paired orals related to careers.

Look at the standard format for a business letter on the opposite page.

Points to note

1 It is no longer considered necessary to use punctuation in addresses. (It is obviously less confusing to leave it out.)
2 It is likewise unnecessary to indent your address. If you do, then the date should be in line with the beginning of the address. It is definitely wrong to indent the business address.
3 The accepted rule about the greeting is that you use the name of the person you are writing to if you know it. Otherwise you use 'Sir' or 'Madam', and 'Sir/Madam' if you are unaware of their gender.
4 The body of the letter should be paragraphed and written in formal English (e.g. using 'you are' instead of 'you're'). The first paragraph should briefly state the topic of the letter. The final paragraph should politely indicate the action you expect.
5 The closing salutation should be 'sincerely' if you know the person you are writing to, or if you are greeting them by name, and 'faithfully' if not.

Your address
Street
Town
County and postcode
Date

Your/their reference number (if known)

Business address
Name or position of individual (e.g. The Manager)
Name of business/organisation
Street
Town
County and postcode

Summary of subject of letter
Re: (subject of letter/Account No., etc.)

Greeting
Dear Sir/Madam,

I am writing . . .

I look forward to hearing from you shortly.

Closing salutation
Yours faithfully/sincerely

Signature
Name

A job application letter and CV

If you are applying for a job, it is customary to write a letter and enclose with it a curriculum vitae (CV).

The purpose of the CV is to provide all the essential information about yourself and your qualifications and career record in standard, easily assimilated form. This involves listing all the basic information about yourself under the following headings:

Name

Address

Telephone number

Marital status

Date of birth

Education:
  Secondary schools attended with dates in chronological sequence
  Public examination results, with grades and years

Work experience:
  Jobs, including promotions gained, starting with the most
  recent and working backwards

Professional courses attended, with month and year

Membership of professional bodies

Membership of clubs and societies

Hobbies and interests

Name(s) and address(es) of referee(s)

There is no need to repeat this information in the letter. The purpose of the letter is to make it clear what you are applying for and why, and to give some impression of yourself as a person. You could elaborate on the aspects of the job which appeal to you, and any ambitions you may have in relation to the job. You could try to describe your personality, and go into some detail about your hobbies and interests. Essentially, you are selling yourself to a prospective employer in your application letter, so you should try to make it as accurate and impressive as possible.

● Now practise writing a letter of application for a job, using the standard format set out above. Do not bother to write out your CV as well.

You could reply to one of the advertisements opposite, or make up your own advertisement.

TABWELL TOOLS LIMITED

is a progressive chain of retail outlets specialising in the sale of Hand and Power Tools to both the professional and DIY markets. We require a Retail Sales assistant for our Christchurch branch.

The ideal candidate will have experience in dealing with customers, preferably within the retail trade, be physically fit and self-motivated.

Please apply with CV and salary details to:

Mr C Buckle,
Branch Manager,
Tabwell Tools Ltd.,
54 Bridge Street,
Christchurch BH23 1EB

IMMEDIATE VACANCIES FOR LARGE AMERICAN COMPANY

Due to the opening of 4 new branches in Poole, Bournemouth, Wimborne & Weymouth the following positions are now available:

SALES/DELIVERY
SET UP & DISPLAY
TRAINEE MANAGERS
DRIVERS

Applications open to both Men and Women. No experience necessary as full training will be given. Age 18–30.

£1,000 per month OTE
+ bonuses + incentives
+ FREE HOLIDAYS ABROAD
Own car essential

Please apply, stating which position you are interested in, to:

Mr. J. Carey
Area Manager,
Matcorp Ltd.,
Fernside Industrial Est.,
Weymouth
DT16 5LB

Paired orals

Pairs of students could be assessed for speaking and listening while the rest of the class are writing letters of application and magazine articles as covered in the section below.

The orals should be prepared for, and should take the form of either 'mock' job interviews or a discussion of career plans, as explained in Unit 2.

Magazine articles

Writing a magazine article may well be a requirement of the examination. It can also cover a coursework writing requirement. The object of the last part of this unit is therefore to explain magazine article writing and to offer coursework suggestions based on the study of articles.

- The article opposite is taken from a January 1997 issue of the magazine *Bella*. Read the article and discuss the viewpoints adopted towards rape trials.

- The article on pages 46–7 was written by a GCSE college student, Val Clarke-Allen. It was based on the style and presentation of a published magazine article. Read the article and comment on the style and presentation.

Should rape victims be shielded in court?

VICTIMS ON TRIAL

Screens in court may ease the ordeal of rape victims. But would they make for fairer trials?

'Not every woman is able to face her attacker in court'

YES *Julia Mason, 34, endured six day's questioning in open court by the man who raped her, Ralston Edwards. He was convicted of the attack last August. Julia now campaigns for change in the way rape trials are conducted.*

In a personal assault the attacker is taking part of your being. That's why it's so important that a screen or video link shields the complainant from intimidation.

When Ralston Edwards held me prisoner for 16 hours and raped me, it took all my strength not to show him any feelings. If he had realised how petrified I was, I wouldn't be alive today.

I was determined not to show any feelings in court either, but I never dreamed he'd represent himself.

He wore the same clothes in court that he had when he raped me, and he clearly got a kick from my distress.

I'm a strong person but, at times, I found it very hard to cope and on one occasion had to leave the courtroom to be physically sick.

Not every woman is strong enough to face her attacker in court. I know of cases where women have not been able to carry on giving evidence — and the defendant has been acquitted.

A screen may have made all the difference. It could be placed on one side of the witness stand so that the judge and jury could still see the woman's reactions but the attacker couldn't.

At the moment the accused has all the rights and the victim has none. Why should a person who has brutalised another be given the right to continue that brutalising in court?

The people who decide on these matters haven't been defendants or victims — they don't know what it's like.

There's no reason why innocent defendants should be worried about a screen. When you're telling the truth you have nothing to fear in a court of law.

No other woman should have to go through what I did during that trial.

If there was an option to safeguard the complainant — like a screen — then perhaps more victims would be willing to give evidence, and more people would be brought to justice.

'If a witness is lying, it might be easier behind a screen'

NO *Katherine Reid, a partner at Kingsley Napley Solicitors in London, deals exclusively with the defence in rape trials.*

As a woman, I appreciate that giving evidence in a rape trial is a traumatic process. But bearing in mind that some allegations of rape are false, it's important to be fair to both sides.

Rape is such a serious crime and can obviously ruin a convicted man's reputation, so the defence should have direct access to the complainant.

If a witness is lying, it might be easier to evade answers behind a screen. And it's also important that the jury sees the complainant in order to assess the credibility of her story.

They do that not by solely listening to her answers, but watching how she presents her evidence and reacts under cross-examination.

Questions like: 'Is she upset or in control? Does she look you in the eye? Does she look comfortable or give evasive or short answers?' can help a jury decide.

Cross-examination is always closely controlled by the trial judge, who can intervene if questioning is repetitive, irrelevant or aggressive. And if the alleged victim is upset, that may help the prosecution.

In so-called 'date rape' cases, or accusations of rape where the victim and accused know each other, the jury really needs to see both sides.

There might be a case for the use of screens in certain cases. If a prosecution witness seems unable to continue, then it might be appropriate to put her behind a screen — just to get her through.

But the problem would be where to draw the line.

As a general rule, it would be much better if rape victims were prepared for what will happen to them when they go to court.

Because at present, most aren't — and that only adds to their trauma.

Nuala Duxbury

Rex Features, Alistair Heap, South Wales Echo

Feeling sluggish? Then it's time you had a nice cup of tea.

There is a whole lot more to drinking tea than simply pouring it out and gulping it back. Tea is a central part of the British way of life. So central, that when someone asks, "Do you want a cuppa", nobody has to verify what substance the cup will contain. Instinctively we know that it will be the result of the infusion of boiling water poured over a selection of dried, crumbled leaves of a plant that was picked some several thousand miles away. Strange? Yes, but strangely enough, we British do take our tea drinking seriously. Or do we!

TEA SPEAK - COLLOQUIALLY.

A cup of tea is commonly known in friendly circles as 'a cuppa', (now a mugga) London's cockneys use rhyming slang, as in 'Rosy Lea', though their version is not as weak and insipid as its fairground, fortune-telling namesake, who feigns knowledgeable insight into your future by staring into the soggy tealeaves at the bottom of your spent teacup! The term 'Cha' comes from the old colonial days when 'char wallers' served tea to their 'Mem Sahibs' in India, to cool their thick British blood on hot sultry afternoons. Northerners drink 'a brew', and let a pot of tea 'mash' (brew). Southerners 'brew' a pot of tea and drink a cuppa.

WHERE TO DRINK TEA.

The act of drinking tea socially has played an important part in our heritage for centuries. It can be 'taken', elegantly, in that epitome of etiquette 'The Ritz', or as humbly as in the plastic cupped variety imbibed on the factory floor. A family picnic on the beach, at the height of the sweltering summer, would never be the same without mother's obligatory cup of tea! Thank God for 'Mr Thermos'! In simplicity, tea can be taken, slurped, sipped or supped anywhere.

TEDIOUSLY TASTEFUL TEA TECHNIQUE ...

To make proper tea follow this proper procedure. Pour cold water into a vessel, especially made for boiling water, called 'a kettle'. For

each person partaking tea, place one spoonful of tea leaves, and one extra spoonful, into a vessel appropriately called 'a teapot'. When the water in the vessel called 'a kettle' has boiled, pour it over the leaves in the vessel called 'a teapot'. Leave to infuse for approximately five minutes. Meanwhile, place a china vessel, called 'a cup', on a flat china object, called 'a saucer', and place a silver stick, called 'a spoon', on the saucer. Pour the infused liquid, from the vessel called 'a teapot', into a vessel called 'a cup'. Add some 'juice of a cow' called 'milk', and, if required to sweeten, the product of the cane plant called sugar. Stir with the object called 'a spoon', and sip gently!

... OR, TEA IN A TICK.

Throw a teabag into a mug, fill with boiling water, splash in some milk, add a spoonful or two of sugar, stir well and drink in huge satisfying gulps.

DESERVING DRINKERS.

Always offer the plumber,

TOTAL

gasman, decorator, carpet-layer, copious cups of the strong, liberally sugared variety. Loose leafed Earl Grey just

ACCOMPANIMENTS, or, befitting companions to specialist teas. One should drink: Darjeeling - to accompany a 'pungent' Indian takeaway. Camomile - definitely on the lawn. China - speaks for itself. Earl Grey - when the aristocracy drop in. Souchong - lean Lapsang - leave the language first, or you might not be drinking what you think you are!

doesn't raise the interest of the thirsty digger-driver who is decimating your daffs to replace the sewerage pipes! The humble tea bag, for some reason, tastes best when the pungent aroma of damp earth and brick-dust abounds! Ply the D.I.Y. enthusiast with tea and your home could be a safer place to live for all concerned

TEA SERVICE.

When we serve tea in china cups it tends to be only on polite occasions usually it's in a mug. The British household should have a good selection of one or more of the following:

● a mug bearing the name of a member of the family that everybody uses.

● a mug bearing the name of nobody in the family which nobody uses. (A good bargain at the time!)

● at least one 'Yukky'

yellow mug with the name of a popular chocolate bar adorning it, that supported last years easter egg.

● an assortment of chipped, cracked, stained and handle-less varieties, used for whatever substance requires a vessel at the time.

● half a set of relatively useable mugs obtained free with petrol tokens.

● a set of fine bone china mugs, only bought into commission when Granny calls, or that posh lady from the W.I. drops in for the 'jumble' and pleads, 'Don't stand on ceremony for me!' Or, for the workmen directly outside your front gate, in case the Jones's are watching your generosity!

WHO MAKES TEA?

The wife or mother of the family makes for the kettle before anyone else can, therefore, she makes the tea. It is her prerogative, unless it is Sunday morning, when the man of the house should go downstairs, collect the newspaper from the mat, put out the cat, and bring a cup of tea back to his wife. Ahh, there's nothing quite like that Sunday morning 'cuppa'.

Val Clarke-Allen

Coursework suggestions

- Write an article for the 'Talking Point' series in *Bella*, presenting conflicting viewpoints on an issue which interests you.
- Write an article for a named magazine whose style and presentation you are familiar with, on a topic which you have researched.

Spelling: the '-y' to '-ie' rule

Most words ending in 'y' drop the 'y' and replace it with 'ie' when an 's' is added.

The rule

Words ending in a vowel plus 'y' just add an 's':

donkey	– donkeys	valley	– valleys
repay	– repays	journey	– journeys

Words ending in a consonant plus 'y' change the 'y' to 'ie':

marry	– marries	tragedy	– tragedies
deny	– denies	party	– parties
enquiry	– enquiries	country	– countries

SYLLABUS REQUIREMENTS COVERED

Letter writing may feature in the examinations of all the syllabuses.

Magazine article writing is a possible examination component in the London, MEG and NEAB examinations, and could provide practice in argumentative writing which is required in the NEAB and SEG examinations.

A magazine article could be offered for the MEG, SEG and WJEC Writing coursework units.

The paired oral work fulfils the requirement of all the syllabuses for speaking and listening assessment in a paired situation. The requirements to 'explain, describe, narrate' and 'explore, analyse, imagine' are covered by the suggested activities.

IMAGERY AND HEIGHTENED WRITING

When you read fiction or poetry or, in fact, any kind of creative writing, you will encounter a range of literary devices. Writers have been using these devices for thousands of years to make their writing more colourful and vivid, and to appeal to the reader's imagination. Such devices are often referred to as 'figures of speech'. There are two main kinds: figures of meaning (or images), and figures of sound.

In the GCSE exam you are quite likely to be asked to comment on the effectiveness of the language used in a poem or prose extract. To do this convincingly, you will need to recognise the writer's use of images and figures of sound, and explain how they add to the impact of the poem or passage. In your coursework also, you may be asked to discuss the language used in a piece of imaginative writing. You will probably also be expected to produce imaginative writing of your own, and your personal writing is likely to be all the more effective if you can create your own figures of speech.

For all of these reasons it is necessary to learn the names of the most commonly used and important figures of speech, and how to identify them.

Images (figures of meaning)

Simile

If you want to create a more precise or vivid impression of something, you can do so by saying it is *like* something else. This is called a simile. A simile always contains the word 'like' or the word 'as'.

> **e.g.** I wandered about like a lost and starving dog. (Charlotte Brontë, *Jane Eyre*)
>
> She wondered what Charlie would think of her pick-up; unquestionably she had landed him, rather as an angler struggling with a heavy catch finds that he has hooked nothing better than an old boot. (Graham Greene, *Cheap in August*)

Metaphor

Like a simile, a metaphor is a comparison of one thing with another, intended to make an idea easier to imagine or visualise. Unlike a simile, the comparison is direct and does not use 'like' or 'as'.

> **e.g.** My wife handed me the box of pills. 'Are these the ones?' I asked with a mask of ice on my face. (Italo Svevo, *Generous Wine*)
>
> It was a town of machinery and tall chimneys, out of which interminable serpents of smoke trailed themselves for ever and ever, and never got uncoiled. (Charles Dickens, *Hard Times*)

Personification

Personification is a form of imagery in which objects which cannot literally experience any sensations are described as though they have human characteristics or feelings.

> **e.g.** The stealthy moon crept slantwise to the shelter of the mountains. (Katherine Anne Porter, *Maria Concepcion*)
>
> The boat blew a long mournful whistle into the mist. (James Joyce, *Eveline*)

- Look again at the images created by Charles Dickens and Katherine Ann Porter. Why is one included as an example of metaphor and the other of personification?

- Here are three further examples of imagery:

He was as quiet as a mouse.

She laughed like a drain.

He was a shadow of his former self.

- What kind of image is each? Do they appeal to your imagination as much as the images used as illustrative examples? If not, why not?

Figures of sound

Another way of making writing more colourful and vivid is through the use of various devices of sound patterning. These devices can heighten the emotional appeal or the sense impressions of a piece of writing. They should be used sparingly, but especially in descriptive passages, or at key moments in a narrative when a particular emotional impact is needed, they can add considerably to the power and effectiveness of writing.

Onomatopoeia

This is the use of a word, or several words in a sequence, in which the sound of the word or words closely resembles the meaning – like 'boom', 'crash', 'bang', 'splash', 'whisper'.

e.g. The two young women … were both in white, and their dresses were rippling and fluttering as if they had just been blown back in after a short flight around the house. I must have stood for a few moments listening to the whip and snap of the curtains and the groan of the picture on the wall. Then there was a boom as Tom Buchanan shut the rear windows and the caught wind died out about the room. (F. Scott Fitzgerald, *The Great Gatsby*)

The lavatories were given over to their own internal rumblings; the cistern gulped now and then. (Nadine Gordimer, *No Place Like*)

Alliteration

Alliteration is the deliberate use of a number of words, placed close together in a sentence or sentences, all beginning with the same consonant sound, or in which the same consonant sound dominates.

A particular effect must be identifiable in the consonant repetition; if no particular sound colouring or emotional impression is created by the repeated consonants, then it is merely coincidence, rather than alliteration, that we are looking at.

Some consonants tend to have a naturally gentle, soothing sound, such as 'f', 'n' or 'l', while others tend to create a much harsher, more intense or even violent sound impression, especially the consonants 'b' and 'd' and the hard 'c' (as in the word 'clasp') and 'k'. The soft 'c' (as in the word 'cygnet') and the 's' consonant can create different sound impressions dependent on the context in which they are used: they can sometimes be soft-sounding, sometimes create a kind of hissing sound, and sometimes sound quite sinister. Repeated 'w' sounds can also sometimes sound soothing and sometimes sinister;

the repetition of the 'r' consonant generally creates an impression of intensity.

e.g. The frozen moisture of its breathing has settled on its fur in a fine powder of frost. (Jack London, *To Build a Fire*)

And then she began to dance, a slow sensuous movement, the smoke of a hundred cigars clinging to her, like the thinnest of veils. (Ralph Ellison, *Invisible Man*)

He could see her legs, protruding from the open bedroom door. Beside her were the bodies of the black-backed gulls, and an umbrella, broken. (Daphne du Maurier, 'The Birds')

Assonance

This is a deliberate use of a number of words, placed close together in a sentence or sentences, all containing the same vowel sound.

If the same vowel sound recurs in a sequence of words then this sound is likely to be dominant. It has to be the same *sound*, however, and not just the same letter. For instance, 'ancient caves' is an example of assonance, but 'ancient caverns' is not, because the 'a' sound is different in the latter phrase.

Some vowel sounds tend to create a light sound impression, especially the short 'i' vowel sound (as in the word 'lift'), while the long 'i' vowel sound (as in the word 'light') often creates an impression of intensity. The longer 'o' vowel sounds (as in the words 'crow' and 'ghoul') tend to create a heavier, more sombre sound impression. The short 'a' vowel sound (as in the word 'cat') often creates a rather harsh sound impression.

e.g. On the lake, the loon lifted its piercing cry into the evening gloom. (Stephen King, *Gerald's Game*)

In the pauses of his impassioned orations the wind sighed quietly aloft, the calm sea unheeded murmured in warning whisper along the ship's side. (Joseph Conrad, *The Nigger of the Narcissus*)

- Write down all the onomatopoeic words in the examples used to illustrate onomatopoeia. Work out what part of speech each of them is. (You may want to look at Unit 2, page 9 before you attempt this.)
- Write down as many onomatopoeic words resembling sounds as you can think of in five minutes. Compare lists. Write six sentences of your own using at least one of the words in each.

- Read through the examples used to illustrate onomatopoeia again, and underline any words or phrases contained in them which also contain examples of simile, metaphor or personification.
- Write a sentence of your own in which one word works as both onomatopoeia and personification.
- Look again at the examples used to illustrate alliteration.
  - Write down all the examples of alliteration in each.
  - Try to comment on the mood or atmosphere created in each sentence, and consider how this is enhanced by the use of alliteration.
- Look again at the examples used to illustrate assonance.
  - Write down all the examples of assonance in each.
  - Find examples of alliteration and personification as well.
  - Comment on the effectiveness of all the literary devices in creating atmosphere.

Detailed analysis of literary devices

Extracts from the works of two of the major American writers of the twentieth century are offered here to give you a chance to test your understanding of the literary devices we have been exploring, and your awareness of their value in certain kinds of writing.

To illustrate how to write an analysis of a passage, commenting on the use of literary devices, we shall explore a brief extract from John Steinbeck's short novel (or novella), *The Pearl*.

The Pearl

Kino was in mid-leap when the gun crashed and the barrel-flash made a picture on his eyes. The great knife swung and crunched hollowly. It bit through neck and deep into chest, and Kino was a terrible machine now. He grasped the rifle as he wrenched free his knife.

His strength and his movement and his speed were a machine. He whirled and struck the head of the seated man like a melon. The third man scrabbled away like a crab, slipped into the pool, and then he began to climb frantically, to climb up the cliff where the water pencilled down.

John Steinbeck, *The Pearl*

Here is a summary of the story up to the point at which the extract appears:

Kino, a pearl diver in a small town in South America, has found a magnificent pearl. He is hurrying through the jungle to the city to sell his pearl and to pay for a doctor to cure his sick baby. He is pursued by three men who intend to kill him and steal the pearl. At night, Kino rests with his baby in a cave. Below him are his pursuers, who are waiting for daylight so that they can pick him out and shoot him. Two of them are sleeping, while the third is awake and watching for any signs of movement in the rocks above. Kino decides that he must creep silently down the mountain face and stab the men before the moon comes up. The moon rises, however, as he is preparing to leap down on his pursuers and stab them with his long knife. At the same moment, his baby cries, and one of the men below cocks his rifle and raises it towards the cave from which the wailing noise is coming. Kino reacts instantly.

Here is a detailed analysis of the use of literary devices in the extract:

In the first sentence, the sound of the gun is captured by onomatopoeia, in the word 'crashed'. The onomatopoeic effect is heightened by assonance in 'barrel-flash', using the same harsh, short 'a' vowel as in the word 'crashed'. A similar effect is produced in the second sentence, with the onomatopoeic effect of the word 'crunched' reinforced by the assonance of 'swung and crunched'.

Assonance is used again in the third sentence to emphasise the violence of the killing, in the repeated short 'e' sounds of 'neck', 'chest' and 'terrible'. Alliteration, using 'r' sounds, creates a similar effect in the sentence which follows, in the words 'grasped', 'rifle' and 'wrenched'. In the next sentence, the power and brutality of the killings are captured by the metaphor of 'a machine'. Similes are used very effectively in the next two sentences, as the man's head is being struck 'like a melon', capturing the sense of its fragility against the violence of the blow, and as the third man 'scrabbled away like a crab', a sense of his desperate panic captured partly by the 'crab' simile, and partly by onomatopoeia in the word 'scrabbled', reinforced by the assonance of 'scrabbled' and 'crab'.

Finally, a sense of the calm indifference of nature is captured in a metaphor, 'the water pencilled down', suggesting a thin, gentle flow of water down the mountainside.

A further literary device is worth mentioning while we are looking at this passage. In the last sentence, we are told: 'he began to climb frantically, to climb up the cliff where the water pencilled down'. Instead of saying simply, 'he began to climb frantically up the cliff ...', Steinbeck repeats 'to climb'. This is a device called **rhetorical**

repetition, and it is usually used, as in this case, to add a sense of intensity, excitement or tension to the writing.

One other feature of the style of this passage is noticeable: the use of short sentences. This aspect of sentence-structure is discussed and illustrated in Unit 15, on page 198. Short sentences generally add punch and extra impact, and often, as in this extract, additional dramatic effect.

Now try your own analysis of Steinbeck's writing in *The Pearl*. Here is a longer extract, which includes the short section we have just explored. You might want to reread the summary of the story on page 53 before you read on.

This extract begins at the point were Kino decides that he must creep down the mountain face under cover of darkness, before the moon comes up, and stab the 'watcher' and his two sleeping companions.

It was the watcher Kino must find – must find quickly and without hesitation. Silently, he drew the amulet string over his shoulder and loosened the loop from the horn handle of his great knife.

He was too late, for as he rose from his crouch the silver edge of the moon slipped above the eastern horizon, and Kino sank back behind his bush.

It was an old and ragged moon, but it threw hard light and hard shadow into the mountain cleft, and now Kino could see the seated figure of the watcher on the little beach beside the pool. The watcher gazed full at the moon, and then he lighted another cigarette, and the match illumined his dark face for a moment. There could be no waiting now; when the watcher turned his head, Kino must leap. His legs were as tight as wound springs.

And then from above came a little murmuring cry. The watcher turned his head to listen, and then he stood up, and one of the sleepers stirred on the ground and awakened and asked quietly: 'What is it?'

'I don't know,' said the watcher. 'It sounded like a cry, almost like a human – like a baby.'

The man who had been sleeping said: 'You can't tell. Some coyote bitch with a litter. I've heard a coyote pup cry like a baby.'

The sweat rolled in drops down Kino's forehead and fell into his eyes and burned them. The little cry came again and the watcher looked up the side of the hill to the dark cave.

'Coyote maybe,' he said, and Kino heard the harsh click as he cocked the rifle. 'If it's a coyote, this will stop it,' the watcher said as he raised the gun. Kino was in mid-leap when the gun crashed and the barrel-flash made a picture on his eyes. The great knife swung and crunched hollowly. It bit through neck and deep into chest, and Kino was a terrible machine now. He grasped the rifle as he wrenched free his knife.

His strength and his movement and his speed were a machine. He whirled and struck the head of the seated man like a melon. The third man scrabbled away like a crab, slipped into the pool, and then he began to climb frantically, to climb up the cliff where the water pencilled down. His hands and feet threshed in the tangle of the wild grapevine, and he whimpered and gibbered as he tried to get up.

But Kino had become as cold and deadly as steel. Deliberately he threw the lever of the rifle, and then he raised the gun and aimed deliberately and fired. He saw his enemy tumble backwards into the pool, and Kino strode to the water. In the moonlight he could see the frantic frightened eyes, and Kino aimed and fired between the eyes.

And then Kino stood uncertainly. Something was wrong, some signal was trying to get through to his brain. Tree frogs and cicadas were silent now. And then Kino's brain cleared from its red concentration and he knew the sound — the keening, moaning, rising, hysterical cry from the little cave in the side of the stone mountain, the cry of death.

John Steinbeck, The Pearl

Here are some suggestions as to how to analyse the various ways in which John Steinbeck creates drama and tension in this passage:

- On a copy of the passage, underline as many examples of different stylistic devices as you can find.
- Then discuss the effectiveness of the devices you have identified, either in small groups or as a class.
- Write an analysis, along the lines illustrated on page 54, commenting on the stylistic features of the passage and the effects created.
- As a short, follow-up exercise, you might try adding an episode of your own, in the style you have just been analysing. Imagine there is a fourth man, and describe how Kino kills him. Alternatively, you could continue the story from where it leaves off.

For further analysis of stylistic devices, read the following essay by Norman Mailer, describing an actual event. It is a description of a World Welterweight Championship boxing match which took place in the 1960s between Benny Paret, who was the world champion, and his challenger, Emile Griffith. For reasons which will become obvious, it was one of the most notorious fights ever.

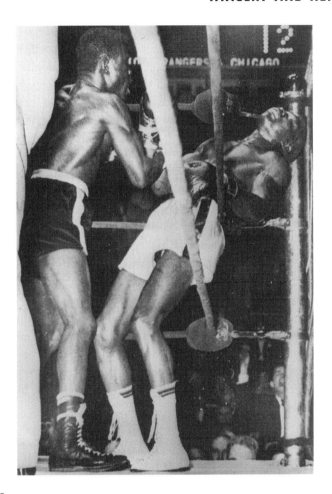

Death

The rage in Emile Griffith was extreme. I was at the fight that night. I had never seen a fight like it. It was scheduled for fifteen rounds, but they fought without stopping from the bell which began the round to the bell which ended it, and then they fought after the bell, sometimes for as much as fifteen seconds before the referee could force them apart.

Paret was a Cuban, a proud club fighter who had become welter-weight champion because of his unusual ability to take a punch. His style of fighting was to take three punches to the head in order to give back two. At the end of ten rounds, he would still be bouncing, his opponent would have a headache. But in the last two years, over the fifteen-round fights, he had started to take some bad maulings.

This fight had its turns. Griffith won most of the early rounds, but Paret knocked Griffith down in the sixth. Griffith had trouble getting up, but made it, came alive and was dominating Paret again before the round was over. Then Paret began to wilt. In the middle of the eighth round, after a clubbing punch had turned his back to Griffith, Paret walked three disgusted steps away, showing his hindquarters. For a champion he took much too long to turn back around. It was the first hint of weakness Paret had ever shown, and it must have inspired a particular shame, because he fought the rest of the fight as if he were seeking to demonstrate that he could take more punishment than any man alive. In the twelfth, Griffith caught him. Paret got trapped in a corner. Trying to duck away, his left arm and his head became tangled on the wrong side of the top rope. Griffith was in like a cat ready to rip the life out of a huge boxed rat. He hit him eighteen right hands in a row, an act which took perhaps three or four seconds, Griffith making a pent-up whimpering sound all the while he attacked, the right hand whipping like a piston rod which had broken through the crankcase, or like a baseball bat demolishing a pumpkin. I was sitting in the second row of that corner – they were not ten feet away from me, and like everybody else, I was hypnotised. I had never seen one man hit another so hard and so many times. Over the referee's face came a look of woe as if some spasm had passed its way through him, and then he leaped on Griffith to pull him away. It was the act of a brave man. Griffith was un-controllable. His trainer leaped into the ring, his manager, his cut man, there were four people holding Griffith, but he was off on an orgy, he had left the Garden, he was back on a hoodlum's street. If he had been able to break loose from his handlers and the referee, he would have jumped Paret to the floor and whaled on him there.

And Paret? Paret died on his feet. As he took those eighteen punches something happened to everyone who was in psychic range of the event. Some part of his death reached out to us. One felt it hover in the air. He was still standing in the ropes, trapped as he had been before, he gave some little half-smile of regret, as if he were saying, 'I didn't know I was going to die just yet,' and then, his head leaning back but still erect, his death came to breathe about him. He began to pass away.

As he passed, so his limbs descended beneath him, and he sank slowly to the floor. He went down more slowly than any fighter had ever gone down, he went down like a large ship which turns on end and slides second by second into its grave. As he went down, the sound of Griffith's punches echoed in the mind like a heavy axe in the distance chopping into a wet log.

Paret lay on the ground, quivering gently, a small froth on his mouth. The house doctor jumped into the ring. He knelt. He pried Paret's eye-lid open. He looked at the eyeball staring out. He let the lid snap shut. He reached into his satchel, took out a needle, jabbed Paret with a stim-ulant. Paret's back rose in a high arch. He writhed in real agony. They were calling him back from death. One wanted to cry out, 'Leave the man alone. Let him die.' But they saved Paret long enough to take him to a hospital where he lingered for days. He was in a coma. He never came out of it. If he lived, he would have been a vegetable. His brain was smashed. But they held him in life for a week, they fed him chemicals, and made exploratory operations into his skull, and fed details of his condition to The Goat. And The Goat kicked clods of mud all over the place, and spoke harshly of prohibiting boxing. There was shock in the land. Children had seen the fight on television. There were editorials, gloomy forecasts that the Game was dead. The managers and the prize fighters got together. Gently, in thick, depressed hypocrisies, they tried to defend their sport. They did not find it easy to explain that they shared an unstated view of life which was religious.

Norman Mailer, 'Death'

● You might again discuss and/or write about the stylistic features of this passage, analysing the effectiveness of the imagery and figures of sound, and the sentence structure.

Vocabulary extension: adjectives of degree

The English language contains an enormous range of adjectives, making it possible to express the subtlest and most precise shades of meaning in descriptive writing.

Here is an exercise in the recognition of variety and degrees of strength of adjectives. This can be done as a class exercise, drawing up a series of lists on the board, and perhaps recording them in a vocabulary book. Think of as many adjectives as you can, indicating degrees of the following:

fat, thin, big, small, hungry, frightened

Re-arrange the list in an ascending order of degree, from least fat, etc. to most fat, etc.

Punctuation: semi-colons, colons and exclamation marks

The semi-colon

The main use of the semi-colon was illustrated in Unit 2, on page 15. It shows that there is a link between two completed statements which could otherwise be written as separate sentences or linked with a joining word or phrase.

For example, the two statements which follow are clearly dependent on one another to make a point:

Life is short. We are fools if we don't make the most of it.

This can be written as two separate sentences, as above. However, to establish the link, the statements can be brought together in a single sentence, by using a joining word, thus:

Life is short, and we are fools if we don't make the most of it.

A more punchy way to make the link, however, would be by using a semi-colon:

Life is short; we are fools if we don't make the most of it.

Semi-colons should not be over-used, and you must be careful not to use them instead of *commas*. Used carefully and occasionally, they can add style and sophistication to your writing.

The colon

The most important use of the colon is to introduce a list, when a pause is required before the list.

An example would be:

You will need to bring several items with you into the exam: a pen, a pencil, an eraser, the pre-release booklet and your brains.

However, in a construction in which the list is fitted into the flow of the sentence, a colon is not needed:

You will need to bring a pen, a pencil, an eraser, the pre-release booklet and your brains into the exam.

A colon is always needed after the phrase 'the following', as in:

You will need to bring the following into the exam: a pen, a pencil, etc.

The colon is also needed when you are introducing an extended quotation. For example:

Hamlet picks up the skull of the old court jester and says: 'Alas, poor Yorick! I knew him, Horatio.'

If (a) brief quotation(s) are simply fitted into a sentence, however, without a pause, you would not need a colon. For example:

Hamlet addresses the skull as 'poor Yorick', and tells Horatio that he 'knew him'.

A further common use of the colon is in a sentence in which a second statement backs up or explains an opening statement. For example:

There can be no doubt about one thing: we're never going to one of Jane's parties again!

In this kind of construction, the colon is an alternative to writing 'that is' or 'namely'.

A capital letter is not needed after a colon.

The exclamation mark

An exclamation mark is needed when strong feeling or shock or surprise is being expressed.

Here are some examples:

My God! My ex-wife's at the door!

I hate Mondays!

Don't do it! You'll kill him!

In formal writing, exclamation marks should be used sparingly, although in informal writing, such as in a letter to a friend, they tend to be used as an expression of intimacy, so that any kind of emotion can be pointed up by an exclamation mark.

SYLLABUS REQUIREMENTS COVERED

This unit is central to the requirements of all syllabuses from 1998 onwards. You are certain to be engaged in analysis of the language of poetry and prose in the examination or coursework, or both, and a proper understanding and appreciation of the uses of imagery and figures of sound is essential if you are going to make a success of this kind of work. The analytical work on prose and poetry in the next three units depends on a knowledge of the features of language use covered in this unit. Some of the subsequent units also depend on this knowledge if they are to be covered adequately.

TWENTIETH-CENTURY FICTION: 'THE BIRDS' BY DAPHNE DU MAURIER

T he focus of this unit is 'The Birds', a short story by Daphne du Maurier. It is her most popular story, and it will give you the chance to read, discuss and write about a fairly extended piece of twentieth-century fiction. You will also be offered the option of producing some imaginative writing of your own, based on the story.

Daphne du Maurier was born in London in 1907. She settled in Cornwall where most of her fiction is set, including her most famous novels, *Rebecca*, *My Cousin Rachel* and *Jamaica Inn*. She died in 1989.

'The Birds' is also set in Cornwall. Daphne du Maurier explains how the idea for the story came to her. " 'The Birds' came about through walking in the fields beyond Menabilly, where I was living at the time, and watching the gulls swarming over the farmer's head as he ploughed the soil. What if they swooped and attacked him? This was all. Then the story formed itself."

Discussion and analysis of the writing style

Six passages in the story (which follows) are highlighted for detailed analysis. You can stop to discuss them while you are reading the story, or read the story straight through, discuss it *as* a story, then come back to them.

The purpose of analysing the highlighted passages is to get a better sense of how a good fiction writer can create atmosphere and drama in her writing, and bring incidents to life by capturing the reader's imagination. You should try to analyse du Maurier's writing *style* in these passages. The passages are on pages 66, 68, 74, 78, 79, and 92.

Here are some suggestions to guide your analysis:

- Underline all the examples you can find of the literary devices (images and figures of sound) that were explored in Unit 6.
- Try to assess how the literary devices add to the atmosphere and dramatic effectiveness of the writing.
- Pick out other words and phrases which create a powerful effect, and explain why you have chosen them.
- Look at the sentence-structure, and try to explain how it enhances the dramatic effect of the writing.

The Birds

On December the third the wind changed overnight and it was winter. Until then the autumn had been mellow, soft. The leaves had lingered on the trees, golden red, and the hedgerows were still green. The earth was rich where the plough had turned it.

Nat Hocken, because of a war-time disability, had a pension and did not work full-time at the farm. He worked three days a week, and they gave him the lighter jobs: hedging, thatching, repairs to the farm buildings.

Although he was married, with children, his was a solitary disposition;

he liked best to work alone. It pleased him when he was given a bank to build up, or a gate to mend at the far end of the peninsula, where the sea surrounded the farm land on either side. Then, at midday, he would pause and eat the pasty that his wife had baked for him, and sitting on the cliff's edge would watch the birds. Autumn was best for this, better than spring. In spring the birds flew inland, purposeful, intent; they knew where they were bound, the rhythm and ritual of their life brooked no delay. In autumn those that had not migrated overseas but remained to pass the winter were caught up in the same driving urge, but because migration was denied them followed a pattern of their own. Great flocks of them came to the peninsula, restless, uneasy, spending themselves in motion; now wheeling, circling in the sky, now settling to feed on the rich new-turned soil, but even when they fed it was as though they did so without hunger, without desire. Restlessness drove them to the skies again.

Black and white, jackdaw and gull, mingled in strange partnership, seeking some sort of liberation, never satisfied, never still. Flocks of starlings, rustling like silk, flew to fresh pasture, driven by the same necessity of movement, and the smaller birds, the finches and the larks, scattered from tree to hedge as if compelled.

Nat watched them, and he watched the sea-birds too. Down in the bay they waited for the tide. They had more patience. Oyster-catchers, redshank, sanderling, and curlew watched by the water's edge; as the slow sea sucked at the shore and then withdrew, leaving the strip of seaweed bare and the shingle churned, the sea-birds raced and ran upon the beaches. Then that same impulse to flight seized upon them too. Crying, whistling, calling, they skimmed the placid sea and left the shore. Make haste, make speed, hurry and begone; yet where, and to what purpose? The restless urge of autumn, unsatisfying, sad, had put a spell upon them and they must flock, and wheel, and cry; they must spill themselves of motion before winter came.

Perhaps, thought Nat, munching his pasty by the cliff's edge, a message comes to the birds in autumn, like a warning. Winter is coming. Many of them perish. And like people who, apprehensive of death before their time, drive themselves to work or folly, the birds do likewise.

The birds had been more restless than ever this fall of the year, the agitation more marked because the days were still. As the tractor traced its path up and down the western hills, the figure of the farmer silhouetted on the driving-seat, the whole machine and the man upon it would be lost momentarily in the great cloud of wheeling, crying birds. There were many more than usual, Nat was sure of this. Always, in autumn, they followed the plough, but not in great flocks like these, nor with such clamour.

Nat remarked upon it, when hedging was finished for the day. 'Yes,' said the farmer, 'there are more birds about than usual; I've noticed it too. And daring, some of them, taking no notice of the tractor. One or two gulls came so close to my head this afternoon I thought they'd knock my cap off! As it was, I could scarcely see what I was doing, when they were overhead and I had the sun in my eyes. I have a notion the weather will change. It will be a hard winter. That's why the birds are restless.'

Nat, tramping home across the fields and down the lane to his cottage, saw the birds still flocking over the western hills, in the last glow of the sun. No wind, and the grey sea calm and full. Campion in bloom yet in the hedges, and the air mild. The farmer was right, though, and it was that night the weather turned. Nat's bedroom faced east. He woke just after two and heard the wind in the chimney. Not the storm and bluster of a sou'westerly gale, bringing the rain, but east wind, cold and dry. It sounded hollow in the chimney, and a loose slate rattled on the roof. Nat listened, and he could hear the sea roaring in the bay. Even the air in the small bedroom had turned chill: a draught came under the skirting of the door, blowing upon the bed. Nat drew the blanket round him, leant closer to the back of his sleeping wife, and stayed wakeful, watchful, aware of misgiving without cause.

Then he heard the tapping on the window. There was no creeper on the cottage walls to break loose and scratch upon the pane. He listened, and the tapping continued until, irritated by the sound, Nat got out of bed and went to the window. He opened it, and as he did so something brushed his hand, jabbing at his knuckles, grazing the skin. Then he saw the flutter of the wings and it was gone, over the roof, behind the cottage.

It was a bird, what kind of bird he could not tell. The wind must have driven it to shelter on the sill.

He shut the window and went back to bed, but feeling his knuckles wet put his mouth to the scratch. The bird had drawn blood. Frightened, he supposed, and bewildered, the bird, seeking shelter, had stabbed at him in the darkness. Once more he settled himself to sleep.

Presently the tapping came again, this time more forceful, more insistent, and now his wife woke at the sound, and turning in the bed said to him, 'See to the window, Nat, it's rattling.'

'I've already seen to it,' he told her, 'there's some bird there, trying to get in. Can't you hear the wind? It's blowing from the east, driving the birds to shelter.'

'Send them away,' she said. 'I can't sleep with that noise.'

He went to the window for the second time, and now when he opened it there was not one bird upon the sill but half a dozen; they flew straight into his face, attacking him.

He shouted, striking out at them with his arms, scattering them; like the first one, they flew over the roof and disappeared. Quickly he let the window fall and latched it.

'Did you hear that?' he said. 'They went for me. Tried to peck my eyes.' He stood by the window, peering into the darkness, and could see nothing. His wife, heavy with sleep, murmured from the bed.

'I'm not making it up,' he said, angry at her suggestion. 'I tell you the birds were on the sill, trying to get into the room.'

Suddenly a frightened cry came from the room across the passage where the children slept.

'It's Jill,' said his wife, roused at the sound, sitting up in bed. 'Go to her, see what's the matter.'

Nat lit the candle, but when he opened the bedroom door to cross the passage the draught blew out the flame.

There was a second cry of terror, this time from both children, and stumbling into their room he felt the beating of wings about him in the darkness. The window was wide open. Through it came the birds, hitting first the ceiling and the walls, then swerving in mid–flight, turning to the children in their beds.

'It's all right, I'm here,' shouted Nat, and the children flung themselves, screaming, upon him, while in the darkness the birds rose and dived and came for him again.

'What is it, Nat, what's happened?' his wife called from the further bedroom, and swiftly he pushed the children through the door to the passage and shut it upon them, so that he was alone now, in their bedroom, with the birds.

He seized a blanket from the nearest bed, and using it as a weapon flung it to right and left about him in the air. He felt the thud of bodies, heard the fluttering of wings, but they were not yet defeated, for again and again they returned to the assault, jabbing his hands, his head, the little stabbing beaks sharp as a pointed fork. The blanket became a weapon of defence; he wound it about his head, and then in greater darkness beat at the birds with his bare hands. He dared not stumble to the door and open it, lest in doing so the birds should follow him.

How long he fought with them in the darkness he could not tell, but at last the beating of the wings about him lessened and then withdrew, and through the density of the blanket he was aware of light. He waited, listened; there was no sound except the fretful crying of one of the children from the bedroom beyond. The fluttering, the whirring of the wings had ceased.

He took the blanket from his head and stared about him. The cold grey morning light exposed the room. Dawn, and the open window, had called the living birds; the dead lay on the floor. Nat gazed at the little corpses, shocked and horrified. They were all small birds, none of any size; there must have been fifty of them lying there upon the floor. There were robins, finches, sparrows, blue tits, larks and bramblings, birds that by nature's law kept to their own flock and their own territory, and now, joining one with another in their urge for battle, had destroyed themselves against the bedroom walls, or in the strife had been destroyed by him. Some had lost feathers in the fight, others had blood, his blood, upon their beaks.

Sickened, Nat went to the window and stared out across his patch of garden to the fields.

It was bitter cold, and the ground had all the hard black look of frost. Not white frost, to shine in the morning sun, but the black frost that the east wind brings. The sea, fiercer now with the turning tide, white-capped and steep, broke harshly in the bay. Of the birds there was no sign. Not a sparrow chattered in the hedge beyond the garden gate, no early missel-thrush or blackbird pecked on the grass for worms. There was no sound at all but the east wind and the sea.

Nat shut the window and the door of the small bedroom, and went back across the passage to his own. His wife sat up in bed, one child asleep beside her, the smaller in her arms, his face bandaged. The curtains were tightly drawn across the window, the candles lit. Her face looked garish in the yellow light. She shook her head for silence.

'He's sleeping now,' she whispered, 'but only just. Something must have cut him, there was blood at the corner of his eyes. Jill said it was the birds. She said she woke up, and the birds were in the room.'

His wife looked up at Nat, searching his face for confirmation. She looked terrified, bewildered, and he did not want her to know that he was also shaken, dazed almost, by the events of the past few hours.

'There are birds in there,' he said, 'dead birds, nearly fifty of them. Robins, wrens, all the little birds from hereabouts. It's as though a madness seized them, with the east wind.' He sat down on the bed beside his wife, and held her hand. 'It's the weather,' he said, 'it must be that, it's the hard weather. They aren't the birds, maybe, from here around. They've been driven down, from up country.'

'But Nat,' whispered his wife, 'it's only this night that the weather turned. There's been no snow to drive them. And they can't be hungry yet. There's food for them, out there, in the fields.'

'It's the weather,' repeated Nat. 'I tell you, it's the weather.'

His face too was drawn and tired, like hers. They stared at one another for a while without speaking.

'I'll go downstairs and make a cup of tea,' he said.

The sight of the kitchen reassured him. The cups and saucers, neatly stacked upon the dresser, the table and chairs, his wife's roll of knitting on her basket chair, the children's toys in a corner cupboard.

He knelt down, raked out the old embers and relit the fire. The glowing sticks brought normality, the steaming kettle and the brown teapot comfort and security. He drank his tea, carried a cup up to his wife. Then he washed in the scullery, and, putting on his boots, opened the back door.

The sky was hard and leaden, and the brown hills that had gleamed in the sun the day before looked dark and bare. The east wind, like a razor, stripped the trees, and the leaves, crackling and dry, shivered and scattered with the wind's blast. Nat stubbed the earth with his boot. It was frozen hard. He had never known a change so swift and sudden. Black winter had descended in a single night.

The children were awake now. Jill was chattering upstairs and young Johnny crying once again. Nat heard his wife's voice, soothing, comforting. Presently they came down. He had breakfast ready for them, and the routine of the day began.

'Did you drive away the birds?' asked Jill, restored to calm because of the kitchen fire, because of day, because of breakfast.

'Yes, they've all gone now,' said Nat. 'It was the east wind brought them in. They were frightened and lost, they wanted shelter.'

'They tried to peck us,' said Jill. 'They went for Johnny's eyes.'

'Fright made them do that,' said Nat. 'They didn't know where they were, in the dark bedroom.'

'I hope they won't come again,' said Jill. 'Perhaps if we put bread for them outside the window they will eat that and fly away.'

She finished her breakfast and then went for her coat and hood, her school books and her satchel. Nat said nothing, but his wife looked at him across the table. A silent message passed between them.

'I'll walk with her to the bus,' he said. 'I don't go to the farm today.'

And while the child was washing in the scullery he said to his wife, 'Keep all the windows closed, and the doors too. Just to be on the safe side. I'll go to the farm. Find out if they heard anything in the night.' Then he walked with his small daughter up the lane. She seemed to have forgotten her experience of the night before. She danced ahead of him, chasing the leaves, her face whipped with the cold and rosy under the pixie hood.

'Is it going to snow, Dad?' she said. 'It's cold enough.'

He glanced up at the bleak sky, felt the wind tear at his shoulders.

'No,' he said, 'it's not going to snow. This is a black winter, not a white one.'

All the while he searched the hedgerows for the birds, glanced over the top of them to the fields beyond, looked to the small wood above the farm where the rooks and jackdaws gathered. He saw none.

The other children waited by the bus-stop, muffled, hooded like Jill, the faces white and pinched with cold.

Jill ran to them, waving. 'My Dad says it won't snow,' she called, 'it's going to be a black winter.'

She said nothing of the birds. She began to push and struggle with another little girl. The bus came ambling up the hill. Nat saw her on to it, then turned and walked back towards the farm. It was not his day for work, but he wanted to satisfy himself that all was well. Jim, the cowman, was clattering in the yard.

'Boss around?' asked Nat.

'Gone to market,' said Jim. 'It's Tuesday, isn't it?'

He clumped off round the corner of a shed. He had no time for Nat. Nat was said to be superior. Read books, and the like. Nat had forgotten it was Tuesday. This showed how the events of the preceding night had shaken him. He went to the back door of the farm-house and heard Mrs Trigg singing in the kitchen, the wireless making a background to her song.

'Are you there, missus?' called out Nat.

She came to the door, beaming, broad, a good-tempered woman.

'Hullo, Mr Hocken,' she said. 'Can you tell me where this cold is coming from? Is it Russia? I've never seen such a change. And it's going on, the wireless says. Something to do with the Arctic circle.'

'We didn't turn on the wireless this morning,' said Nat. 'Fact is, we had trouble in the night.'

'Kiddies poorly?'

'No . . .' He hardly knew how to explain it. Now, in daylight, the battle of the birds would sound absurd.

He tried to tell Mrs Trigg what had happened, but he could see from her eyes that she thought his story was the result of a nightmare.

'Sure they were real birds,' she said, smiling, 'with proper feathers and all? Not the funny-shaped kind, that the men see after closing hours on a Saturday night?'

'Mrs Trigg,' he said, 'there are fifty dead birds, robins, wrens, and such, lying low on the floor of the children's bedroom. They went for me; they tried to go for young Johnny's eyes.'

Mrs Trigg stared at him doubtfully.

'Well there, now,' she answered, 'I suppose the weather brought them. Once in the bedroom, they wouldn't know where they were to. Foreign birds maybe, from that Arctic circle.'

'No,' said Nat, 'they were the birds you see about here every day.'

'Funny thing,' said Mrs Trigg, 'no explaining it, really. You ought to

69

write up and ask the *Guardian*. They'd have some answer for it. Well, I must be getting on.'

She nodded, smiled, and went back into the kitchen.

Nat, dissatisfied, turned to the farm-gate. Had it not been for those corpses on the bedroom floor, which he must now collect and bury somewhere, he would have considered the tale exaggeration too.

Jim was standing by the gate.

'Had any trouble with the birds?' asked Nat.

'Birds? What birds?'

'We got them up our place last night. Scores of them, came in the chil-dren's bedroom. Quite savage they were.'

'Oh?' It took time for anything to penetrate Jim's head. 'Never heard of birds acting savage,' he said at length. 'They get tame, like, sometimes. I've seen them come to the windows for crumbs.'

'These birds last night weren't tame.'

'No? Cold maybe. Hungry. You put out some crumbs.'

Jim was no more interested than Mrs Trigg had been. It was, Nat thought, like air-raids in the war. No one down this end of the country knew what the Plymouth folk had seen and suffered. You had to endure something yourself before it touched you. He walked back along the lane and crossed the stile to his cottage. He found his wife in the kitchen with young Johnny.

'See anyone?' she asked.

'Mrs Trigg and Jim,' he answered. 'I don't think they believed me. Anyway, nothing wrong up there.'

'You might take the birds away,' she said. 'I daren't go into the room to make the beds until you do. I'm scared.'

'Nothing to scare you now,' said Nat. 'They're dead, aren't they?'

He went up with a sack and dropped the stiff bodies into it, one by one. Yes, there were fifty of them, all told. Just the ordinary common birds of the hedgerow, nothing as large even as a thrush. It must have been fright that made them act the way they did. Blue tits, wrens, it was incredible to think of the power of their small beaks, jabbing at his face and hands the night before. He took the sack out into the garden and was faced now with a fresh problem. The ground was too hard to dig. It was frozen solid, yet no snow had fallen, nothing had happened in the past hours but the coming of the east wind. It was unnatural, queer. The weather prophets must be right. The change was something connected with the Arctic circle.

The wind seemed to cut him to the bone as he stood there, uncer-tainly, holding the sack. He could see the white-capped seas breaking down under in the bay. He decided to take the birds to the shore and bury them.

When he reached the beach below the headland he could scarcely stand, the force of the east wind was so strong. It hurt to draw breath, and his bare hands were blue. Never had he known such cold, not in all the bad winters he could remember. It was low tide. He crunched his way over the shingle to the softer sand and then, his back to the wind, ground a pit in the sand with his heel. He meant to drop the birds into it, but as he opened up the sack the force of the wind carried them, lifted them, as though in flight again, and they were blown away from him along the beach, tossed like feathers, spread and scattered, the bodies of the fifty frozen birds. There was something ugly in the sight. He did not like it. The dead birds were swept away from him by the wind.

'The tide will take them when it turns,' he said to himself.

He looked out to sea and watched the crested breakers, combing green. They rose stiffly, curled, and broke again, and because it was ebb tide the roar was distant, more remote, lacking the sound and thunder of the flood.

Then he saw them. The gulls. Out there, riding the seas.

What he had thought at first to be the white caps of the waves were gulls. Hundreds, thousands, tens of thousands . . . They rose and fell in the trough of the seas, heads to the wind, like a mighty fleet at anchor, wait-ing on the tide. To eastward, and to the west, the gulls were there. They stretched as far as his eye could reach, in close formation, line upon line. Had the sea been still they would have covered the bay like a white cloud, head to head, body packed to body. Only the east wind, whipping the sea to breakers, hid them from the shore.

Nat turned, and leaving the beach climbed the steep path home. Someone should know of this. Someone should be told. Something was happening, because of the east wind and the weather, that he did not understand. He wondered if he should go to the call-box by the bus-stop and ring up the police. Yet what could they do? What could anyone do? Tens and thousands of gulls riding the sea there, in the bay, because of storm, because of hunger. The police would think him mad, or drunk, or take the statement from him with great calm. 'Thank you. Yes, the matter has already been reported. The hard weather is driving the birds inland in great numbers.' Nat looked about him. Still no sign of any other bird. Perhaps the cold had sent them all from up country? As he drew near to the cottage his wife came to meet him, at the door. She called to him, excited. 'Nat,' she said, 'it's on the wireless. They've just read out a special news bulletin. I've written it down.'

'What's on the wireless?' he said.

'About the birds,' she said. 'It's not only here, it's everywhere. In London, all over the country. Something has happened to the birds.'

Together they went into the kitchen. He read the piece of paper lying on the table.

'Statement from the Home Office at eleven a.m. today. Reports from all over the country are coming in hourly about the vast quantity of birds flocking above towns, villages, and outlying districts, causing obstruction and damage and even attacking individuals. It is thought that the Arctic air stream, at present covering the British Isles, is causing birds to migrate south in immense numbers, and that intense hunger may drive these birds to attack human beings. Householders are warned to see to their windows, doors, and chimneys, and to take reasonable precautions for the safety of their children. A further statement will be issued later.'

A kind of excitement seized Nat; he looked at his wife in triumph.

'There you are,' he said, 'let's hope they'll hear that at the farm. Mrs Trigg will know it wasn't any story. It's true. All over the country. I've been telling myself all morning there's something wrong. And just now, down on the beach, I looked out to sea and there are gulls, thousands of them, tens of thousands, you couldn't put a pin between their heads, and they're all out there, riding on the sea, waiting.'

'What are they waiting for, Nat?' she asked.

He stared at her, then looked down again at the piece of paper.

'I don't know,' he said slowly. 'It says here the birds are hungry.'

He went over to the drawer where he kept his hammer and tools.

'What are you going to do, Nat?'

'See to the windows and the chimneys too, like they tell you.'

'You think they would break in, with the windows shut? Those sparrows and robins and such? Why, how could they?'

He did not answer. He was not thinking of the robins and the sparrows. He was thinking of the gulls. . . .

He went upstairs and worked there the rest of the morning, boarding the windows of the bedrooms, filling up the chimney bases. Good job it was his free day and he was not working at the farm. It reminded him of the old days, at the beginning of the war. He was not married then, and he had made all the blackout boards for his mother's house in Plymouth. Made the shelter too. Not that it had been of any use, when the moment came. He wondered if they would take these precautions up at the farm. He doubted it. Too easy-going, Harry Trigg and his missus. Maybe they'd laugh at the whole thing. Go off to a dance or a whist drive.

'Dinner's ready,' she called him, from the kitchen.

'All right. Coming down.'

He was pleased with his handiwork. The frames fitted nicely over the little panes and at the base of the chimneys.

When dinner was over and his wife was washing up, Nat switched on the one o'clock news. The same announcement was repeated, the one which she had taken down during the morning, but the news bulletin enlarged upon it. 'The flocks of birds have caused dislocation in all areas,' read the announcer, 'and in London the sky was so dense at ten o'clock this morning that it seemed as if the city was covered by a vast black cloud.

'The birds settled on roof-tops, on window ledges and on chimneys. The species included blackbird, thrush, the common house-sparrow, and, as might be expected in the metropolis, a vast quantity of pigeons and starlings, and that frequenter of the London river, the black-headed gull. The sight has been so unusual that the traffic came to a standstill in many thoroughfares, work was abandoned in shops and offices, and the streets and pavements were crowded with people standing about to watch the birds.'

Various incidents were recounted, the suspected reason of cold and hunger stated again, and warnings to householders repeated. The announcer's voice was smooth and suave. Nat had the impression that this man, in particular, treated the whole business as he would an elaborate joke. There would be others like him, hundreds of them, who did not know what it was to struggle in darkness with a flock of birds. There would be parties tonight in London, like the ones they gave on election nights. People standing about, shouting and laughing, getting drunk. 'Come and watch the birds!'

Nat switched off the wireless. He got up and started work on the kitchen windows. His wife watched him, young Johnny at her heels.

'What, boards for down here too?' she said. 'Why, I'll have to light up before three o'clock. I see no call for boards down here.'

'Better be sure than sorry,' answered Nat. 'I'm not going to take any chances.'

'What they ought to do,' she said, 'is to call the army out and shoot the birds. That would soon scare them off.'

'Let them try,' said Nat. 'How'd they set about it?'

'They have the army to the docks,' she answered, 'when the dockers strike. The soldiers go down and unload the ships.'

'Yes,' said Nat, 'and the population of London is eight million or more. Think of all the buildings, and the flats, and houses. Do you think they've enough soldiers to go round shooting birds from every roof?'

'I don't know. But something should be done. They ought to do something.'

Nat thought to himself that 'they' were no doubt considering the problem at that very moment, but whatever 'they' decided to do in London and the big cities would not help the people here, three hundred miles away. Each householder must look after his own.

'How are we off for food?' he said.

'Now, Nat, whatever next?'

'Never mind. What have you got in the larder?'

'It's shopping day tomorrow, you know that. I don't keep uncooked food hanging about, it goes off. Butcher doesn't call till the day after. But I can bring back something when I go in tomorrow.'

Nat did not want to scare her. He thought it possible that she might not go to town tomorrow. He looked in the larder for himself, and in the cupboard where she kept her tins. They would do, for a couple of days. Bread was low.

'What about the baker?'

'He comes tomorrow too.'

He saw she had flour. If the baker did not call she had enough to bake one loaf.

'We'd be better off in the old days,' he said, 'when the women baked twice a week, and had pilchards salted, and there was food for a family to last a siege, if need be.'

'I've tried the children with tinned fish, they don't like it,' she said.

Nat went on hammering the boards across the kitchen windows. Candles. They were low in candles too. That must be another thing she meant to buy tomorrow. Well, it could not be helped. They must go early to bed tonight. That was, if . . .

He got up and went out of the back door and stood in the garden, looking down towards the sea. There had been no sun all day, and now, at barely three o'clock, a kind of darkness had already come, the sky sullen, heavy, colourless like salt. He could hear the vicious sea drumming on the rocks. He walked down the path, half-way to the beach. And then he stopped. He could see the tide had turned. The rock that had shown in mid-morning was now covered, but it was not the sea that held his eyes. The gulls had risen. They were circling, hundreds of them, thousands of them, lifting their wings against the wind. It was the gulls that made the darkening of the sky. And they were silent. They made not a sound. They just went on soaring and circling, rising, falling, trying their strength against the wind.

Nat turned. He ran up the path, back to the cottage.

'I'm going for Jill,' he said. 'I'll wait for her, at the bus-stop.'

'What's the matter?' asked his wife. 'You've gone quite white.'

'Keep Johnny inside,' he said. 'Keep the door shut. Light up now, and draw the curtains.'

'It's only just gone three,' she said.

'Never mind. Do what I tell you.'

He looked inside the toolshed, outside the back door. Nothing there of much use. A spade was too heavy, and a fork no good. He took the hoe. It was the only possible tool, and light enough to carry.

He started walking up the lane to the bus-stop, and now and again glanced back over his shoulder.

The gulls had risen higher now, their circles were broader, wider, they were spreading out in huge formation across the sky.

He hurried on; although he knew the bus would not come to the top of the hill before four o'clock he had to hurry. He passed no one on the way. He was glad of this. No time to stop and chatter.

At the top of the hill he waited. He was much too soon. There was half an hour still to go. The east wind came whipping across the fields from the higher ground. He stamped his feet and blew upon his hands. In the distance he could see the clay hills, white and clean, against the heavy pallor of the sky. Something black rose from behind them, like a smudge at first, then widening, becoming deeper, and the smudge became a cloud, and the cloud divided again into five other clouds, spreading north, east, south and west, and they were not clouds at all; they were birds. He watched them travel across the sky, and as one section passed overhead, within two or three hundred feet of him, he knew, from their speed, they were bound inland, up country, they had no business with the people here on the peninsula. They were rooks, crows, jackdaws, magpies, jays, all birds that usually preyed upon the smaller species; but this afternoon they were bound on some other mission.

'They've been given the towns,' thought Nat, 'they know what they have to do. We don't matter so much here. The gulls will serve for us. The others go to the towns.'

He went to the call-box, stepped inside and lifted the receiver. The exchange would do. They would pass the message on.

'I'm speaking from Highway,' he said, 'by the bus-stop. I want to report large formations of birds travelling up country. The gulls are also forming in the bay.'

'All right,' answered the voice, laconic, weary.

'You'll be sure and pass this message on to the proper quarter?'

'She's another,' thought Nat, 'doesn't care. Maybe she's had to answer calls all day. She hopes to go to the pictures tonight. She'll squeeze some fellow's hand, and point up at the sky, and "Look at all them birds!" She doesn't care.'

The bus came lumbering up the hill. Jill climbed out and three or four other children. The bus went on towards the town.

'What's the hoe for, Dad?'

They crowded around him, laughing, pointing.

'I just brought it along,' he said. 'Come on now, let's get home. It's cold, no hanging about. Here, you. I'll watch you across the fields, see how fast you can run.'

He was speaking to Jill's companions who came from different families, living in the council houses. A short cut would take them to the cottages.

'We want to play a bit in the lane,' said one of them.

'No, you don't. You go off home, or I'll tell your mammy.'

They whispered to one another, round-eyed, then scuttled off across the fields. Jill stared at her father, her mouth sullen.

'We always play in the lane,' she said.

'Not tonight, you don't,' he said. 'Come on now, no dawdling.'

He could see the gulls now, circling the fields, coming in towards the land. Still silent. Still no sound.

'Look, Dad, look over there, look at all the gulls.'

'Yes. Hurry, now.'

'Where are they flying to? Where are they going?'

'Up country, I dare say. Where it's warmer.'

He seized her hand and dragged her after him along the lane.

'Don't go so fast. I can't keep up.'

The gulls were copying the rooks and crows. They were spreading out in formation across the sky. They headed, in bands of thousands, to the four compass points.

'Dad, what is it? What are the gulls doing?'

They were not intent upon their flight, as the crows, as the jackdaws had been. They still circled overhead. Nor did they fly so high. It was as though they waited upon some signal. As though some decision had yet to be given. The order was not clear.

'Do you want me to carry you, Jill? Here, come pick-a-back.'

This way he might put on speed; but he was wrong. Jill was heavy. She kept slipping. And she was crying too. His sense of urgency, of fear, had communicated itself to the child.

'I wish the gulls would go away. I don't like them. They're coming closer to the lane.'

He put her down again. He started running, swinging Jill after him. As they went past the farm turning he saw the farmer backing his car out of the garage. Nat called to him.

'Can you give us a lift?' he said.

'What's that?'

Mr Trigg turned in the driving seat and stared at them. Then a smile came to his cheerful, rubicund face.

'It looks as though we're in for some fun,' he said. 'Have you seen the gulls? Jim and I are going to take a crack at them. Everyone's gone bird crazy, talking of nothing else. I hear you were troubled in the night. Want a gun?'

Nat shook his head.

The small car was packed. There was just room for Jill, if she crouched on top of petrol tins on the back seat.

'I don't want a gun,' said Nat, 'but I'd be obliged if you'd run Jill home. She's scared of the birds.'

He spoke briefly. He did not want to talk in front of Jill.

'O.K.,' said the farmer, 'I'll take her home. Why don't you stop behind and join the shooting match? We'll make the feathers fly.'

Jill climbed in, and turning the car the driver sped up the lane. Nat followed after. Trigg must be crazy. What use was a gun against a sky of birds?

Now Nat was not responsible for Jill he had time to look about him. The birds were circling still, above the fields. Mostly herring gull, but the black-backed gull amongst them. Usually they kept apart. Now they were united. Some bond had brought them together. It was the black-backed gull that attacked the smaller birds, and even new-born lambs, so he'd heard. He'd never seen it done. He remembered this now, though, looking above him in the sky. They were coming in towards the farm. They were circling lower in the sky, and the black-backed gulls were to the front, the black-backed gulls were leading. The farm, then, was their target. They were making for the farm.

Nat increased his pace towards his own cottage. He saw the farmer's car turn and come back along the lane. It drew up beside him with a jerk.

'The kid has run inside,' said the farmer. 'Your wife was watching for her. Well, what do you make of it? They're saying in town the Russians have done it. The Russians have poisoned the birds.'

'How could they do that?' asked Nat.

'Don't ask me. You know how stories get around. Will you join my shooting match?'

'No, I'll get along home. The wife will be worried else.'

'My missus says if you could eat gull, there'd be some sense in it,' said Trigg. 'We'd have roast gull, baked gull, and pickle 'em into the bargain. You wait until I let off a few barrels into the brutes. That'll scare 'em.'

'Have you boarded your windows?' asked Nat.

'No. Lot of nonsense. They like to scare you on the wireless. I've had more to do today than to go round boarding up my windows.'

'I'd board them now, if I were you.'

'Garn. You're windy. Like to come to our place to sleep?'

'No, thanks all the same.'

'All right. See you in the morning. Give you a gull breakfast.'

The farmer grinned and turned his car to the farm entrance.

Nat hurried on. Past the little wood, past the old barn, and then across the stile to the remaining field.

As he jumped the stile he heard the whirr of wings. A black-backed gull dived down at him from the sky, missed, swerved in flight, and rose to dive again. In a moment it was joined by others, six, seven, a dozen, black-backed and herring mixed. Nat dropped his hoe. The hoe was useless. Covering his head with his arms he ran towards the cottage. They kept coming at him from the air, silent save for the beating wings. The terrible, fluttering wings. He could feel the blood on his hands, his wrists, his neck. Each stab of a swooping beak tore his flesh. If only he could keep them from his eyes. Nothing else mattered. He must keep them from his eyes. They had not learnt yet how to cling to a shoulder, how to rip clothing, how to dive in mass upon the head, upon the body. But with each dive, with each attack, they became bolder. And they had no thought for themselves. When they dived low and missed, they crashed, bruised and broken, on the ground. As Nat ran he tumbled, kicking their spent bodies in front of him.

He found the door, he hammered upon it with his bleeding hands. Because of the boarded windows no light shone. Everything was dark.

'Let me in,' he shouted, 'it's Nat. Let me in.'

He shouted loud to make himself heard above the whirr of the gulls' wings.

Then he saw the gannet, poised for the dive, above him in the sky. The gulls circled, retired, soared, one with another, against the wind. Only the gannet remained. One single gannet, above him in the sky. The wings folded suddenly to its body. It dropped, like a stone. Nat screamed, and the door opened. He stumbled across the threshold, and his wife threw her weight against the door.

They heard the thud of the gannet as it fell.

His wife dressed his wounds. They were not deep. The backs of his hands had suffered most, and his wrists. Had he not worn a cap they would have reached his head. As to the gannet . . . the gannet could have split his skull.

The children were crying, of course. They had seen the blood on their father's hands.

'It's all right now,' he told them. 'I'm not hurt. Just a few scratches. You play with Johnny, Jill. Mammy will wash these cuts.'

He half shut the door to the scullery, so that they could not see. His wife was ashen. She began running water from the sink.

'I saw them overhead,' she whispered. 'They began collecting just as Jill ran in with Mr Trigg. I shut the door fast, and it jammed. That's why I couldn't open it at once, when you came.'

'Thank God they waited for me,' he said. 'Jill would have fallen at once. One bird alone would have done it.'

Furtively, so as not to alarm the children, they whispered together, as she bandaged his hands and the back of his neck.

'They're flying inland,' he said, 'thousands of them. Rooks, crows, all the bigger birds. I saw them from the bus-stop. They're making for the towns.'

'But what can they do, Nat?'

'They'll attack. Go for everyone out in the streets. Then they'll try the windows, the chimneys.'

'Why don't the authorities do something? Why don't they get the army, get machine-guns, anything?'

'There's been no time. Nobody's prepared. We'll hear what they have to say on the six o'clock news.'

Nat went back into the kitchen, followed by his wife. Johnny was playing quietly on the floor. Only Jill looked anxious.

'I can hear the birds,' she said. 'Listen, Dad.'

Nat listened. Muffled sounds came from the windows, from the door. Wings brushing the surface, sliding, scraping, seeking a way of entry. The sound of many bodies, pressed together, shuffling on the sills. Now and again a thud, a crash, as some bird dived and fell. 'Some of them will kill themselves that way,' he thought, 'but not enough. Never enough.'

'All right,' he said aloud, 'I've got boards over the windows, Jill. The birds can't get in.'

He went and examined all the windows. His work had been thorough. Every gap was closed. He would make extra certain, however. He found wedges, pieces of old tin, strips of wood and metal, and fastened them at the sides to reinforce the boards. His hammering helped to deafen the sound of the birds, the shuffling, the tapping, and more ominous – he did not want his wife or the children to hear it – the splinter of cracked glass.

'Turn on the wireless,' he said, 'let's have the wireless.'

This would drown the sound also. He went upstairs to the bedrooms and reinforced the windows there. Now he could hear the birds on the roof, the scraping of claws, a sliding, jostling sound.

He decided they must sleep in the kitchen, keep up the fire, bring down the mattresses and lay them out on the floor. He was afraid of the bedroom chimneys. The boards he had placed at the chimney bases might give way. In the kitchen they would be safe, because of the fire. He would have to make a joke of it. Pretend to the children they were play-ing at camp. If the worst happened, and the birds forced an entry down the bedroom chimneys, it would be hours, days perhaps, before they could break down the doors. The birds would be imprisoned in the bedrooms. They could do no harm there. Crowded together, they would stifle and die.

He began to bring the mattresses downstairs. At sight of them his wife's eyes widened in apprehension. She thought the birds had already broken in upstairs.

'All right,' he said cheerfully, 'we'll all sleep together in the kitchen tonight. More cosy here by the fire. Then we shan't be worried by those silly old birds tapping at the windows.'

He made the children help him rearrange the furniture, and he took the precaution of moving the dresser, with his wife's help, across the window. It fitted well. It was an added safeguard. The mattresses could now be lain, one beside the other, against the wall where the dresser had stood.

'We're safe enough now,' he thought, 'we're snug and tight, like an air-raid shelter. We can hold out. It's just the food that worries me. Food, and coal for the fire. We've enough for two or three days, not more. By that time . . .'

No use thinking ahead as far as that. And they'd be giving directions on the wireless. People would be told what to do. And now, in the midst of many problems, he realized that it was dance music only coming over the air. Not Children's Hour, as it should have been. He glanced at the dial. Yes, they were on the Home Service all right. Dance records. He switched to the Light programme. He knew the reason. The usual programmes had been abandoned. This only happened at exceptional times. Elections, and such. He tried to remember if it had happened in the war, during the heavy raids on London. But of course. The B.B.C. was not stationed in London during the war. The programmes were broadcast from other, temporary quarters. 'We're better off here,' he thought, 'we're better off here in the kitchen, with the windows and the doors boarded, than they are up in the towns. Thank God we're not in the towns.'

At six o'clock the records ceased. The time signal was given. No matter if it scared the children, he must hear the news. There was a pause after the pips. Then the announcer spoke. His voice was solemn, grave. Quite different from midday.

'This is London,' he said. 'A National Emergency was proclaimed at four o'clock this afternoon. Measures are being taken to safeguard the lives and property of the population, but it must be understood that these are not easy to effect immediately, owing to the unforeseen and unparalleled nature of the present crisis. Every householder must take precautions to his own building, and where several people live together, as in flats and apartments, they must unite to do the utmost they can to prevent entry. It is absolutely imperative that every individual stays indoors tonight, and that no one at all remains on the streets, or roads, or anywhere without doors. The birds, in vast numbers, are attacking anyone on sight, and have already begun an assault upon buildings; but these, with due care, should be impenetrable. The population is asked to remain calm, and not to panic. Owing to the exceptional nature of the emergency, there will be no further transmission from any broadcasting station until seven a.m. tomorrow.'

They played the National Anthem. Nothing more happened. Nat switched off the set. He looked at his wife. She stared back at him.

'What's it mean?' said Jill. 'What did the news say?'

'There won't be any more programmes tonight,' said Nat. 'There's been a breakdown at the B.B.C.'

'Is it the birds?' asked Jill. 'Have the birds done it?'

'No,' said Nat, 'it's just that everyone's very busy, and then of course they have to get rid of the birds, messing everything up, in the towns. Well, we can manage without the wireless for one evening.'

'I wish we had a gramophone,' said Jill, 'that would be better than nothing.'

She had her face turned to the dresser, backed against the windows. Try as they did to ignore it, they were all aware of the shuffling, the stabbing, the persistent beating and sweeping of wings.

'We'll have supper early,' suggested Nat, 'something for a treat. Ask Mammy. Toasted cheese, eh? Something we all like?'

He winked and nodded at his wife. He wanted the look of dread, of apprehension, to go from Jill's face.

He helped with the supper, whistling, singing, making as much clatter as he could, and it seemed to him that the shuffling and the tapping were not so intense as they had been at first. Presently he went up to the bedrooms and listened, and he no longer heard the jostling for place upon the roof.

'They've got reasoning powers,' he thought, 'they know it's hard to break in here. They'll try elsewhere. They won't waste their time with us.'

Supper passed without incident, and then, when they were clearing away, they heard a new sound, droning, familiar, a sound they all knew and understood.

His wife looked up at him, her face alight. 'It's planes,' she said, 'they're sending out planes after the birds. That's what I said they ought to do, all along. That will get them. Isn't that gun-fire? Can't you hear guns?'

It might be gun-fire, out at sea. Nat could not tell. Big naval guns might have an effect upon the gulls out at sea, but the gulls were inland now. The guns couldn't shell the shore, because of the population.

'It's good, isn't it,' said his wife, 'to hear the planes?'

And Jill, catching her enthusiasm, jumped up and down with Johnny. 'The planes will get the birds. The planes will shoot them.'

Just then they heard a crash about two miles distant, followed by a second, then a third. The droning became more distant, passed away out to sea.

'What was that?' asked his wife. 'Were they dropping bombs on the birds?'

'I don't know,' answered Nat. 'I don't think so.'

He did not want to tell her that the sound they had heard was the crashing of aircraft. It was, he had no doubt, a venture on the part of the authorities to send out reconnaissance forces, but they might have known the venture was suicidal. What could aircraft do against birds that flung themselves to death against propeller and fuselage, but hurtle to the ground themselves? This was being tried now, he supposed, over the whole country. And at a cost. Someone high up had lost his head.

'Where have the planes gone, Dad?' asked Jill.

'Back to base,' he said. 'Come on, now, time to tuck down for bed.'

It kept his wife occupied, undressing the children before the fire, seeing to the bedding, one thing and another, while he went round the cottage again, making sure that nothing had worked loose. There was no further drone of aircraft, and the naval guns had ceased. 'Waste of life and effort,' Nat said to himself. 'We can't destroy enough of them that way. Cost too heavy. There's always gas. Maybe they'll try spraying with gas, mustard gas. We'll be warned first, of course, if they do. There's one thing, the best brains of the country will be on to it tonight.'

Somehow the thought reassured him. He had a picture of scientists, naturalists, technicians, and all those chaps they called the back-room boys, summoned to a council; they'd be working on the problem now. This was not a job for the government, for the chiefs-of-staff – they would merely carry out the orders of the scientists.

'They'll have to be ruthless,' he thought. 'Where the trouble's worst they'll have to risk more lives, if they use gas. All the livestock, too, and the soil – all contaminated. As long as everyone doesn't panic. That's the trouble. People panicking, losing their heads. The B.B.C. was right to warn us of that.'

Upstairs in the bedrooms all was quiet. No further scraping and stabbing at the windows. A lull in battle. Forces regrouping. Wasn't that what they called it, in the old war-time bulletins? The wind hadn't dropped, though. He could still hear it, roaring in the chimneys. And the sea breaking down on the shore. Then he remembered the tide. The tide would be on the turn. Maybe the lull in battle was because of the tide. There was some law the birds obeyed, and it was all to do with the east wind and the tide.

He glanced at his watch. Nearly eight o'clock. It must have gone high water an hour ago. That explained the lull: the birds attacked with the flood tide. It might not work that way inland, up country, but it seemed as if it was so this way, on the coast. He reckoned the time limit in his head. They had six hours to go, without attack. When the tide turned again, around one-twenty in the morning, the birds would come back. . . .

There were two things he could do. The first to rest, with his wife and the children, and all of them snatch what sleep they could, until the small hours. The second to go out, see how they were faring at the farm, see if the telephone was still working there, so that they might get news from the exchange.

He called softly to his wife, who had just settled the children. She came half-way up the stairs and he whispered to her.

'You're not to go,' she said at once, 'you're not to go and leave me alone with the children. I can't stand it.'

Her voice rose hysterically. He hushed her, calmed her.

'All right,' he said, 'all right. I'll wait till morning. And we'll get the wireless bulletin then too, at seven. But in the morning, when the tide ebbs again, I'll try for the farm, and they may let us have bread and potatoes, and milk too.'

His mind was busy again, planning against emergency. They would not have milked, of course, this evening. The cows would be standing by the gate, waiting in the yard, with the household inside, battened behind boards, if they were at the cottage. That is, if they had time to take precautions. He thought of the farmer, Trigg, smiling at him from the car. There would have been no shooting party, not tonight.

The children were asleep. His wife, still clothed, was sitting on her mattress. She watched him, her eyes nervous.

'What are you going to do?' she whispered.

He shook his head for silence. Softly, stealthily, he opened the back door and looked outside.

It was pitch dark. The wind was blowing harder than ever, coming in steady gusts, icy, from the sea. He kicked at the step outside the door. It was heaped with birds. There were dead birds everywhere. Under the windows, against the walls. These were the suicides, the divers, the ones with broken necks. Wherever he looked he saw dead birds. No trace of the living. The living had flown seaward with the turn of the tide. The gulls would be riding the seas now, as they had done in the forenoon.

In the far distance, on the hill where the tractor had been two days before, something was burning. One of the aircraft that had crashed; the fire, fanned by the wind, had set light to a stack.

He looked at the bodies of the birds, and he had a notion that if he heaped them, one upon the other, on the window sills, they would make added protection for the next attack. Not much, perhaps, but something. The bodies would have to be clawed at, pecked, and dragged aside, before the living birds gained purchase on the sills and attacked the panes. He set to work in the darkness. It was queer; he hated touching them. The bodies were still warm and bloody. The blood matted their feathers. He felt his stomach turn, but he went on with his work. He noticed, grimly, that every window-pane was shattered. Only the boards had kept the birds from breaking in. He stuffed the cracked panes with the bleeding bodies of the birds.

When he had finished he went back into the cottage. He barricaded the kitchen door, made it doubly secure. He took off his bandages, sticky with the birds' blood, not with his own cuts, and put on fresh plaster.

His wife had made him cocoa and he drank it thirstily. He was very tired.

'All right,' he said, smiling, 'don't worry. We'll get through.'

He lay down on his mattress and closed his eyes. He slept at once. He dreamt uneasily, because through his dreams there ran a thread of something forgotten. Some piece of work, neglected, that he should have done. Some precaution that he had known well but had not taken, and he could not put a name to it in his dreams. It was connected in some way with the burning aircraft and the stack upon the hill. He went on sleeping, though; he did not awake. It was his wife shaking his shoulder that awoke him finally.

'They've begun,' she sobbed, 'they've started this last hour. I can't listen to it any longer, alone. There's something smelling bad too, something burning.'

Then he remembered. He had forgotten to make up the fire. It was smouldering, nearly out. He got up swiftly and lit the lamp. The hammering had started at the windows and the doors, but it was not that he minded now. It was the smell of singed feathers. The smell filled the kitchen. He knew at once what it was. The birds were coming down the chimney, squeezing their way down to the kitchen range.

He got sticks and paper and put them on the embers, then reached for the can of paraffin.

'Stand back,' he shouted to his wife, 'we've got to risk this.'

He threw the paraffin on to the fire. The flame roared up the pipe, and down upon the fire fell the scorched, blackened bodies of the birds.

The children woke, crying. 'What is it?' said Jill. 'What's happened?'

Nat had no time to answer. He was raking the bodies from the chimney, clawing them out on to the floor. The flames still roared, and the danger of the chimney catching fire was one he had to take. The flames would send away the living birds from the chimney top. The lower joint was the difficulty, though. This was choked with the smouldering help-less bodies of the birds caught by fire. He scarcely heeded the attack on the windows and the door: let them beat their wings, break their beaks, lose their lives, in the attempt to force an entry into his home. They would not break in. He thanked God he had one of the old cottages, with small windows, stout walls. Not like the new council houses. Heaven help them up the lane, in the new council houses.

'Stop crying,' he called to the children. 'There's nothing to be afraid of, stop crying.'

He went on raking at the burning, smouldering bodies as they fell into the fire.

'This'll fetch them,' he said to himself, 'the draught and the flames together. We're all right, as long as the chimney doesn't catch. I ought to be shot for this. It's all my fault. Last thing I should have made up the fire. I knew there was something.'

Amid the scratching and tearing at the window boards came the sudden homely striking of the kitchen clock. Three a.m. A little more than four hours yet to go. He could not be sure of the exact time of high water. He reckoned it would not turn much before half past seven, twenty to eight.

'Light up the primus,' he said to his wife. 'Make us some tea, and the kids some cocoa. No use sitting around doing nothing.'

That was the line. Keep her busy, and the children too. Move about, eat, drink; always best to be on the go.

He waited by the range. The flames were dying. But no more black-ened bodies fell from the chimney. He thrust his poker up as far as it could go and found nothing. It was clear. The chimney was clear. He wiped the sweat from his forehead.

'Come on now, Jill,' he said, 'bring me some more sticks. We'll have a good fire going directly.' She wouldn't come near him, though. She was staring at the heaped, singed bodies of the birds.

'Never mind them,' he said. 'We'll put those in the passage when I've got the fire steady.'

The danger of the chimney was over. It could not happen again, not if the fire was kept burning day and night.

'I'll have to get more fuel from the farm tomorrow,' he thought. 'This will never last. I'll manage, though. I can do all that with the ebb tide. It can be worked, fetching what we need, when the tide's turned. We've just got to adapt ourselves, that's all.'

They drank tea and cocoa and ate slices of bread and Bovril. Only half a loaf left, Nat noticed. Never mind though, they'd get by.

'Stop it,' said young Johnny, pointing to the windows with his spoon, 'stop it, you old birds.'

'That's right,' said Nat, smiling, 'we don't want the old beggars, do we? Had enough of 'em.'

They began to cheer when they heard the thud of the suicide birds.

'There's another, Dad,' cried Jill, 'he's done for.'

'He's had it,' said Nat. 'There he goes, the blighter.'

This was the way to face up to it. This was the spirit. If they could keep this up, hang on like this until seven, when the first news bulletin came through, they would not have done too badly.

'Give us a fag,' he said to his wife. 'A bit of a smoke will clear away the smell of the scorched feathers.'

'There's only two left in the packet,' she said. 'I was going to buy you some from the Co-op.'

'I'll have one,' he said. 'T'other will keep for a rainy day.'

No sense trying to make the children rest. There was no rest to be got while the tapping and the scratching went on at the windows. He sat with one arm round his wife and the other round Jill, with Johnny on his mother's lap and the blankets heaped about them on the mattress.

'You can't help admiring the beggars,' he said. 'They've got persistence. You'd think they'd tire of the game, but not a bit of it.'

Admiration was hard to sustain. The tapping went on and on and a new rasping note struck Nat's ear, as though a sharper beak than any hitherto had come to take over from its fellows. He tried to remember the names of birds, he tried to think which species would go for this particular job. It was not the tap of the woodpecker. That would be light and frequent. This was more serious, because if it continued long the wood would splinter as the glass had done. Then he remembered the hawks. Could the hawks have taken over from the gulls? Were there buzzards now upon the sills, using talons as well as beaks? Hawks, buzzards, kestrels, falcons – he had forgotten the birds of prey. He had forgotten the gripping power of the birds of prey. Three hours to go, and while they waited the sound of the splintering wood, the talons tearing at the wood.

Nat looked about him, seeing what furniture he could destroy to fortify the door. The windows were safe, because of the dresser. He was not certain of the door. He went upstairs, but when he reached the landing he paused and listened. There was a soft patter on the floor of the children's bedroom. The birds had broken through ... He put his ear to the door. No mistake. He could hear the rustle of wings, and the light patter as they searched the floor. The other bedroom was still clear. He went into it and began bringing out the furniture, to pile at the head of the stairs should the door of the children's bedroom go. It was a preparation. It might never be needed. He could not stack the furniture against the door, because it opened inward. The only possible thing was to have it at the top of the stairs.

'Come down, Nat, what are you doing?' called his wife.

'I won't be long,' he shouted. 'Just making everything shipshape up here.'

He did not want her to come; he did not want her to hear the pattering of the feet in the children's bedroom, the brushing of those wings against the door.

At five-thirty he suggested breakfast, bacon and fried bread, if only to stop the growing look of panic in his wife's eyes and to calm the fretful children. She did not know about the birds upstairs. The bedroom, luckily, was not over the kitchen. Had it been so she could not have failed to hear the sound of them, up there, tapping the boards. And the silly, senseless thud of the suicide birds, the death-and-glory boys, who flew into the bedroom, smashing their heads against the walls. He knew them of old, the herring gulls. They had no brains. The black-backs were different, they knew what they were doing. So did the buzzards, the hawks. . . .

He found himself watching the clock, gazing at the hands that went so slowly round the dial. If his theory was not correct, if the attack did not cease with the turn of the tide, he knew they were beaten. They could not continue through the long day without air, without rest, without more fuel, without . . . his mind raced. He knew there were so many things they needed to withstand siege. They were not fully prepared. They were not ready. It might be that it would be safer in the towns after all. If he could get a message through, on the farm telephone, to his cousin, only a short journey by train up country they might be able to hire a car. That would be quicker – hire a car between tides. . . .

His wife's voice, calling his name, drove away the sudden, desperate desire for sleep.

'What is it? What now?' he said sharply.

'The wireless,' said his wife. 'I've been watching the clock. It's nearly seven.'

'Don't twist the knob,' he said, impatient for the first time. 'It's on the Home where it is. They'll speak from the Home.'

They waited. The kitchen clock struck seven. There was no sound. No chimes, no music. They waited until a quarter past, switching to the Light. The result was the same. No news bulletin came through.

'We've heard wrong,' he said, 'they won't be broadcasting until eight o'clock.'

They left it switched on, and Nat thought of the battery, wondered how much power was left in it. It was generally recharged when his wife went shopping in the town. If the battery failed they would not hear the instructions.

'It's getting light,' whispered his wife. 'I can't see it, but I can feel it. And the birds aren't hammering so loud.'

She was right. The rasping, tearing sound grew fainter every moment. So did the shuffling, the jostling for place upon the step, upon the sills. The tide was on the turn. By eight there was no sound at all. Only the wind. The children, lulled at last by the stillness, fell asleep. At half past eight Nat switched the wireless off.

'What are you doing? We'll miss the news,' said his wife.

'There isn't going to be any news,' said Nat. 'We've got to depend upon ourselves.'

He went to the door and slowly pulled away the barricades. He drew the bolts, and kicking the bodies from the step outside the door breathed the cold air. He had six working hours before him, and he knew he must reserve his strength for the right things, not waste it in any way. Food, and light, and fuel; these were the necessary things. If he could get them in sufficiency, they could endure another night.

He stepped into the garden, and as he did so he saw the living birds. The gulls had gone to ride the sea, as they had done before; they sought sea food, and the buoyancy of the tide, before they returned to the attack. Not so the land birds. They waited and watched. Nat saw them, on the hedgerows, on the soil, crowded in the trees, outside in the field, line upon line of birds, all still, doing nothing.

He went to the end of his small garden. The birds did not move. They went on watching him.

'I've got to get food,' said Nat to himself, 'I've got to go to the farm to find food.'

He went back to the cottage. He saw to the windows and the doors. He went upstairs and opened the children's bedroom. It was empty, except for the dead birds on the floor. The living were out there, in the garden, in the fields. He went downstairs.

'I'm going to the farm,' he said.

His wife clung to him. She had seen the living birds from the open door.

'Take us with you,' she begged. 'We can't stay here alone. I'd rather die than stay here alone.'

He considered the matter. He nodded.

'Come on, then,' he said, 'bring baskets, and Johnny's pram. We can load up the pram.'

They dressed against the biting wind, wore gloves and scarves. His wife put Johnny in the pram. Nat took Jill's hand.

'The birds,' she whimpered, 'they're all out there, in the fields.'

'They won't hurt us,' he said, 'not in the light.'

They started walking across the field towards the stile, and the birds did not move. They waited, their heads turned to the wind.

When they reached the turning to the farm, Nat stopped and told his wife to wait in the shelter of the hedge with the two children.

'But I want to see Mrs Trigg,' she protested. 'There are lots of things we can borrow, if they went to market yesterday; not only bread, and...'

'Wait here,' Nat interrupted. 'I'll be back in a moment.'

The cows were lowing, moving restlessly in the yard, and he could see a gap in the fence where the sheep had knocked their way through, to roam unchecked in the front garden before the farm-house. No smoke came from the chimneys. He was filled with misgiving. He did not want his wife or the children to go down to the farm.

'Don't jib now,' said Nat, harshly, 'do what I say.'

She withdrew with the pram into the hedge, screening herself and the children from the wind.

He went down alone to the farm. He pushed his way through the herd of bellowing cows, which turned this way and that, distressed, their udders full. He saw the car standing by the gate, not put away in the garage. The windows of the farm-house were smashed. There were many dead gulls lying in the yard and around the house. The living birds perched on the group of trees behind the farm and on the roof of the house. They were quite still. They watched him.

Jim's body lay in the yard ... what was left of it. When the birds had finished, the cows had trampled him. His gun was beside him. The door of the house was shut and bolted, but as the windows were smashed it was easy to lift them and climb through. Trigg's body was close to the telephone. He must have been trying to get through to the exchange when the birds came for him. The receiver was hanging loose, the instrument torn from the wall. No sign of Mrs Trigg. She would be upstairs. Was it any use going up? Sickened, Nat knew what he would find.

'Thank God,' he said to himself, 'there were no children.'

He forced himself to climb the stairs, but half-way he turned and descended again. He could see her legs, protruding from the open bedroom door. Beside her were the bodies of the black-backed gulls, and an umbrella, broken.

'It's no use,' thought Nat, 'doing anything. I've only got five hours, less than that. The Triggs would understand. I must load up with what I can find.'

He tramped back to his wife and children.

'I'm going to fill up the car with stuff,' he said. 'I'll put coal in it, and paraffin for the primus. We'll take it home and return for a fresh load.'

'What about the Triggs?' asked his wife.

'They must have gone to friends,' he said.

'Shall I come and help you, then?'

'No; there's a mess down there. Cows and sheep all over the place. Wait, I'll get the car. You can sit in it.'

Clumsily he backed the car out of the yard and into the lane. His wife and the children could not see Jim's body from there.

'Stay here,' he said, 'never mind the pram. The pram can be fetched later. I'm going to load the car.'

Her eyes watched his all the time. He believed she understood, otherwise she would have suggested helping him to find the bread and groceries.

They made three journeys altogether, backwards and forwards between their cottage and the farm, before he was satisfied they had everything they needed. It was surprising, once he started thinking, how many things were necessary. Almost the most important of all was planking for the windows. He had to go round searching for timber. He wanted to renew the boards on all the windows at the cottage. Candles, paraffin, nails, tinned stuff; the list was endless. Besides all that, he milked three of the cows. The rest, poor brutes, would have to go on bellowing.

On the final journey he drove the car to the bus-stop, got out, and went to the telephone box. He waited a few minutes, jangling the receiver. No good, though. The line was dead. He climbed on to a bank and looked over the countryside, but there was no sign of life at all, nothing in the fields but the waiting, watching birds. Some of them slept – he could see the beaks tucked into the feathers.

'You'd think they'd be feeding,' he said to himself, 'not just standing in that way.'

Then he remembered. They were gorged with food. They had eaten their fill during the night. That was why they did not move this morning. . . .

No smoke came from the chimneys of the council houses. He thought of the children who had run across the fields the night before.

'I should have known,' he thought, 'I ought to have taken them home with me.'

He lifted his face to the sky. It was colourless and grey. The bare trees on the landscape looked bent and blackened by the east wind. The cold did not affect the living birds, waiting out there in the fields.

'This is the time they ought to get them,' said Nat, 'they're a sitting target now. They must be doing this all over the country. Why don't our aircraft take off now and spray them with mustard gas? What are all our chaps doing? They must know, they must see for themselves.'

He went back to the car and got into the driver's seat.

'Go quickly past that second gate,' whispered his wife. 'The postman's lying there. I don't want Jill to see.'

He accelerated. The little Morris bumped and rattled along the lane. The children shrieked with laughter.

'Up-a-down, up-a-down,' shouted young Johnny.

It was a quarter to one by the time they reached the cottage. Only an hour to go.

'Better have cold dinner,' said Nat. 'Hot up something for yourself and the children, some of that soup. I've no time to eat now. I've got to unload all this stuff.'

He got everything inside the cottage. It could be sorted later. Give them all something to do during the long hours ahead. First he must see to the windows and the doors.

He went round the cottage methodically, testing every window, every door. He climbed on to the roof also, and fixed boards across every chimney, except the kitchen. The cold was so intense he could hardly bear it, but the job had to be done. Now and again he would look up, searching the sky for aircraft. None came. As he worked he cursed the inefficiency of the authorities.

'It's always the same,' he muttered, 'they always let us down. Muddle, muddle, from the start. No plan, no real organization. And we don't matter, down here. That's what it is. The people up country have priority. They're using gas up there, no doubt, and all the aircraft. We've got to wait and take what comes.'

He paused, his work on the bedroom chimney finished, and looked out to sea. Something was moving out there. Something grey and white amongst the breakers.

'Good old Navy,' he said, 'they never let us down. They're coming down channel, they're turning in the bay.'

He waited, straining his eyes, watering in the wind, towards the sea. He was wrong, though. It was not ships. The Navy was not there. The gulls were rising from the sea. The massed flocks in the fields, with ruffled feathers, rose in formation from the ground, and wing to wing soared upwards to the sky.

The tide had turned again.

Nat climbed down the ladder and went inside the kitchen. The family were at dinner. It was a little after two. He bolted the door, put up the barricade, and lit the lamp.

'It's night-time,' said young Johnny.

His wife had switched on the wireless once again, but no sound came from it.

'I've been all round the dial,' she said, 'foreign stations, and that lot. I can't get anything.'

'Maybe they have the same trouble,' he said, 'maybe it's the same right through Europe.'

She poured out a plateful of the Triggs' soup, cut him a large slice of the Triggs' bread, and spread their dripping upon it.

They ate in silence. A piece of the dripping ran down young Johnny's chin and fell on to the table.

'Manners, Johnny,' said Jill, 'you should learn to wipe your mouth.'

The tapping began at the windows, at the door. The rustling, the jostling, the pushing for position on the sills. The first thud of the suicide gulls upon the step.

'Won't America do something?' said his wife. 'They've always been our allies, haven't they? Surely America will do something?'

Nat did not answer. The boards were strong against the windows, and on the chimneys too. The cottage was filled with stores, with fuel, with all they needed for the next few days. When he had finished dinner he would put the stuff away, stack it neatly, get everything shipshape, handy-like. His wife could help him, and the children too. They'd tire themselves out, between now and a quarter to nine, when the tide would ebb; then he'd tuck them down on their mattresses, see that they slept good and sound until three in the morning.

He had a new scheme for the windows, which was to fix barbed wire in front of the boards. He had brought a great roll of it from the farm. The nuisance was, he'd have to work at this in the dark, when the lull came between nine and three. Pity he had not thought of it before. Still, as long as the wife slept, and the kids, that was the main thing.

The smaller birds were at the window now. He recognized the light tap-tapping of their beaks, and the soft brush of their wings. The hawks ignored the windows. They concentrated their attack upon the door. Nat listened to the tearing sound of splintering wood, and wondered how many million years of memory were stored in those little brains, behind the stabbing beaks, the piercing eyes, now giving them this instinct to destroy mankind with all the deft precision of machines.

'I'll smoke that last fag,' he said to his wife. 'Stupid of me, it was the one thing I forgot to bring back from the farm.'

He reached for it, switched on the silent wireless. He threw the empty packet on the fire, and watched it burn.

Daphne du Maurier, 'The Birds'

Discussion of the story

Here are some possible discussion points on 'The Birds'.

- How does Daphne du Maurier try to explain why the birds attack only during certain periods of the day? How would the story have been different if there were no periods of respite from the birds' attacks?

- At the end of the story the narrator reflects on the birds' newly discovered 'instinct to destroy mankind'. At what point did you realise that the attacks *were* happening worldwide? Do the Hockens realise it at the same time?
- Looked at rationally, this story is completely unbelievable. Does this spoil it for you? How does du Maurier try to make it *seem* believable? Try to think of an episode that was particularly lifelike.
- Do you find the behaviour of the Triggs believable?
- How would you describe the character of Nat? Is he a likeable character? Does this matter?
- We are never given physical descriptions of any of the characters. Would it have been better if we had?
- Can you think of any way that the story could have been improved?

Wider reading programme

As part of the wider reading programme, it is suggested that you read *The Birds and Other Stories* by Daphne du Maurier. The last two coursework suggestions for this unit are based on your reading of the whole short story collection, and a deadline of a month is suggested for the submission of a coursework piece based on your wider reading of du Maurier's work.

Coursework suggestions

- Daphne du Maurier left the ending of 'The Birds' open. Supply an ending that she might have written. Make sure that your ending reflects the style in which the story is written, and that it makes complete sense in terms of the characters and events of Daphne du Maurier's story.
- Write a critique of Daphne du Maurier's style of writing in 'The Birds', showing how she creates atmosphere and drama in her writing.
- Write a critical assessment of 'The Birds', showing what you liked or disliked about the story and the way it builds up. Refer to particular incidents to back up your answer.
- Choose your favourite story from *The Birds and Other Stories*, and write an analysis of it, showing why you enjoyed it. You should refer to particular details and episodes to back up your judgements.
- Write a comparative evaluation of 'The Birds' and any other story

from *The Birds and Other Stories.* Explain why you prefer the one story to the other. You could write about, and illustrate, the creation of atmosphere, dramatic writing, sense of character, sense of setting, build up of suspense.

Punctuation: inverted commas

The main use of inverted commas (or quotation marks as they are sometimes called) is in punctuating dialogue.

When you are writing dialogue, you put inverted commas round the words that someone is speaking, like this:

'I hope you won't forget to buy Amy's present.'

'Do you think I'm a complete idiot? Of course I won't!'

'You forgot last year, and I had to rush out on Christmas Eve and get it myself.'

As the above passage indicates, you begin each spoken sentence with a capital letter, and start a new line each time the speaker changes.

If you include a verb of saying with the spoken sentence (he *said,* she *whispered,* they *shouted,* etc.) you must put a *comma* between the spoken words and the verb of saying:

'I hope you won't forget to buy Amy's present,' he said.

The comma must come *before* the inverted commas. Make sure it *is* clearly before and not *under* the inverted commas.

If the spoken sentence is a question, then you use a question mark before the verb of saying, instead of a comma. You should never put a question mark first and then a comma:

'Do you think I'm a complete idiot?' she replied.

Notice that 'she' begins with a small letter even though it comes after a question mark. This is because 'she replied' is part of the complete sentence. The same applies with an exclamation mark.

If the verb of saying comes between two spoken sentences, it is followed by a full stop, and the second spoken sentence begins with a capital letter:

'Do you think I'm a complete idiot?' she replied. 'Of course I won't!'

However, if the verb of saying comes in the *middle* of a spoken sentence, it is followed by a comma, and the second half of the spoken sentence begins with a small letter:

'You forgot last year,' he retorted, 'and I had to rush out on Christmas Eve and get it myself.'

To make sure that you are quite clear about punctuating dialogue, look at the following passage and answer the question:

'I hope it won't cost too much,' she said. 'If it's more than ten pounds I can't afford it.'

'You're so stingy,' he scoffed, 'that it's a wonder you bought anybody any presents!'

- Why is the first verb of saying followed by a capital 'I' and the second verb of saying followed by a small 't'?

Quotation marks are also used for the following:

1 Quotations from books, plays, speeches, etc. For example: A famous play by Shakespeare begins: 'If music be the food of love, play on.'
2 The titles of books, plays, films, TV programmes, newspapers, magazines, etc. and the names of pubs, restaurants, ships, etc., such as Shakespeare's 'Twelfth Night', the 'Sunday Mirror'; 'EastEnders', 'HMS Invincible'.

Inverted commas exercise

- Rewrite the following sentences putting in inverted commas, capital letters, commas and any other necessary punctuation.

Can I have some of your crisps the boy asked I'm ever so hungry.

We saw the film the long kiss goodnight one evening when we were crossing the atlantic in the queen elizabeth.

I would like to know he said why you insist on humiliating me in public. I don't she replied its just your paranoid imagination.

Spelling: the prefix rule

There is a simple way of remembering how to spell words which begin with a prefix like 'un-', 'mis-', 'ir-' 'dis-', etc.

Write the prefix, then add the *complete* word that goes with it, e.g., u*nn*atural, mi*ss*pell, i*rr*elevant, di*ss*atisfied.

To check your understanding of this rule, write down the *opposite* of the following words:

appear   necessary

legal   regular

moral   mature

logical   rational

SYLLABUS REQUIREMENTS COVERED

This unit covers the requirement to study a work or works by a writer or writers with a well-established critical reputation, who were published after 1900.

The coursework suggestions relate to the coursework requirements of the various syllabuses as follows:

Suggestion 1

London: Personal and imaginative writing

MEG: Unit 2: Writing to explore, imagine, entertain

         Unit 3: Reading in the English literary heritage

NEAB: Original writing

SEG: Personal writing – fiction

         Response to one author published after 1900

WJEC: Best writing

Suggestions 2, 3, 4 and 5

MEG: Unit 3 (reading in the English literary heritage)

SEG: Response to one author whose works were published post 1900

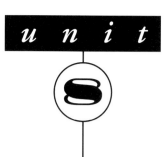

FILM, TELEVISION AND POETRY

In this unit alternative options are offered for the main activity. For those syllabuses which include media analysis as part of the coursework, there are two options: watching and discussing Alfred Hitchcock's film of *The Birds*, and watching and discussing episodes from television soap operas. Practice in writing reviews is included as a follow-up or as an alternative activity.

The other main option is poetry analysis. Poems feature in the next unit, and an analysis of the *nature* of poetry features there, but if additional work on poetry, either as coursework or exam preparation, is needed, then this can be the focus of the unit.

Alfred Hitchcock's The Birds

As a follow-up to the previous unit, you could watch the film version of *The Birds* which is loosely based on the central idea behind Daphne du Maurier's story.*

The film was made in 1963, originally in black and white, but is now available in colour on video. The director, Alfred Hitchcock, was one of the great innovators in world cinema, and *The Birds* is one of his major films.

You could watch the whole film and then discuss it, or focus the discussion on scenes which come closest to episodes from the du Maurier story.

* *The Birds* is available on Video Plus Direct video, number VC727. It lasts 113 minutes.

Whole group discussion

Here are some discussion suggestions on the success or otherwise of the film.

- Did the story of Mitch and Melanie create an effective framework for the horror story?
- What was the purpose of the episode in the bird shop at the beginning?
- What, if anything, did the relationships between Mitch and his mother and Annie add to the film?
- Choose some of the episodes in which birds attack people. What made them effective? How were the effects created?

- How effectively is the scepticism of the townspeople suggested?
- How do the scenes in the bar and the back room of the diner add to the dramatic impact of the film?
- Do you think the final scene of the film is effective?

Small group discussion

In groups of three or four, work out the main differences between the film and the story. What is gained or lost by Hitchcock's treatment of the story?

Think of the scenes which correspond most closely with episodes from the story. What are the basic differences between the two media in their treatment of these episodes? In what ways did you prefer the film, and in what ways did you prefer the story?

Writing a film review

As a potential media coursework piece, you may wish to write a re-view of a film of your own choice. The best approach to this might be to watch a film at the cinema or on television or video, with a checklist of aspects of film reviewing in mind while you are watch-ing. Here is a possible checklist:

- Give the title of the film and an idea of what *kind* of film it is (thriller, romance, comedy, etc).
- Make a personal evaluation of how good the film is.
- Give a *basic* outline of the plot, without going into too much de-tail.
- Write about the main characters, the actors who play them and how good the performance is.
- Make comparisons with other films with a similar theme, if you have seen any.
- Discuss other aspects of the film, such as who directed it, how good the direction is, camera work, special effects, use of music, pace of the film, etc.
- Make your final judgement on the film, its strengths and weak-nesses and on the kind of audience it would be likely to appeal to.

You may find it useful to study reviews of recent films in newspapers and magazines as further guidance. An example of a film review from a newspaper follows.

It's January. Our critic has already chosen his film of the year

By Philip French

It is a pleasure to start the year by greeting a movie that is as good as anything we're likely to see in the course of 1997. *Shine* is the story of the Australian concert pianist David Helfgott, and in several ways Scott Hicks's warm and inspiring film recalls Jane Campion's biopic of the New Zealand writer Janet Frame. Both are about gifted artists from working-class backgrounds who win scholarships to study in England, suffer extended periods of madness, spend years in institutions, and are helped by kind and forbearing people. In both movies, the central character is played by three actors, and while at times harrowing and painful, both films manage to be lyrical and exuberant without ever becoming sentimental.

We first meet David (Geoffrey Rush) in his thirties, lost one rainy night in downtown Adelaide and seeking refuge in a wine bar. He jabbers compulsively and semi-coherently, rhyming, punning, making weird connections. Sylvia (Sonia Todd), the bar's kindly owner, takes him home, and in a series of flashbacks we meet David as a nine-year-old musical prodigy (Alex Rafalowicz) and as a brilliantly accomplished teenager (Noah Taylor). It is to the credit of Hicks, his casting director and the three actors that they convince as the same person at different stages in his troubled development.

Looming over these flashbacks is David's father Peter, a proud, tormented, overbearing man played with immense authority by Armin Mueller-Stahl. Helfgott Senior wants his son to be a great musician, but he doesn't want anyone's help and is determined that the boy will never leave home.

Peter and his wife are Jewish survivors of the Holocaust, who lost all their family in Europe. This we only learn through a brief, oblique exchange, for the movie deliberately steers clear of providing the kind of information that would enable us to make a pat diagnosis of either David or his father.

What we do know is that David retreats into himself and, while growing as a musician, remains not merely immature but infantile. Like Blanche in *A Streetcar Named Desire*, he comes to depend on the kindness of strangers, and while his father casts him into outer darkness, a succession of people are there to comfort and assist. Along the way there are encounters with sweet-natured, selfless men and women, all memorably realised – a piano teacher (Nicholas Bell) who gives him free lessons; an elderly left-wing woman writer (Googie Withers), who introduces him to literature; a demanding, inspiring professor (John Gielgud) at the Royal College of Music in London; Sylvia, the owner of the wine bar where he starts playing the piano again after years in a home; and Gillian (Lynn Redgrave), the Sydney astrologer with a PhD who is encouraged by their joint charts to marry the wild, unpredictable David, and lead him back to the concert hall.

There is, more than incidentally, an important distinction to be made between this film and a recent series of pictures, stories about holy fools, mostly but not entirely from Hollywood, such as *Ryan's Daughter, Rain Man, Forrest Gump* and *The Eighth Day*, in which the central characters suffer from some form of mental illness or brain damage. This has led to the suggestion that there ought to be a special Oscar category for such roles. *Shine* steers clear of the old cliché about there being a thin line between genius and madness, and it doesn't suggest that David's suffering has made him into a superior person or given him a peculiar insight into the human condition.

Shine is a marvellous story about an extraordinary man being brought back into society by ordinary people. The movie gives a good name to the concept of care in the community. It is not about being cured, it's about learning to function and to understand. But for the audience, the film is ultimately exuberant and therapeutic. The music is pretty good, too.

Source: the *Observer*, 5 January 1997

Coursework suggestions

- Write a comparative analysis of 'The Birds' by Daphne du Maurier and the film version by Alfred Hitchcock. You should write about the special qualities of the film and the story, and illustrate your points by quoting from/describing especially effective episodes/ scenes from both the story and the film. You should analyse scenes from the film which are drawn from episodes in the story, and make comparative judgements as to their effectiveness.
- Compare and contrast the treatment of the horror motif in the story and the film *The Birds*.
- Write a film review of Alfred Hitchcock's *The Birds*.
- Write a review of a recent film which you have particularly enjoyed.

Soap operas

Soap operas are the most popular form of drama in Britain. British and Australian 'soaps' command daily audiences of millions. The objective of this section is to compare British and Australian soap operas, and to take an objective look at particular soap opera episodes.

Discussion of British and Australian 'soaps'

Discuss each of these differences between soap operas dealing with life in Britain and those set in Australia. You should give examples from soap operas that you watch.

* realism of the characters/range of characters

* social mix of the characters/turnover of characters

* treatment of family relationships

* exploration of controversial issues

* use of comic situations and characters

* use of strong language

* range of settings

* pace of plot development/rapidity of episode changes

* use of dramatic effects

CORONATION STREET

HOME AND AWAY

EASTENDERS

Episodes from soap operas

Perhaps the best way to analyse soap operas is to watch episodes or parts of episodes on video. You could choose one episode from both a British and an Australian 'soap' and discuss and compare them.

You might consider these questions:

- How realistic were the situations?
- How believable were the characters?
- How convincing was the dialogue?
- How good was the acting?
- Which characters, if any, did you sympathise or empathise with? Why?
- Consider one of the story lines followed up in one of the episodes you watched. What makes the development of that particular story line, over the whole period since it was first introduced, interesting and entertaining?
- Did you gain any insights into human life or behaviour from either of the episodes you watched?
- Of all the soap operas currently shown on British television, which do you think is best? Why?

Writing a television review

On the next page is an example of a newspaper review of the whole range of British soap operas over the Christmas and New Year period 1996/97. It is from the *Observer*. Read it through and identify passages dealing with each of the discussion questions under the heading 'Episodes of soap operas', above.

SOAP OPERA

By Andy Medhurst

An overload of neuroses and crises: anything for attention

Keen to play their part in the nation's annual surrender to excess and indulgence, the Christmas and New Year soaps were stuffed to bursting point with intrigue and crisis.

Between them, they clocked up one death, one suicide attempt, two fires (one accidental, the other the result of a lover scorned), a wedding, a widowing, an abortion, two proposals, several marriages on the rocks and one gay relationship not far from it, two best friends seduced by betrayal to lifelong enmity, a succession of unexpected alcohol-fuelled couplings (even *Emmerdale*'s Butch Dingle lost his virginity), and both a Christmas dinner and a New Year party were destroyed by the surfacing of long-simmering conflicts. Pretty much like the real thing then.

Soaps flourish at Christmas, often sprouting extra and/or longer episodes, relishing the chance to perform in front of an even larger than usual public – the record viewing figure for a single slice of soap remains the 30 million who watched *EastEnders* on Christmas Day 1986 to see Dirty Den serve divorce papers on the errant Angie.

This year's ratings were not such good news for *Coronation Street*, which pulled in its lowest Christmas audience on record, a 'mere' nine million. That statistic propelled the tabloids into another flurry of *Corrie*-on-the-rocks stories, speculating on the reasons for the *Street's* apparent decline, but conveniently overlooking the fact that the episode in question was scheduled opposite *Jurassic Park* – even Hilda Ogden and Elsie Tanner, those twin velociraptors of the soap's Golden Age, might have had trouble facing such heavyweight competition.

Christmas week in *Corrie* featured a bravely adult storyline – the plight of those left miserably alone during a period of convivial togetherness – but these good intentions were rather undermined by the choice of Don Brennan, Weatherfield's least likeable man, as the intended object of our sympathies. Was mine the only household to regret his last-minute rescue from the fume-filled car? Surely the point about the festive desperation of the lonely would have been better made with Don's successful suicide – think of all the juicy scenes of recrimination that would have followed, rather than having to put up with his bilious whinges for another year.

The soap that did risk a Christmas death was *Emmerdale*, which celebrated its promotion to thrice weekliness with an ebulliently confident performance. Heart-throb Dave was killed saving his baby from a burning building, but the apparent heroism of this was productively complicated by his decision, minutes earlier, to abandon his wife Kathy for his mistress Kim.

Such moral messiness promised much in the way of subsequent conflict, but the chance has been squandered by Kim's tearful departure from the village. This distressingly clears the way for an overdose of self-righteousness from Kathy, a chance for sanctimonious hammering sure to be relished by the grating Malandra Burrows. Worse still, just before Kim left, we also lost Tina, her understudy in feline scheming. This is a vacuum in urgent need of filling, since no post-*Dynasty* soap can afford to be a bitch-free zone.

Brookside, true to form, had the darkest of Christmases, with all the Corkhills looking at the gloomiest New Year imaginable: Jimmy driven from the Close by unforgivingly small-minded neighbours, Lindsey realising how idle and deceitful the atrociously-bearded Mike can be, Jackie still unable to assert herself against Ron's insensitive misconceptions.

There's an atmosphere of sombre exhaustion hanging over *Brookside* at the moment, not surprising given how fraught 1996 was for every one of its inhabitants, but some new blood and some light relief would be very welcome in the coming months.

The real Christmas cracker was *EastEnders*, especially its brilliant New Year episodes, where Grant and Tiffany's skirmishes escalated into full-scale war.

Their scenes together were taut, intense and utterly believable, with special credit going to Martine McCutcheon's Tiffany – hard-faced madam and terrified child rolled into one confused and contradictory package.

All she wants, which is all she's never had, is reciprocated love, and to watch her going about getting it in a way which guarantees it can never happen is to see a heart breaking before your very eyes. It's a performance to rank with the genre's finest and a truly wonderful way to usher in a soapy new year.

Andy Medhurst, the *Observer*, 5 January 1997

Discussion of the review

Discuss the points made in the review about the characters, situations, social issues, acting, etc., in the various soaps.

Coursework suggestions

- Choose a social issue, such as adultery, racism or unemployment, which is dealt with in more than one soap opera. Write about the way it is treated in the different 'soaps', referring to the characters involved and the extent to which we are encouraged to sympathise with them, the attitudes of other members of the community who are not directly involved, the degree of depth in which the issue is explored, and the moral stance, if any, which the programme encourages us to take. Give your own view of the characters and situation.
- Write a review of a week's episodes of a soap opera, using the newspaper review quoted above as a guide.
- Write a comparison between British and Australian soap operas.

Poetry: aspects of love

The six poems which follow, three written before 1900 and three after, explore different aspects of love.

Read each of the poems and try to work out *what* the poet is saying, *how* he/she is saying it, and what you like about the poem.

You might ask yourself:

- What aspect of love is the poet writing about? What is he/she saying about it?
- What is interesting/unusual about the way the ideas are expressed?
- What words or phrases particularly captured your imagination?
- What uses does the poet make of imagery and figures of sound?
- How does the poet create sense impressions?
- How would you describe the tone of the poem and the 'voice' adopted by the poet?
- What is interesting about the structure and rhythm of the poem?
- What did you like/dislike about the poem?

'Song', John Donne (1572–1631)

John Donne was a contemporary of William Shakespeare. He was born in London, and wrote secular poems, many of them exploring different aspects of love, for most of his life. In his later years, however, after his ordination for the priesthood in 1615, he concentrated more on spiritual themes and also became famous for his published sermons.

> Go, and catch a falling star,
>   Get with child a mandrake root,
> Tell me where all past years are,
>   Or who cleft the Devil's foot,
> Teach me to hear mermaids singing,
> Or to keep off envy's stinging,
>   And find
>   What wind
> Serves to advance an honest mind.
>
> If thou be'st born to strange sights,
>   Things invisible to see,
> Ride ten thousand days and nights
>   Till Age snow white hairs on thee.
> Thou, when thou return'st, wilt tell me
> All strange wonders that befell thee.
>   And swear
>   No where
> Lives a woman true, and fair.
>
> If thou find'st one, let me know,
>   Such a pilgrimage were sweet;
> Yet do not; I would not go,
>   Though at next door we might meet.
> Though she were true, when you met her,
> And last, till you write your letter,
>   Yet she
>   Will be
> False, ere I come, to two, or three.

John Donne

'O My Luve's Like a Red, Red Rose', Robert Burns (1759–96)

Robert Burns is Scotland's most famous poet. He was born in Ayrshire, and wrote poems both in standard English and in Scottish dialect. It is for his dialect poems that he is best remembered, and the poem which follows is an example.

> O my Luve's like a red, red rose
>   That's newly sprung in June:
> O my Luve's like the melodie
>   That's sweetly played in tune.
>
> As far art thou, my bonnie lass,
>   So deep in luve am I:
> And I will luve thee still, my dear,
>   Till a' the seas gang dry.
>
> Till a' the seas gang dry, my dear,
>   And the rocks melt wi' the sun;
> I will luve thee still, my dear,
>   While the sands o' life shall run.
>
> And fare thee weel, my only Luve,
>   And fare thee weel a while!
> And I will come again, my Luve,
>   Tho' it were ten thousand mile.

Robert Burns

'Meeting at Night', Robert Browning (1812–89)

Robert Browning was born in London, and devoted his life to writing poetry. His elopement with Elizabeth Barrett in 1846 was one of the most celebrated real-life romances of the nineteenth century.

> THE gray sea and the long black land;
>   And the yellow half-moon large and low;
>   And the startled little waves that leap
>   In fiery ringlets from their sleep,
>   As I gain the cove with pushing prow,
> And quench its speed i' the slushy sand.
>
> Then a mile of warm sea-scented beach;
>   Three fields to cross till a farm appears;
>   A tap at the pane, the quick sharp scratch
>   And blue spurt of a lighted match,
>   And a voice less loud, thro' its joys and fears,
> Than the two hearts beating each to each!

Robert Browning

'Love without Hope', Robert Graves (1895–1985)

Robert Graves was born in London. He saw himself primarily as a poet but was also an academic, and wrote many novels and works of biography and autobiography.

> Love without hope, as when the young bird-catcher
> Swept off his tall hat to the Squire's own daughter,
> So let the imprisoned larks escape and fly
> Singing about her head, as she rode by.

Robert Graves

'Song', W. H. Auden (1907–73)

W. H. Auden was born in Birmingham. He travelled widely, living in Germany in the 1930s and settling in the USA for the duration of the Second World War (1939–45). He was an academic as well as a poet.

> Stop all the clocks, cut off the telephone,
> Prevent the dog from barking with a juicy bone,
> Silence the pianos and with muffled drum
> Bring out the coffin, let the mourners come.
>
> Let aeroplanes circle moaning overhead
> Scribbling on the sky the message He Is Dead,
> Put crêpe bows round the white necks of the public doves,
> Let the traffic policemen wear black cotton gloves.
>
> He was my North, my South, my East and West,
> My working week and my Sunday rest,
> My noon, my midnight, my talk, my song;
> I thought that love would last for ever: I was wrong.
>
> The stars are not wanted now; put out every one,
> Pack up the moon and dismantle the sun,
> Pour away the ocean and sweep up the wood;
> For nothing now can ever come to any good.

W. H. Auden

'Loveact', Grace Nichols (born 1950)

Grace Nichols was born in Guyana, moving to Britain in 1977. She writes in both standard English and West Indian dialect, as this poem illustrates. She now lives in Brighton.

She enter into his Great House
her see-far looking eyes
unassuming

He fix her with his glassy stare
and feel the thin fire in his blood
awakening

Soon she is the fuel
that keep them all going

He/his mistresswife/and his
children who take to her breasts
like leeches

He want to tower above her
want her to raise her ebony
haunches and when she does
he think she can be trusted
and drinks her in

and his mistresswife
spending her days in rings
of vacant smiling
is glad to be rid of the
loveact

But time pass/es

Her sorcery cut them
like a whip

She hide her triumph
and slowly stir the hate
of poison in

Grace Nichols

Coursework suggestions

- Write a magazine article entitled 'Aspects of Love', using some of the poems studied in this unit. You should comment on what the poet is saying and how he/she captures ideas and feelings through his/her use of language.
- Write a comparison of the poems by Donne, Burns and Browning, showing how each poet conveys his particular perspective on love by his use of language, imagery and poetic structure.
- Write a comparison of the poems by Graves, Auden and Nichols, showing how each poet conveys his/her particular perspective on love by his/her use of language, imagery and poetic structure.

Further coursework titles, making use of poems studied in this unit, are suggested in Unit 21 (suggestion 2 on p. 286) and Unit 24 (p. 308).

You may wish to read/study Unit 24 before you attempt an answer to any of these questions.

Preparation for individual orals

One of the requirements for speaking and listening assessment is to make an individual oral presentation to other members of the class. These presentations can take place early in the spring term.

Over the next few weeks you should choose a work of literature to talk about. The talk should last about five minutes. The idea of the talk is to 'sell' the book to the rest of the class so that they want to read it as well. A good way to do this would be to pick out brief extracts to read aloud, to show what is good about the book and the way it is written.

You should make notes to refer to, and mark the pages in the book that you are going to read from. You can refer to these notes while you are giving your speech, but you must *not* simply read a pre-prepared speech. You must also avoid simply telling the story. What you are trying to do is explain and illustrate the qualities of the book that made you choose it. This involves a lot more than just explaining the plot.

Spelling rule: adding suffixes to words ending in a silent 'e'

Another spelling rule which may be worth learning is the suffix rule governing words ending with a silent 'e' (like 'hope', 'safe', 'manage').

The rule

When you add a suffix beginning with a *consonant* (like '-less', '-ly', '-ment') the 'e' is kept.

When you add a suffix beginning with a vowel or 'y' (like '-ing', '-able', '-y') the 'e' is dropped.

e.g. hope + less   hope + ing
     sincere + ly   subtle + y
     arrange + ment   arrange + ing
     complete + ly   complete + ing

There are exceptions, of course, such as: argument, truly, awful, duly, wholly, saleable, rateable.

Exercise

Make words by adding the bracketed suffixes to the words below:

care (-less, -ing)   peace (-ful, -able)
improve (-ment, -ing)   argue (-ment, -ing)
laze (-y, -ing)   hope (-ful, -ing)

Revision of sentence structure

Here are two exercises to test your understanding of basic sentence structure, and as a revision of Unit 2.

● Write out the sentences below. Tick the correctly constructed ones, and add words to those which are incorrect, to make them into proper sentences.

Dogs barking and howling in their pens.

He went home.

Laughing and joking and having a wonderful time.

She is eating far too much.

The car coughed and spluttered up the hill.

Men and women wandering round in the dark, searching for somewhere to rest.

● Correct the following passages, either by changing the punctuation or adding conjunctions:

1 The little girl was looking for her mother, they had become separated in the crowd, she began to cry, a tall man with horn-rimmed spectacles spoke to her, he asked her what the matter was, 'I've lost my mummy,' the little girl sobbed, the kind-hearted man took her to the nearby police station.

2 The police were looking for a brown Jaguar, suddenly they saw it, they immediately accelerated and chased the car, it also accelerated, both cars were travelling at twice the speed limit, the Jaguar roared through a red traffic light, it smashed into the side of a yellow Datsun, with a sickening crash, the police car arrived seconds later, to drag the victims from the smash, the Datsun driver was badly hurt, bleeding from wounds to the head and wrist, the Jaguar driver was concussed, they had caught him.

SYLLABUS REQUIREMENTS COVERED

'Alfred Hitchcock's 'The Birds' and 'Soap operas''

The coursework suggestions relate to the coursework requirements of the syllabuses as follows:

MEG: Unit 1

NEAB: Media

SEG: Personal writing – non-fiction

WJEC: Best writing

'Poetry: aspects of love'

Poetry analysis is an important part of the examinations for the London and NEAB syllabuses. The coursework suggestions relate to the syllabuses as follows:

MEG: Unit 3 (all 3 suggestions)

SEG: Units 4 or 5 (suggestions 2 and 3)

WJEC: Poetry unit (suggestions 1 and 2)

LONDON IN LITERATURE

The main focus of this unit is short poems and prose extracts written over the last two hundred years or so, all relating to the same theme: perceptions of London. You will be looking in detail both at *what* the various writers are saying about London and *how* they are saying it. In order to be adequately prepared for the exam, as well as for the coursework requirements, you will almost certainly need to look critically at short poems and prose pieces, and learn how to analyse the various ways in which writers convey their ideas to the readers through their use of language, as well as showing that you can understand those ideas and explain them in your own words.

The poems chosen for study are from the late eighteenth century and the early nineteenth century, with two from the late twentieth century, and the prose extracts are from the mid-nineteenth century and the late twentieth century. You may wish to read Unit 24 and Unit 25 before you attempt coursework poetry and prose analysis.

What is a poem?

Before beginning an analysis of the poems, we should consider what constitutes a poem.

Try to answer these questions:

- Does a poem have to rhyme?
- Does a poem have to have a rhythm?
- Why are poems set out in lines?
- What is a poem?
- Why would someone choose to express his/her ideas in the form of a poem rather than in prose?

Rhythm and rhyme

As you may have decided by now, a poem must have *some* form of rhythm, or else there would be no point in setting the ideas out in lines of poetry at all. This does not mean that it has to have a *regular* rhythm, although just about all poetry written before the twentieth century does. Many modern poets choose to write in free verse, without any regular patterning of either rhyme or rhythm.

As regards rhyme, poets as far back as Shakespeare and earlier have written poetry with a regular rhythm (also known as a **metrical pattern**) but no rhyme. What you *don't* ever find are published poems written in rhyme but without a metrical pattern. Students often write rhyming poems without a regular metre, however, and this merely comes across as awkward and careless. If you choose to write a poem yourself as a possible coursework piece, you must make sure that you *do* impose a rigidly consistent rhythm on your poetry if you are going to use rhyme, or else write in free verse, without a regular metre or rhyme.

Poetry which rhymes must also have a **rhyme scheme**. The most basic rhyme scheme is called rhyming (or rhymed) couplets. This means that pairs of lines rhyme (the first two lines rhyming, the next two, and so on).

There are all kinds of rhyme schemes. The poem by William Blake on page 116 is an example of another common rhyme scheme. Look at it now. What do you notice about the pattern of the rhyming lines?

The Blake poem is also written in a series of sections, called **verses** (or **stanzas**). If you look at the verses you will see that they are all of four lines, with a consistent pattern of rhyming lines between one verse and the next. There is a specific term for such four-line verses. They are called **quatrains**.

The poem by Wordsworth which follows the Blake poem is in a different rhyme pattern. How is it different?

Wordsworth's poem is an example of a poetic form called a **sonnet**. This is a poem of fourteen lines, with ten syllables per line. In Wordsworth's poem there is one rhyming pattern in the first eight lines (called the **octave**) and a different rhyming pattern in the last six lines (called the **sestet**.) The rhythm of Wordsworth's sonnet is called **iambic pentameters**. For an explanation of the iambic pentameter, see Unit 19, page 264.

We shall look at the rhythmic patterns of the other poems as we work through this unit. As you study the pieces which follow, you will be asked to analyse the language and tone in which they are written. This will include a discussion of literary devices: imagery and figures of sound. It will be useful to look back at Unit 6 before/while analysing the pieces.

'London', William Blake

The first impression of London in poetic form is William Blake's poem entitled 'London'. It was part of a collection of poems, called *Songs of Experience*, which was published in 1794.

William Blake (1757–1827) is one of the most original of the English poets, and was also a major artist. He produced engravings to illustrate most of his poems.

Blake was a highly original thinker as well as an innovative poet, questioning the conventions and orthodox ideas of the society in which he lived, and developing a political and religious ideology of his own. His beliefs and his poetry were so radical and different from the norms of his time that he was widely considered by his contemporaries to be mad.

'London' is an angry poem, conveying a series of impressions of the people that the poet sees as he walks through the streets of the capital. Through these wonderfully concise sense impressions, a passionate condemnation of an entire society emerges.

The period when Blake wrote the poem was one in which small children were employed to climb up the insides of rich people's chimneys to clean them, and sometimes got stuck there and suffocated to death. The established church supported the political and military establishment. There were many more prostitutes ('harlots') in London then than there are now, and married men commonly sought their pleasure with them.

London

I wander thro' each charter'd street,
Near where the charter'd Thames does flow,
And mark in every face I meet,
Marks of weakness, marks of woe.

In every cry of every Man,
In every Infant's cry of fear,
In every voice, in every ban,
The mind-forg'd manacles I hear.

How the chimney-sweeper's cry,
Every black'ning Church appals,
And the hapless Soldier's sigh,
Runs in blood down Palace walls.

But most thro' midnight streets I hear,
How the youthful Harlot's curse,
Blasts the new born Infant's tear,
And blights with plagues the Marriage hearse.

William Blake

- Here are some features of the poem which you might discuss:

The use of repetition in the first two verses, and balanced phrases in lines 4 and 7.

The double-meaning of 'charter'd' in lines 1 and 2.

The imagery in line 8.

The significance of the connections ('chimney-sweeper'/'church' etc.) in the last two verses.

The use of emotive language (words conveying intense emotion).

The use of alliteration and assonance.

The meaning of the last line and its connections with the rest of the final verse.

- What do you notice about the rhythm of the poem? How many syllables do the lines contain? How do you explain the rhythmic change in verse 3?

'Composed upon Westminster Bridge', William Wordsworth

The next pre-twentieth-century poem, 'Composed Upon Westminster Bridge', was written by William Wordsworth in 1802.

William Wordsworth (1770–1850) is best known as a nature poet. He is one of the so-called Lake Poets, spending most of his life in the English Lake District. His poem 'Daffodils' has bored generations of schoolchildren and has probably done more to create the popular impression of poetry as being 'soppy' than any other poem ever written. However, Wordsworth was capable of evoking the sense impressions of a natural scene with rare power, and many of his best poems convey his feelings about the Lake District.

This poem, however, is about a London scene. The poet is standing on Westminster Bridge, very early in the morning, before the city has come to life, looking out over the Thames and the city scene before him. The emotions this time are of wonder and delight and a feeling of awe.

Composed Upon Westminster Bridge

Earth has not anything to show more fair:
Dull would he be of soul who could pass by
A sight so touching in its majesty:
This City now doth, like a garment, wear
The beauty of the morning; silent, bare,
Ships, towers, domes, theatres and temples lie
Open unto the fields, and to the sky;
All bright and glittering in the smokeless air.
Never did sun more beautifully steep
In his first splendour, valley, rock, or hill;
Ne'er saw I, never felt, a calm so deep!
The river glideth at his own sweet will:
Dear God! the very houses seem asleep;
And all that mighty heart is lying still!

William Wordsworth

- What is Wordsworth saying about London in this poem?
- A useful way of looking at the poem in detail might be to compare it with Blake's 'London'. You might discuss 'Composed Upon Westminster Bridge', in contrast with 'London' in the following respects:

uses of language

uses of imagery

uses of alliteration

uses of balanced phrases (line 7 in Wordsworth) and rhetorical repetition (line 11 in Wordsworth)

the effects of the last line of each poem.

- You might also comment on Wordsworth's use of sentence-structure (or syntax).
- Which was your favourite line in 'Composed Upon Westminster Bridge?' Why?
- How would you describe the tone and mood of this poem, compared with Blake's 'London'?

'Island Man', Grace Nichols

The first of the two twentieth-century poems in this unit, 'Island Man', appeared in Grace Nichols's 1984 volume, *The Fat Black Woman's Poems*.

Grace Nichols (born 1950) grew up in Guyana and came to Britain in 1977. She has written several children's books and volumes of poetry. Many of her poems cast a questioning eye on Britain from a Caribbean perspective.

This free verse poem presents the waking moments of a man who has settled in London having come from a Caribbean island.

Island Man

(for a Caribbean island man in London who still wakes up to the sound of the sea)

Morning
and island man wakes up
to the sound of blue surf
in his head
the steady breaking and wombing

wild seabirds
and fishermen pushing out to sea
the sun surfacing defiantly

from the east
of his small emerald island

he always comes back   groggily, groggily

Comes back to sands
of a grey metallic soar   to surge of wheels
to dull North Circular roar

muffling, muffling
his crumpled pillow waves
island man heaves himself

Another London day

Grace Nichols

- How does Grace Nichols capture the sense impressions of a Caribbean island through her choice of words and literary devices in the first three verses?
- At what moment in the poem do you think the island man begins to realise where he is?
- What is strange about the fourth verse ('Comes . . . roar')? How do you explain it?
- What impression of London does the poem create? How?
- Can you see any reasons for Grace Nichols starting the lines of poetry where she does?
- Why do you think there is no punctuation in the poem?

Translating the English, 1989, Carol Ann Duffy

This poem is from a volume entitled *The Other Country*, published in 1990.

Carol Ann Duffy was born in Glasgow in 1955, and grew up in Staffordshire. She has had several collections of poetry published since the mid-1980s.

In this comic poem a tour operator, with an imperfect command of English, 'sells' London, and England, to foreign tourists.

Translating the English, 1989

'. . . and much of the poetry, alas, is lost in translation . . .'

Welcome to my country! We have here Edwina Currie
and The Sun newspaper. Much excitement.
Also the weather has been most improving
even in February. Daffodils. (Wordsworth. Up North.) If you like
Shakespeare or even Opera we have too the Black Market.
For two hundred quids we are talking Les Miserables,
nods being as good as winks. Don't eat the eggs.

Wheel-clamp. Dogs. Vagrants. A tour of our wonderful
capital city is not to be missed. The Fergie,
The Princess Di and the football hooligan, truly you will
like it here, Squire. Also we can be talking crack, smack
and Carling Black Label if we are so inclined. Don't
drink the H_2O. All very proud we now have
a green Prime Minister. What colour yours? Binbags.
You will be knowing of Charles Dickens and Terry Wogan
and Scotland. All this can be arranged for cash no questions.
Ireland not on. Fish and chips and the Official Secrets Act
second to none. Here we go. We are liking
a smashing good time like estate agents and Neighbours,
also Brookside for we are allowed four Channels.
How many you have? Last night of Proms. Andrew
Lloyd-Webber. Jeffrey Archer. Plenty culture you will be agreeing.
Also history and buildings. The Houses of Lords. Docklands.
Many thrills and high interest rates for own good. Muggers.
Much lead in petrol. Filth. Rule Britannia and child abuse.
Electronic tagging, Boss, ten pints and plenty rape. Queen Mum.
Channel Tunnel. You get here fast no problem to my country
my country my country welcome welcome welcome.

Carol Ann Duffy

- What picture of London emerges in this poem?
- What do you think is the effect of writing the poem in un-idiomatic English? Choose some phrases to illustrate the effect.
- The poem mixes references to tourist attractions and people and things which foreigners identify with Britain, with unpleasant aspects of British life. What do you think is the effect of this?
- Two of the other writers in this unit are mentioned in the poem. What use is the poet making of them?
- What is the effect of the last line?

Little Dorrit and *Sketches by Boz* (extracts), Charles Dickens

The first of the prose writers whose impressions of London we shall look at is Charles Dickens. The extracts are taken from his novel *Little Dorrit*, published in 1857, and his series of short pieces about English life, entitled *Sketches by Boz*, published in 1839.

Charles Dickens (1812–70) is regarded as one of the greatest English novelists. Much of his writing is comic in style and tone, but beneath the high-spirited humour for which he is famous lies a genuine anger at the indifference of the civil authorities to the vice, poverty and misery which afflicted a large proportion of the population in early Victorian England, and London in particular.

The first extract is the opening paragraph of Chapter 3 of *Little Dorrit*. It is a little mood picture of the city.

It was a Sunday evening in London, gloomy, close and stale. Maddening church bells of all degrees of dissonance, sharp and flat, cracked and clear, fast and slow, made the brick-and-mortar echoes hideous. Melancholy streets in a penitential garb of soot, steeped the souls of the people who were condemned to look at them out of windows, in dire despondency. In every thoroughfare, up almost every alley and down almost every turning, some doleful bell was throbbing, jerking, tolling, as if the Plague were in the city and the dead-carts were going round. Everything was bolted and barred that could by possibility furnish relief to an overworked people. No pictures, no unfamiliar animals, no rare plants or flowers, no natural or artificial wonders of the ancient world – all *taboo* with that en-lightened strictness, that the ugly South Sea gods in the British Museum might have supposed themselves at home again. Nothing to see but streets, streets, streets. Nothing to breathe but streets, streets, streets. Nothing to change the brooding mind, or raise it up. Nothing for the spent toiler to do, but to compare the monotony of his seventh day with the monotony of his six days, think what a weary life he led, and make the best of it – or the worst, according to the probabilities.

Charles Dickens, *Little Dorrit*

- What impression of London is Dickens trying to convey?
- How does he use language to convey the impression? You might find and discuss as many examples as you can of emotive language, combined with onomatopoeia, alliteration, simile and rhetorical repetition.

The second extract is a section of the sketch entitled 'Gin Shops' from *Sketches by Boz*.

We will endeavour to sketch the bar of a large gin shop, and its ordinary customers, for the edification of such of our readers as may not have had opportunities of observing such scenes; and on the chance of finding one, well suited to our purpose, we will make for Drury Lane, through the narrow streets and dirty courts which divide it from Oxford Street, and that classical spot adjoining the brewery at the bottom of Tottenham Court Road, best known to the initiated as the 'Rookery'.

The filthy and miserable appearance of this part of London can hardly be imagined by those (and there are many such) who have not witnessed it. Wretched houses with broken windows patched with rags and paper: every room let out to a different family and in many instances to two or even three; fruit and 'sweet stuff' manufacturers in the cellars, barbers and red-herring vendors in the front parlours, and cobblers in the back; a bird-fancier in the first floor, three families on the second, starvation in the attics, Irishmen in the passage; a 'musician' in the front kitchen, and a charwoman and five hungry children in the back one – filth everywhere – a gutter before the houses and a drain behind them – clothes drying and slops emptying from the windows: girls of fourteen or fifteen with matted hair walking about barefooted, and in white greatcoats, almost their only covering; boys of all ages, in coats of all sizes and no coats at all; men and women, in every variety of scanty and dirty apparel, lounging, scolding, drinking, smoking, squabbling, fighting and swearing.

You turn the corner, what a change! All is light and brilliancy. The hum of many voices issues from that splendid gin shop which forms the commencement of the two streets opposite, and the gay building with the fantastically ornamented parapet, the illuminated clock, the plate-glass windows surrounded by stucco rosettes, and its profusion of gaslights in richly-gilt burners, is perfectly dazzling when contrasted with the darkness and dirt we have just left. The interior is even gayer than the exterior. A bar of French-polished mahogany, elegantly carved, extends the whole width of the place; and there are two side-aisles of great casks, painted green and gold, enclosed within a light brass rail, and bearing such inscriptions as 'Old Tom, 549'; 'Young Tom, 360'; 'Samson, 1421'. Beyond the bar is a lofty and spacious saloon, full of the same enticing vessels, with a gallery running round it, equally well furnished.

It is growing late, and the throng of men, women, and children, who have been constantly going in and out, dwindles down to two or three occasional stragglers – cold, wretched-looking creatures, in the last stage of emaciation and disease. The knot of Irish labourers at the lower end of the place, who have been alternately shaking hands with, and threatening the life of, each other for the last hour, become furious in their disputes, and finding it impossible to silence one man, who is particularly anxious to adjust the difference, they resort to the infallible expedient of knocking him down and jumping on him afterwards. The man in the fur cap, and the potboy rush out: a scene of riot and confusion ensues; half the Irishmen get shut out, and the other half get shut in, the potboy is knocked among the tubs in no time; the landlord hits everybody, and everybody hits the landlord, the barmaids scream, the police come in; and the rest is a confused mixture of arms, legs, staves, torn coats, shouting and struggling. Some of the party are borne off to the station-house, and

The Gin Shop

the remainder slink home to beat their wives for complaining, and kick the children for daring to be hungry.

We have sketched this subject very slightly, not only because our limits compel us to do so, but because, if it were pursued further, it would be painful and repulsive. Well-disposed gentlemen, and charitable ladies, would alike turn with coldness and disgust from a description of the drunken besotted men, and wretched broken-down miserable women, who form no inconsiderable portion of the frequenters of these haunts; forgetting, in the pleasant consciousness of their own high rectitude, the poverty of the one, and the temptation of the other. Gin-drinking is a great vice in England, but poverty is a greater; and until you can cure it, or persuade a half-famished wretch not to seek relief in the temporary oblivion of his own misery, with the pittance which, divided among his family, would just furnish a morsel of bread for each, gin shops will increase in number and splendour. If Temperance Societies could suggest an antidote against hunger and distress, or establish dispensaries for the gratuitous distribution of bottles of Lethe-water, gin palaces would be numbered among the things that were. Until then, their decrease may be despaired of.

Charles Dickens, Sketches by Boz

- In the opening three paragraphs, what is Dickens trying to tell us about the houses in which people live and the gin shops in which they drink? How does he capture the difference in his uses of language and sentence-structure?
- Is the second section (the last two paragraphs) meant to be funny or serious? Try to analyse the way it is written, to justify your answer.

Notes from a Small Island (extracts), Bill Bryson

Finally, we shall look at some impressions of contemporary London through the eyes of Bill Bryson, in Chapter 3 of his travel book, *Notes from a Small Island*.

Bill Bryson is a travel writer and journalist who was born in the USA in 1951, and lived for two decades in Britain. In 1995, he decided to move back to the States for a while, and before he left he went on a journey by pubic transport around his adopted country, which provided the material for his book.

In the extracts which follow, he charts some of the recent changes which have occurred in parts of London.

I came up now at Tower Hill and there wasn't a tower and there wasn't a hill. There isn't even any longer a Royal Mint (which I always preferred to imagine as a very large chocolate wrapped in green foil) as it has been moved somewhere else and replaced with a building with lots of smoked glass. Much of what once stood in this noisy corner of London has been swept away and replaced with big buildings with lots of smoked glass. It was only eight years since I'd last been here, but were it not for the fixed reference points of London Bridge and the Tower I'd scarcely have recognised the neighbourhood.

I walked along the painfully noisy street called The Highway, quietly agog at all the new development. It was like being in the midst of an ugly building competition. For the better part of a decade, architects had been arriving in the area and saying, 'You think *that*'s bad? Wait'll you see what *I* can do.' And there, towering proudly above all the clunky new offices, was the ugliest piece of bulk in London, the News International complex, looking like the central air-conditioning unit for the planet. When I last saw it, in 1986, it stood forlornly amid acres of empty warehouses and puddly wasteground. The Highway, as I recalled it, was a comparatively sedate throughway. Now heavy lorries pounded along it, making the pavements tremble and giving the air an unhealthy bluish tinge. The News International compound was still surrounded with sinister fencing and electronic gates, but there was a new maximum security reception centre that looked like something you'd expect to find at a plutonium depot at Sellafield.

. . .

At the old Times building on Gray's Inn Road, the canteen had been in a basement room that had the charm and ambience of a submarine and the food had been slopped out by humourless drones who always brought to mind moles in aprons, but this was bright and spacious, with a wide choice of tempting dishes served by chirpy cockney girls in bright, clean uniforms. The dining area itself was unchanged except for the view. Where formerly had sprawled a muddy swamp criss-crossed with neglected water channels full of bedsteads and shopping trolleys, there now stood row upon row of designer houses and jaunty blocks of flats of the kind you always find around redeveloped waterfronts in Britain, the sort of buildings where all the balconies and exterior trim are made from lengths of tubular metal painted red.

Bill Bryson, *Notes from a Small Island*

- What changes does Bryson regret, and what changes does he appreciate?
- How does he convey his feelings of displeasure and satisfaction through his use of language?

Coursework suggestions

- Write an article for a magazine, entitled 'London in Literature', using the poems and prose extracts studied as illustrations, and commenting on how the language and style convey the writers' feelings.
- Write about how each of the four poets conveys his or her feelings about London through language, tone and imagery.

- Write a detailed comparison between Blake's 'London' and Wordsworth's 'Composed Upon Westminster Bridge', showing how each writer uses language to express his feelings.

For further coursework suggestions see those in Unit 24, page 308. You may wish to study Unit 24 before attempting to answer these.

Punctuation and sentence-structure

Write out the following passage, correcting all the mistakes.

A Trip in the Country

We set off at ten thirty am. I had a nap for an hour, I awoke to the sound of twittering swallows. We were driving along country lanes lined with huge oak trees. Which were shedding their leaves onto the road. The cool, fresh, morning was exhilarating. On the left of us as we passed through a small village, cows were being herded for milking. With the farmer, a small well-built man following behind with a pipe in his mouth and a stick in his hand.

Spelling

Write the correct spellings of these words in your spelling book.

independant	developement	enviroment
absolutley	unconcious	theorys
exagerate	carefull	sucessfull
unecessery	imediatley	reciept
differant	beleif	fulfill

SYLLABUS REQUIREMENTS COVERED

Poetry analysis features prominently in the examinations of the London and NEAB boards.

The coursework suggestions relate to syllabuses as follows:

Suggestion 1: MEG Unit 3

Suggestion 2: MEG Unit 3

       WJEC Pre-1900

Suggestion 3: SEG Unit 4 or 5

       WJEC Pre-1900

NEWSPAPERS

Media analysis is a feature of the exam syllabuses and also fulfils the non-fiction writing coursework requirements of most syllabuses. This unit is concerned specifically with newspaper analysis.

As most people are at least vaguely aware, there is a world of difference between a newspaper like the *Sun* and a newspaper like *The Times*.

● How would you describe the difference?

There are, in fact, special terms for the general *types* of newspaper in Britain. Papers like the *Sun* are called **tabloids**. All that the term actually means is that they are comparatively small in size.

● What are the names of the other tabloid daily and Sunday newspapers?

The other category, covering newspapers like *The Times*, is **broadsheets**. They are so-called because they are larger and wider in size than the tabloids.

● What are the other broadsheets?

In fact, as you may already have decided, there are two broad categories of tabloids. The *Mail* and the *Express* are often referred to as 'middle-brow' papers, as distinct from the 'high-brow' broadsheets and the other tabloids (which are sometimes disparagingly referred to as the 'gutter press').

One of the main objectives of this unit will be to study the complete range of British national newspapers and to work out to what extent and in what ways they differ. You will be looking at the style, the presentation, the balance and the concerns of the different newspapers.

As a way of illustrating how different the approach of newspapers to an issue can be, and as a way of understanding *how* to analyse the language, style and bias in newspapers, we shall look at four articles dealing with the same news item.

The break-up of the hippie convoy

The articles which follow all deal with events which took place in June 1986, in Hampshire, England. A so-called 'hippie convoy', attempting to camp near Stonehenge at the time of the summer solstice, was forcefully broken up and dispersed by police.

The background to these events is described in the first article. This is a report which appeared in a weekly newspaper.

1/ Police 'victory' over hippies

For almost three weeks British newspapers and television screens have been full of reports, commentaries and even 'research' articles on a rather unusual subject – the struggle between a group of homeless and aimless people denoted in the press here by the vague term 'hippies', and the British authorities.

The reason for the confrontation was the intention by representatives of this group to hold their traditional song festival in the Stonehenge area, where there is a concentration of structures dating back to the Neolithic era.

The hippies have been organising such festivals every year since 1977. Last year, however, the attempts to organise it came up against a ban by the authorities. On arriving there the hippies were met by the police and bloody clashes ensued.

The same thing happened this year as well. Driven out of Stonehenge, the homeless people, many of them with small children, tried to set up camp on vacant land belonging to a local farmer.

A few days later, however, the Supreme Court issued an edict prohibiting them from staying there and the hippies, under pressure from the law and order forces, ended up on the road once again.

About a week ago they made yet another attempt to set up camp – this time on a disused airfield near the village of Stoney Cross in Hampshire. Nor on this occasion, however, did they manage to hold out for longer than a week.

At dawn on June 9 about 500 policemen arrived in special vehicles, surrounded the camp and once and for all broke up the hippies' refuge. Reporting the successful completion of 'Operation Dawn', as the police raid is bombastically named in official documents, the newspapers wrote that as result of it, 42 persons were arrested and the rest were 'dispersed' and 'sent home' – to homes which they simply do not have.

Of course, the government can ban and even break up song festivals set up by the hippies. But the root of the problem lies elsewhere.

The hippies are first and foremost homeless and deprived people who can find no place for themselves in contemporary British society, and the more unemployment grows and the other social problems intensify, as is happening at present, the more frequently will arise similar types of conflicts reflecting the overall sick state of contemporary Western society.

The second extract was written by a columnist in a Sunday newspaper.

2/NO HIPPY ENDING THEN

HOME SECRETARY Douglas Hurd describes the hippy 'peace convoy' as 'a band of medieval brigands'.

But in the Middle Ages brigands did not have half so cushy a time as these bums, beggars, vandals, and thieves, with whom grovelling TV personalities like Frank Bough and Desmond Morris, both of whom should know better, choose to sympathise.

Medieval brigands would swiftly have found themselves set upon by the vassals and hounds of baron landlords, or by royal servants or by local freemen. They would have found their lives to be not only nasty and brutish, but decidedly short.

What is more, they would not have been followed around by clerks from the exchequer dishing out substantial sums of cash each Thursday to enable them to carry on marauding through the countryside.

The hippies claim, with arrant humbug, to be living 'an alternative life style'. The claim would be marginally less fraudulent if they had found an alternative to the dole we so foolishly give them, and they so eagerly take.

The third extract was written by a columnist in a provincial newspaper.

3/

THE HIPPY saga has gone on since my comments last week, and part of the lovely New Forest has been spoiled by this scruffy bunch of layabouts. All at our expense, of course.

We continue to dole out state benefits to law-breakers (one newspaper even reported that the social security employs special staff to wander round the country servicing these vagabonds).

I wonder if the state is equally careful about ensuring that hippies are up to date with their taxes, road fund licences and MoT testing of their raggle-taggle vehicles?

TALKING about the hippies, television news one night showed a wild-eyed, tangle-haired harpie spit at a policeman seeing them off the New Forest site: 'Have you got a home to go to?' – followed by a companion bawling 'We haven't, we haven't a home'.

The policeman resisted the provocation. He did not reply. So I will reply for him.

'Yes, ducks, I do have a home which I pay for, care for, and look after. I keep it clean, pay my way, and don't offend my neighbours. I don't doss down on anybody else's land and I don't leave it looking like a tip. How about you?'

The fourth extract is another daily newspaper report.

4

SO WHERE DOES HE GO NOW?

Innocent on the road of rejection

HUNCHED against the wind in the security of a borrowed blanket, the child stumbled across the land that had briefly been his home.

The boy looked bewildered against the background of the three unmoved policemen.

Confusion

The man with him, a ragged symbol of the hippies, plunged his hands into the empty pockets of his tattered jeans and the stones on the ground bit into his feet. His bedding hung over his arm.

The child burrowed deeper into the blanket and stared back with innocent confusion at the towering, impassive policemen. Little emotion flickered from their eyes.

The only friendship, the only token of parting affection, the only hint of kindness to a child came from a free-running dog. An old Labrador sniffed the child amiably and licked gently.

The Child and The Man With Nowhere to Go looked at one another with despair. He plunged his hands even more deeply into his pockets – and the three of them set off together.

A confused child, a ragged, hope-crushed man and a friendly old dog.

All on the Road of Rejection.

We shall now look in detail at the four articles, with several objectives in mind:

To recognise the difference between fact and opinion.

To identify bias in the use of language.

To recognise how news can be slanted.

To develop skills in summarising articles.

You must have noticed, just by reading the articles, that the attitudes towards the 'hippies' and the police taken by the various writers are poles apart. We are now going to identify *how* the writers have presented their particular viewpoints.

First, though, it might be a good idea to do some work on distinguishing fact from opinion.

Fact and opinion

One of the distinguishing and perhaps disquieting features of newspaper journalism is the way that writers *slant* their stories to fit in with the social and political viewpoint of the newspaper in general. One of the ways they do this is to present opinions masquerading as facts. It is important to be able to recognise when this is happening.

● How would you define the difference between a fact and an opinion?
● Look at two statements describing a person called John:

John is 42 years old,

John is old.

Assuming that the information about John's age is correct, the first statement must be a fact. What about the second?

● Now look at these two statements. Are they fact or opinion?

The theatre is an old listed building, dating from the late seventeenth century, and is therefore safe from the threat of destruction from planners who want to build a fly-over through the area.

The ugly old theatre is an eyesore, and ought to be knocked down.

Perhaps the simplest way of distinguishing between fact and opinion would be to say that if a statement is incontestable and verifiable it is a fact; if it could be challenged or disagreed with it is an opinion.

Now let us look at the *first* of the 'hippies' articles and see how far it is factual.

In the opening sentence the so-called 'hippies' are described as 'homeless and aimless'.

● Is this a factual statement?

The article goes on to describe how they made various attempts to set up camp, and were moved on each time. It is reasonable to assume, therefore, that they do not have a settled home.

But what about 'aimless?'

Is it not possible that the aim of some of them is to live a life free from the ties of a settled home and job? If so, they cannot be 'aimless'. This part of the statement, therefore, although it is presented as if it is a fact, is actually an opinion.

The paragraphs which follow explain the events leading up to 'Operation Dawn'. The information is verifiable and therefore, as long as it isn't invented (which is another common aspect of journalism!), it is factual.

The word 'bombastically' in the paragraph, describing the police raid, is clearly an opinion.

The final paragraph is a comment on the implications of the events described in the rest of the article.

● Is any of this paragraph factual?

Discussion or writing exercise

● Re-read the third article. Work out how much of it is fact and how much is opinion.

Now we shall look at all the articles and consider how the journalists attempt to influence our views of a story by their uses of language and their selection of aspects of the story on which to focus.

Here is a checklist of typical features of journalistic language:

the use of puns, especially in headlines

the use of alliteration, especially in headlines

the use of 'loaded' words: expressions which convey a strong impression of support or condemnation

the use of emotive words: words conveying strong positive or negative emotion

the use of derisory slang

the use of 'tabloidese': words which are generally used only in tabloid newspapers, like 'blasts' (meaning 'strongly criticises'), 'axed' ('dismissed' or 'made redundant'), 'quit' ('resigned'), which have a tendency to exaggerate a situation in a negative way.

Bias in the 'hippie' articles

Now we shall look at each of the articles in turn, and dissect them. The best way of doing this might be to allow yourself time to think about the questions, perhaps underlining words and phrases on a copy of the article and jotting down notes, followed by class discussion, leading eventually, perhaps, to an extended written piece.

1 Police 'victory' over hippies

- What is the effect of putting 'victory' in inverted commas?
- What is the effect of specifying the places where the 'hippies' attempted to camp?
- Pick out phrases in the last paragraph which indicate where the writer's sympathies lie in the conflict.

2 No hippie ending then

- Does the pun in the title carry any hint of which side the writer is on?
- Pick out examples of 'loaded' words. Which words do you think are particularly biased?
- Look at the fourth paragraph. Is the writer showing bias here? How?

3 Untitled extract

- What is the effect of the use of slang in this piece?
- Discuss the other ways in which the writer shows his or her bias.

4 So where does he go now?

- What is the effect of the sub-heading?
- How would you describe the tone of this article: angry, compassionate, scornful, despairing, or what?
- Look at the descriptions of the man, the child and the policeman. How does the reporter show on which side his sympathies lie by his use of language?
- How does the use of rhetorical repetition in the fifth paragraph (about the dog) add to the effect the writer is attempting to create?
- How do sentence and paragraph structure add to the overall effect in the last two paragraphs?
- Articles 3 and 4 both make use of an incident between an individual policeman and some 'hippies'. Compare the uses they make of the incident they describe.

One of the exercises which you may be required to complete in the exam is summary writing. Before leaving the 'hippie convoy', we shall use it to study and practise this skill.

Summary work

Summary writing involves rewriting a passage in abbreviated form to meet a specific word limit. It may also involve focusing on a particular theme or aspect of the passage and summarising only those sections which relate to that theme.

Probably the best way to tackle a summary is to read through the passage, underlining what you consider to be the *key points*, and keeping the word limit in mind. You can then write a first draft of your summary, explaining the basic points as concisely as you possibly can, and then reduce your summary further, if necessary, in a second draft.

As an illustration, here is an answer to a summary question on the first of the four 'hippie convoy' articles.

The question

Summarise the factual information about the incidents at Stoney Cross, in the article 'Police "victory" over hippies', in no more than 50 words.

A possible answer

A group of homeless hippies set up camp at a disused airfield at Stoney Cross, Hampshire, in early June. A dawn raid on June 9, by about 500 police, resulted in about 42 arrests and the breaking up of the camp and the dispersal of the remainder of the hippies. (50 words)

● Now try answering this question:

Summarise the complaints against the hippies in article 3, in no more than 35 words, using standard English.

Coursework suggestion

● Write a comparative analysis of the presentation of a news issue in four different newspapers.

Comparison of newspapers

To get a sense of the range and diversity of the British press, it is necessary to make a comparative study of the nation's daily or Sunday newspapers.

The best way to do this is probably to attempt to bring in copies of all the newspapers published on a single day.

Working in pairs or groups of three, choose a newspaper to work on so that all the different newspapers are covered. Attempt the following tasks. It might be a good idea to make notes and write down quotations from the other newspapers as well as your own, in preparation for a possible coursework assignment.

- Each pair or group reads out the front page headline. Discuss what the headlines reveal about the priorities of the different newspapers.
- Hold up the front page of your newspaper. Work out the proportion of the entire page taken up with each of the following:

the main item

the headline

the photograph

the main story itself.

- Compare the papers in this respect and discuss the significance of the differences you have noticed between the papers.
- Working through your paper, mark all the items H, G or S, according to whether they deal with any of the following:

'hard news': stories dealing with serious national or international news ('H')

gossip stories about celebrities or popular media personalities ('G')

sport ('S').

- Work out the percentage of the paper devoted to each. Discuss the significance of your findings with reference to each of the papers.
- Choose a 'broadsheet' front page story. Try to find the same story in the paper you are working on. Compare the paper's treatment of the story in terms of its position in the paper and the amount of space devoted to it. Discuss the significance of the different papers in this respect.
- Using either the same news item, or another one of your choice, make brief notes, with illustrative examples, on the following:

length and difficulty of words

length of sentences

length of paragraphs

style and tone of the article.

Compare the papers in terms of these features, and discuss what your findings show about the papers and the market at which they are aimed.

- Find an editorial in your paper. Study it and try to draw conclusions about the following:

the use of biased language

the use of slang and/or 'tabloidese'

the depth of analysis

the political line taken by the paper.

   Highlight examples of each.
- Compare the papers in terms of the editorials, reading out examples to illustrate the points you are making.

- Discuss your overall conclusions about the differences between Britain's national newspapers.

Coursework suggestions

- Write a report on the differences between British national newspapers, giving illustrations of the points you make.
- Write a newspaper story of your own, imitating the style of the newspaper of your choice.
- Design and write a front page in the style of a named tabloid newspaper.

Punctuation and sentence-structure

One of the activities that takes place before a newspaper goes on sale is proof reading. People are employed to check the accuracy of the English in the articles chosen for publication, although this does not always seem to be done with football programmes. You have the job of proof reading the manager's notes for a programme of a Division One football club. The extract that follows is taken, unaltered, from an actual football programme. On a copy, correct all the inaccuracies in the use of commas and full stops.

From The Boss

Good afternoon ladies and gentlemen and welcome to today's very important game against Black Country rivals Wolverhampton Wanderers.

My notes for the Reading game dwelt on the unexplainable result against Colchester, fortunately our performances since then haven't been influenced by that experience. Tuesday's victory over Reading was particularly pleasing, it was our first game at the Hawthorns since we entertained Colchester and it is a tribute to the players that they took the game by the scruff of the neck and converted the pressure into an early goal. We could have scored five or six, but in the end it was a bit of a nail biter as Reading came back at us, however the lads showed excellent discipline and obviously everyone was very pleased for Andy Hunt who scored a superb hat-trick.

Albion News, 15 September 1996

SYLLABUS REQUIREMENTS COVERED

Media analysis features in the examinations of all the boards. The various activities covered in this unit relate to the different boards' examination requirements as follows:

Identifying fact and opinion: MEG, NEAB

Summarising: MEG, SEG, WJEC

Evaluating information and argument: London, MEG, WJEC

Commenting on methods of persuasion: MEG, NEAB, SEG, WJEC

Identifying bias: London, MEG

Layout and presentation of articles: London, MEG, WJEC

Writing a newspaper article: NEAB

The coursework suggestions relate to the coursework units of the syllabuses as follows:

MEG Non-fiction

NEAB Media

SEG Personal writing – non-fiction

WJEC Best writing (coursework suggestions 2 and 3)

PRE-TWENTIETH CENTURY FICTION: THOMAS HARDY'S 'ON THE WESTERN CIRCUIT'

A written piece relating to a complete work of literature published before 1900 is a coursework requirement of all the syllabuses except NEAB Post-16. The main text chosen is a short story called 'On the Western Circuit' by Thomas Hardy.

Thomas Hardy was born in a village near Dorchester, Dorset, in 1840. He trained as an architect and pursued this profession until 1874, when his novel *Far From the Madding Crowd* achieved such success that he was able to devote himself to writing. He lived almost all his life in Dorset, where most of his many novels and short stories are set. Hardy revived the ancient name of Wessex as a fictional name for Dorset, and created his own names for the towns and villages of the county where his stories are set.

Hardy gave up writing fiction in 1895, after his novel *Jude the Obscure* was condemned in reviews as an immoral attack on the institution of marriage. He devoted the rest of his life to writing poetry. He died in 1928.

Most of Hardy's fiction presents a rather bleak view of human life, focusing on the ironies and sufferings of life and love. 'On the Western Circuit' was, in fact, published in a collection of stories called *Life's Little Ironies*, in 1894. The story centres on Salisbury which is given the fictional name of Melchester.

As the story is divided into six sections, it might be a good idea to discuss each section before moving on. The questions, designed to guide the discussion, which appear at the end of the story, are divided into the same six sections as the story, with this in mind. Alternatively, of course, you can read the whole story through, and then discuss it.

On the Western Circuit

I

THE man who played the disturbing part in the two quiet feminine lives hereunder depicted – no great man, in any sense, by the way – first had knowledge of them on an October evening, in the city of Melchester. He had been standing in the Close, vainly endeavouring to gain amid the darkness a glimpse of the most homogeneous pile of mediæval architecture in England,[1] which towered and tapered from the damp and level sward in front of him. While he stood the presence of the Cathedral walls was revealed rather by the ear than by the eyes; he could not see them, but they reflected sharply a roar of sound which entered the Close by a street leading from the city square, and, falling upon the building, was flung back upon him.

He postponed till the morrow his attempt to examine the deserted edifice, and turned his attention to the noise. It was compounded of steam barrel-organs, the clanging of gongs, the ringing of hand-bells, the clack of rattles, and the undistinguishable shouts of men. A lurid light hung in the air in the direction of the tumult. Thitherward he went, passing under the arched gateway, along a straight street, and into the square.

He might have searched Europe over for a greater contrast between juxtaposed scenes. The spectacle was that of the eighth chasm of the Inferno[2] as to colour and flame, and, as to mirth, a development of the Homeric heaven. A smoky glare, of the complexion of brass-filings, ascended from the fiery tongues of innumerable naptha lamps affixed to booths, stalls, and other temporary erections which crowded the spacious market-square. In front of this irradiation scores of human figures, more or less in profile, were darting athwart and across, up, down, and around, like gnats against a sunset.

Their motions were so rhythmical that they seemed to be moved by machinery. And it presently appeared that they were moved by machinery indeed; the figures being those of the patrons of swings, see-saws, flying-leaps, above all of the three steam roundabouts which occupied the

---

[1] Salisbury Cathedral, which is, unusually, almost completely in the style (Early English Gothic) of one period.
[2] Dante's account of Hell in his *Divine Comedy*.

centre of the position. It was from the latter that the din of steam-organs came.

Throbbing humanity in full light was, on second thoughts, better than architecture in the dark. The young man, lighting a short pipe, and putting his hat on one side and one hand in his pocket, to throw himself into harmony with his new environment, drew near to the largest and most patronized of the steam circuses, as the roundabouts were called by their owners. This was one of brilliant finish, and it was now in full revolution. The musical instrument around which and to whose tones the riders revolved, directed its trumpet-mouths of brass upon the young man, and the long plate-glass mirrors set at angles, which revolved with the machine, flashed the gyrating personages and hobby-horses kaleidoscopically into his eyes.

It could now be seen that he was unlike the majority of the crowd. A gentlemanly young fellow, one of the species found in large towns only, and London particularly, built on delicate lines, well, though not fashionably dressed, he appeared to belong to the professional class; he had nothing square or practical about his look, much that was curvilinear and sensuous. Indeed, some would have called him a man not altogether typical of the middle-class male of a century wherein sordid ambition is the master-passion that seems to be taking the time-honoured place of love.

The revolving figures passed before his eyes with an unexpected and quiet grace in a throng whose natural movements did not suggest gracefulness or quietude as a rule. By some contrivance there was imparted to each of the hobby-horses a motion which was really the triumph and perfection of roundabout inventiveness – a galloping rise and fall, so timed that, of each pair of steeds, one was on the spring while the other was on the pitch. The riders were quite fascinated by these equine undulations in this most delightful holiday-game of our times. There were riders as young as six, and as old as sixty years, with every age between. At first it was difficult to catch a personality, but by and by the observer's eyes centred on the prettiest girl out of the several pretty ones revolving.

It was not that one with the light frock and light hat whom he had been at first attracted by; no, it was the one with the black cape, grey skirt, light gloves and – no, not even she, but the one behind her; she with the crimson skirt, dark jacket, brown hat and brown gloves. Unmistakably that was the prettiest girl.

Having finally selected her, this idle spectator studied her as well as he was able during each of her brief transits across his visual field. She was absolutely unconscious of everything save the act of riding: her features were rapt in an ecstatic dreaminess; for the moment she did not know her age or her history or her lineaments, much less her troubles. He himself was full of vague latter-day glooms and popular melancholies, and it was a refreshing sensation to behold this young thing then and there, absolutely as happy as if she were in a Paradise.

Dreading the moment when the inexorable stoker, grimily lurking behind the glittering rococo-work,[3] should decide that this set of riders had had their pennyworth, and bring the whole concern of steam-engine, horses, mirrors, trumpets, drums, cymbals, and such-like to pause and silence, he waited for her every reappearance, glancing indifferently over the intervening forms, including the two plainer girls, the old woman and child, the two youngsters, the newly-married couple, the old man with a clay pipe, the sparkish youth with a ring, the young ladies in the chariot, the pair of journeyman-carpenters, and others, till his select country beauty followed on again in her place. He had never seen a fairer product of nature, and at each round she made a deeper mark in his sentiments. The stoppage then came, and the sighs of the riders were audible.

He moved round to the place at which he reckoned she would alight; but she retained her seat. The empty saddles began to refill, and she plainly was deciding to have another turn. The young man drew up to the side of her steed, and pleasantly asked her if she had enjoyed her ride.

'O yes!' she said, with dancing eyes. 'It has been quite unlike anything I have ever felt in my life before!'

It was not difficult to fall into conversation with her. Unreserved – too unreserved – by nature, she was not experienced enough to be reserved by art, and after a little coaxing she answered his remarks readily. She had come to live in Melchester from a village on the Great Plain, and this was the first time that she had ever seen a steam-circus; she could not understand how such wonderful machines were made. She had come to the city on the invitation of Mrs. Harnham, who had taken her into her household to train her as a servant, if she showed any aptitude. Mrs. Harnham was a young lady who before she married had been Miss Edith White, living in the country near the speaker's cottage; she was now very kind to her through knowing her in childhood so well. She was even taking the trouble to educate her. Mrs. Harnham was the only friend she had in the world, and being without children had wished to have her near her in preference to anybody else, though she had only lately come; allowed her to do almost as she liked, and to have a holiday whenever she asked for it. The husband of this kind young lady was a rich wine-merchant of the town, but Mrs. Harnham did not care much about him. In the daytime you could see the house from where they were talking. She, the speaker, liked Melchester better than the lonely country, and she was going to have a new hat for next Sunday that was to cost fifteen and ninepence.

[3] Exuberant decoration.

Then she inquired of her acquaintance where he lived, and he told her in London, that ancient and smoky city, where everybody lived who lived at all, and died because they could not live there. He came into Wessex two or three times a year for professional reasons; he had arrived from Wintoncester yesterday, and was going on into the next county in a day or two. For one thing he did like the country better than the town, and it was because it contained such girls as herself.

Then the pleasure-machine started again, and, to the light-hearted girl, the figure of the handsome young man, the market-square with its lights and crowd, the houses beyond, and the world at large, began moving round as before, countermoving in the revolving mirrors on her right hand, she being as it were the fixed point in an undulating, dazzling, lurid universe, in which loomed forward most prominently of all the form of her late interlocutor. Each time that she approached the half of her orbit that lay nearest him they gazed at each other with smiles, and with that unmistakable expression which means so little at the moment, yet so often leads up to passion, heart-ache, union, disunion, devotion, over-population, drudgery, content, resignation, despair.

When the horses slowed anew he stepped to her side and proposed another heat. 'Hang the expense for once,' he said. 'I'll pay!'

She laughed till the tears came.

'Why do you laugh, dear?' said he.

'Because – you are so genteel that you must have plenty of money, and only say that for fun!' she returned.

'Ha-ha!' laughed the young man in unison, and gallantly producing his money she was enabled to whirl on again.

As he stood smiling there in the motley crowd, with his pipe in his hand, and clad in the rough pea-jacket and wideawake that he had put on for his stroll, who would have supposed him to be Charles Bradford Raye, Esquire, stuff-gownsman, educated at Wintoncester, called to the Bar at Lincoln's-Inn, now going the Western Circuit, merely detained in Melchester by a small arbitration after his brethren had moved on to the next county-town?

II

THE square was overlooked from its remoter corner by the house of which the young girl had spoken, a dignified residence of considerable size, having several windows on each floor. Inside one of these, on the first floor, the apartment being a large drawing-room, sat a lady, in appearance from twenty-eight to thirty years of age. The blinds were still undrawn, and the lady was absently surveying the weird scene without, her cheek resting on her hand. The room was unlit from within, but enough of the glare from the market-place entered it to reveal the lady's face. She was what is called an interesting creature rather than a handsome woman; dark-eyed, thoughtful, and with sensitive lips.

A man sauntered into the room from behind and came forward.

'O, Edith, I didn't see you,' he said. 'Why are you sitting here in the dark?'

'I am looking at the fair,' replied the lady in a languid voice.

'Oh? Horrid nuisance every year! I wish it could be put a stop to.'

'I like it.'

'H'm. There's no accounting for taste.'

For a moment he gazed from the window with her, for politeness sake, and then went out again.

In a few minutes she rang.

'Hasn't Anna come in?' asked Mrs. Harnham.

'No m'm.'

'She ought to be in by this time. I meant her to go for ten minutes only.'

'Shall I go and look for her, m'm?' said the housemaid alertly.

'No. It is not necessary: she is a good girl and will come soon.'

However, when the servant had gone Mrs. Harnham arose, went up to her room, cloaked and bonneted herself, and proceeded downstairs, where she found her husband.

'I want to see the fair,' she said; 'and I am going to look for Anna. I have made myself responsible for her, and must see she comes to no harm. She ought to be indoors. Will you come with me?'

'Oh, she's all right. I saw her on one of those whirligig things, talking to her young man as I came in. But I'll go if you wish, though I'd rather go a hundred miles the other way.'

'Then please do so. I shall come to no harm alone.'

She left the house and entered the crowd which thronged the market-place, where she soon discovered Anna, seated on the revolving horse. As soon as it stopped Mrs. Harnham advanced and said severely, 'Anna, how can you be such a wild girl? You were only to be out for ten minutes.'

Anna looked blank, and the young man, who had dropped into the background, came to help her alight.

'Please don't blame her,' he said politely. 'It is my fault that she has stayed. She looked so graceful on the horse that I induced her to go round again. I assure you that she has been quite safe.'

'In that case I'll leave her in your hands,' said Mrs. Harnham, turning to retrace her steps.

But this for the moment it was not so easy to do. Something had attracted the crowd to a spot in their rear, and the wine-merchant's wife, caught by its sway, found herself pressed against Anna's acquaintance without power to move away. Their faces were within a few inches of each other, his breath fanned her cheek as well as Anna's. They could do no other than smile at the accident; but neither spoke, and each waited passively. Mrs. Harnham then felt a man's hand clasping her fingers, and from the look of consciousness on the young fellow's face she knew the hand to be his: she also knew that from the position of the girl he had no other thought than that the imprisoned hand was Anna's. What prompted her to refrain from undeceiving him she could hardly tell. Not content with holding the hand, he playfully slipped two of his fingers inside her glove, against her palm. Thus matters continued till the pressure lessened; but several minutes passed before the crowd thinned sufficiently to allow Mrs. Harnham to withdraw.

'How did they get to know each other, I wonder?' she mused as she retreated. 'Anna is really very forward – and he very wicked and nice.'

She was so gently stirred with the stranger's manner and voice, with the tenderness of his idle touch, that instead of re-entering the house she turned back again and observed the pair from a screened nook. Really she argued (being little less impulsive than Anna herself) it was very excusable in Anna to encourage him, however she might have contrived to make his acquaintance; he was so gentlemanly, so fascinating, had such beautiful eyes. The thought that he was several years her junior produced a reasonless sigh.

At length the couple turned from the roundabout towards the door of Mrs. Harnham's house, and the young man could be heard saying that he would accompany her home. Anna, then, had found a lover, apparently a very devoted one. Mrs. Harnham was quite interested in him. When they drew near the door of the wine-merchant's house, a comparatively deserted spot by this time, they stood invisible for a little while in the shadow of a wall, where they separated, Anna going on to the entrance, and her acquaintance returning across the square.

'Anna,' said Mrs. Harnham, coming up. 'I've been looking at you! That young man kissed you at parting, I am almost sure.'

'Well,' stammered Anna; 'he said, if I didn't mind – it would do me no harm, and, and, him a great deal of good!'

'Ah, I thought so! And he was a stranger till tonight?'

'Yes ma'am.'

'Yet I warrant you told him your name and everything about yourself?'

'He asked me.'

'But he didn't tell you his?'

'Yes ma'am, he did!' cried Anna victoriously. 'It is Charles Bradford, of London.'

'Well, if he's respectable, of course I've nothing to say against your knowing him,' remarked her mistress, prepossessed, in spite of general principles, in the young man's favour. 'But I must reconsider all that, if he attempts to renew your acquaintance. A country-bred girl like you, who has never lived in Melchester till this month, who had hardly ever seen a black-coated man till you came here, to be so sharp as to capture a young Londoner like him!'

'I didn't capture him. I didn't do anything,' said Anna, in confusion.

When she was indoors and alone Mrs. Harnham thought what a well-bred and chivalrous young man Anna's companion had seemed. There had been a magic in his wooing touch of her hand; and she wondered how he had come to be attracted by the girl.

The next morning the emotional Edith Harnham went to the usual week-day service in Melchester cathedral. In crossing the Close through the fog she again perceived him who had interested her the previous evening, gazing up thoughtfully at the high-piled architecture of the nave: and as soon as she had taken her seat he entered and sat down in a stall opposite hers.

He did not particularly heed her; but Mrs. Harnham was continually occupying her eyes with him, and wondered more than ever what had attracted him in her unfledged maid-servant. The mistress was almost as unaccustomed as the maiden herself to the end-of-the-age young man, or she might have wondered less. Raye, having looked about him awhile, left abruptly, without regard to the service that was proceeding; and Mrs. Harnham – lonely, impressionable creature that she was – took no further interest in praising the Lord. She wished she had married a London man who knew the subtleties of love-making as they were evidently known to him who had mistakenly caressed her hand.

III

THE calendar at Melchester had been light, occupying the court only a few hours; and the assizes at Casterbridge, the next county-town on the Western Circuit, having no business for Raye, he had not gone thither. At the next town after that they did not open till the following Monday, trials to begin on Tuesday morning. In the natural order of things Raye would have arrived at the latter place on Monday afternoon; but it was not till the middle of Wednesday that his gown and grey wig, curled in tiers, in the best fashion of Assyrian bas-reliefs, were seen blowing and bobbing behind him as he hastily walked up the High Street from his lodgings. But though he entered the assize building there was nothing for him to do, and sitting at the blue baize table in the well of the court, he mended pens with a mind far away from the case in progress. Thoughts of unpremeditated conduct, of which a week earlier he would not have believed himself capable, threw him into a mood of dissatisfied depression.

He had contrived to see again the pretty rural maiden Anna, the day after the fair, had walked out of the city with her to the earthworks of Old Melchester,[1] and feeling a violent fancy for her, had remained in Melchester all Sunday, Monday, and Tuesday; by persuasion obtaining walks and meetings with the girl six or seven times during the interval; had in brief won her, body and soul.

He supposed it must have been owing to the seclusion in which he had lived of late in town that he had given way so unrestrainedly to a passion for an artless creature whose inexperience had, from the first, led her to place herself unreservedly in his hands. Much he deplored trifling with her feelings for the sake of a passing desire; and he could only hope that she might not live to suffer on his account.

She had begged him to come to her again; entreated him; wept. He had promised that he would do so, and he meant to carry out that promise. He could not desert her now. Awkward as such unintentional connections were, the interspace of a hundred miles – which to a girl of her limited capabilities was like a thousand – would effectually hinder this summer fancy from greatly encumbering his life; while thought of her simple love might do him the negative good of keeping him from idle pleasures in town when he wished to work hard. His circuit journeys would take him to Melchester three or four times a year; and then he could always see her.

The pseudonym, or rather partial name, that he had given her as his before knowing how far the acquaintance was going to carry him, had been spoken on the spur of the moment, without any ulterior intention whatever. He had not afterwards disturbed Anna's error, but on leaving her he had felt bound to give her an address at a stationer's not far from his chambers, at which she might write to him under the initials of 'C. B.'

In due time Raye returned to his London abode, having called at Melchester on his way and spent a few additional hours with his fascinating child of nature. In town he lived monotonously every day. Often he and his rooms were enclosed by a tawny fog from all the world besides, and when he lighted the gas to read or write by, his situation seemed so unnatural that he would look into the fire and think of that trusting girl at Melchester again and again. Often, oppressed by absurd fondness for her, he would enter the dim religious nave of the Law Courts by the north door, elbow other juniors[2] habited like himself, and like him un-retained;[3] edge himself into this or that crowded court where a sen-

---

[1] Old Sarum, on a low hill a mile and a half north of Salisbury, the deserted site of a British fort and later of a Saxon and then Norman town.

[2] Young 'apprentice' barristers.

[3] Not yet engaged to appear in a case.

sational case was going on, just as if he were in it, though the police officers at the door knew as well as he knew himself that he had no more concern with the business in hand than the patient idlers at the gallery-door outside, who had waited to enter since eight in the morning because, like him, they belonged to the classes that live on expectation. But he would do these things to no purpose, and think how greatly the characters in such scenes contrasted with the pink and breezy Anna.

An unexpected feature in that peasant maiden's conduct was that she had not as yet written to him, though he had told her she might do so if she wished. Surely a young creature had never before been so reticent in such circumstances. At length he sent her a brief line, positively requesting her to write. There was no answer by the return post, but the day after a letter in a neat feminine hand, and bearing the Melchester postmark, was handed to him by the stationer.

The fact alone of its arrival was sufficient to satisfy his imaginative sentiment. He was not anxious to open the epistle, and in truth did not begin to read it for nearly half-an-hour, anticipating readily its terms of passionate retrospect and tender adjuration. When at last he turned his feet to the fireplace and unfolded the sheet, he was surprised and pleased to find that neither extravagance nor vulgarity was there. It was the most charming little missive he had ever received from a woman. To be sure the language was simple and the ideas were slight; but it was so self-possessed; so purely that of a young girl who felt her womanhood to be enough for her dignity that he read it through twice. Four sides were filled, and a few lines written across, after the fashion of former days; the paper, too, was common, and not of the latest shade and surface. But what of those things? He had received letters from women who were fairly called ladies, but never so sensible, so human a letter as this. He could not single out any one sentence and say it was at all remarkable or clever; the *ensemble* of the letter[4] it was which won him; and beyond the one request that he would write or come to her again soon there was nothing to show her sense of a claim upon him.

To write again and develop a correspondence was the last thing Raye would have preconceived as his conduct in such a situation; yet he did send a short, encouraging line or two, signed with his pseudonym, in which he asked for another letter, and cheeringly promised that he would try to see her again on some near day, and would never forget how much they had been to each other during their short acquaintance.

---

[4] The letter as a whole, its total effect.

IV

To return now to the moment at which Anna, at Melchester, had received Raye's letter.

It had been put into her own hand by the postman on his morning rounds. She flushed down to her neck on receipt of it, and turned it over and over. 'It is mine?' she said.

'Why, yes, can't you see it is?' said the postman, smiling as he guessed the nature of the document and the cause of the confusion.

'O yes, of course!' replied Anna, looking at the letter, forcedly tittering, and blushing still more.

Her look of embarrassment did not leave her with the postman's departure. She opened the envelope, kissed its contents, put away the letter in her pocket, and remained musing till her eyes filled with tears.

A few minutes later she carried up a cup of tea to Mrs. Harnham in her bed-chamber. Anna's mistress looked at her, and said: 'How dismal you seem this morning, Anna. What's the matter?'

'I'm not dismal, I'm glad; only I——' She stopped to stifle a sob.

'Well?'

'I've got a letter – and what good is it to me, if I can't read a word in it!'

'Why, I'll read it, child, if necessary.'

'But this is from somebody – I don't want anybody to read it but myself!' Anna murmured.

'I shall not tell anybody. Is it from that young man?'

'I think so.' Anna slowly produced the letter, saying: 'Then will you read it to me, ma'am?'

This was the secret of Anna's embarrassment and flutterings. She could neither read nor write. She had grown up under the care of an aunt by marriage, at one of the lonely hamlets on the Great Mid-Wessex Plain where, even in days of national education, there had been no school within a distance of two miles. Her aunt was an ignorant woman; there had been nobody to investigate Anna's circumstances, nobody to care about her learning the rudiments; though, as often in such cases, she had been well fed and clothed and not unkindly treated. Since she had come to live at Melchester with Mrs. Harnham, the latter, who took a kindly interest in the girl, had taught her to speak correctly, in which accomplishment Anna showed considerable readiness, as is not unusual with the illiterate; and soon became quite fluent in the use of her mistress's phraseology. Mrs. Harnham also insisted upon her getting a spelling and copy book, and beginning to practise in these. Anna was slower in this branch of her education, and meanwhile here was the letter.

Edith Harnham's large dark eyes expressed some interest in the contents, though, in her character of mere interpreter, she threw into her tone as much as she could of mechanical passiveness. She read the short epistle on to its concluding sentence, which idly requested Anna to send him a tender answer.

'Now – you'll do it for me, won't you, dear mistress?' said Anna eagerly. 'and you'll do it as well as ever you can, please? Because I couldn't bear him to think I am not able to do it myself. I should sink into the earth with shame if he knew that!'

From some words in the letter Mrs. Harnham was led to ask questions, and the answers she received confirmed her suspicions. Deep concern filled Edith's heart at perceiving how the girl had committed her happiness to the issue of this new-sprung attachment. She blamed herself for not interfering in a flirtation which had resulted so seriously for the poor little creature in her charge; though at the time of seeing the pair together she had a feeling that it was hardly within her province to nip young affection in the bud. However, what was done could not be undone, and it behoved her now, as Anna's only protector, to help her as much as she could. To Anna's eager request that she, Mrs. Harnham, should compose and write the answer to this young London man's letter, she felt bound to accede, to keep alive his attachment to the girl if possible; though in other circumstances she might have suggested the cook as an amanuensis.

A tender reply was thereupon concocted, and set down in Edith Harnham's hand. This letter it had been which Raye had received and delighted in. Written in the presence of Anna it certainly was, and on Anna's humble note-paper, and in a measure indited by the young girl; but the life, the spirit, the individuality, were Edith Harnham's.

'Won't you at least put your name yourself?' she said. 'You can manage to write that by this time?'

'No, no,' said Anna, shrinking back. 'I should do it so bad. He'd be ashamed of me, and never see me again!'

The note, so prettily requesting another from him, had, as we have seen, power enough in its pages to bring one. He declared it to be such a pleasure to hear from her that she must write every week. The same process of manufacture was accordingly repeated by Anna and her mistress, and continued for several weeks in succession; each letter being penned and suggested by Edith, the girl standing by; the answer read and commented on by Edith, Anna standing by and listening again.

Late on a winter evening, after the dispatch of the sixth letter, Mrs. Harnham was sitting alone by the remains of her fire. Her husband had retired to bed, and she had fallen into that fixity of musing which takes no count of hour or temperature. The state of mind had been brought about in Edith by a strange thing which she had done that day. For the first time since Raye's visit Anna had gone to stay over a night or two with her cottage friends on the Plain, and in her absence had arrived, out of its time, a letter from Raye. To this Edith had replied on her own responsibility, from the depths of her own heart, without waiting for her maid's collaboration. The luxury of writing to him what would be known to no consciousness but his was great, and she had indulged herself therein.

Why was it a luxury?

Edith Harnham led a lonely life. Influenced by the belief of the British parent that a bad marriage with its aversions is better than free womanhood with its interests, dignity, and leisure, she had consented to marry the elderly wine-merchant as a *pis aller*,[1] at the age of seven-and-twenty – some three years before this date – to find afterwards that she had made a mistake. That contract had left her still a woman whose deeper nature had never been stirred.

She was now clearly realizing that she had become possessed to the bottom of her soul with the image of a man to whom she was hardly so much as a name. From the first he had attracted her by his looks and voice; by his tender touch; and, with these as generators, the writing of letter after letter and the reading of their soft answers had insensibly developed on her side an emotion which fanned his; till there had resulted a magnetic reciprocity between the correspondents, notwithstanding that one of them wrote in a character not her own. That he had been able to seduce another woman in two days was his crowning though unrecognized fascination for her as the she-animal.

They were her own impassioned and pent-up ideas – lowered to monosyllabic phraseology in order to keep up the disguise – that Edith put into letters signed with another name, much to the shallow Anna's delight, who, unassisted, could not for the world have conceived such pretty fancies for winning him, even had she been able to write them. Edith found that it was these, her own foisted-in sentiments, to which the young barrister mainly responded. The few sentences occasionally added from Anna's own lips made apparently no impression upon him.

The letter-writing in her absence Anna never discovered; but on her return the next morning she declared she wished to see her lover about something at once, and begged Mrs. Harnham to ask him to come.

There was a strange anxiety in her manner which did not escape Mrs. Harnham, and ultimately resolved itself into a flood of tears. Sinking down at Edith's knees, she made confession that the result of her relations with her lover it would soon become necessary to disclose.

Edith Harnham was generous enough to be very far from inclined to cast Anna adrift at this conjuncture. No true woman ever is so inclined

---

[1] A last resource – when nothing better can be done or found.

from her own personal point of view, however prompt she may be in taking such steps to safeguard those dear to her. Although she had written to Raye so short a time previously, she instantly penned another Anna-note hinting clearly though delicately the state of affairs.

Raye replied by a hasty line to say how much he was concerned at her news: he felt that he must run down to see her almost immediately.

But a week later the girl came to her mistress's room with another note, which on being read informed her that after all he could not find time for the journey. Anna was broken with grief; but by Mrs. Harnham's counsel strictly refrained from hurling at him the reproaches and bitterness customary from young women so situated. One thing was imperative: to keep the young man's romantic interest in her alive. Rather therefore did Edith, in the name of her *protégée*,[2] request him on no account to be distressed about the looming event, and not to inconvenience himself to hasten down. She desired above everything to be no weight upon him in his career, no clog upon his high activities. She had wished him to know what had befallen: he was to dismiss it again from his mind. Only he must write tenderly as ever, and when he should come again on the spring circuit it would be soon enough to discuss what had better be done.

It may well be supposed that Anna's own feelings had not been quite in accord with these generous expressions; but the mistress's judgment had ruled, and Anna had acquiesced. 'All I want is that *niceness* you can so well put into your letters, my dear, dear mistress, and that I can't for the life o' me make up out of my own head; though I mean the same thing and feel it exactly when you've written it down!'

When the letter had been sent off, and Edith Harnham was left alone, she bowed herself on the back of her chair and wept.

'I wish his child was mine – I wish it was!' she murmured. 'Yet how can I say such a wicked thing!'

V

THE letter moved Raye considerably when it reached him. The intelligence itself had affected him less than her unexpected manner of treating him in relation to it. The absence of any word of reproach, the devotion to his interests, the self-sacrifice apparent in every line, all made up a nobility of character that he had never dreamt of finding in womankind.

'God forgive me!' he said tremulously. 'I have been a wicked wretch. I did not know she was such a treasure as this!'

He reassured her instantly; declaring that he would not of course desert

---

[2] The girl she 'protected'; one whose interests a person guards and advances.

her, that he would provide a home for her somewhere. Meanwhile she was to stay where she was as long as her mistress would allow her.

But a misfortune supervened in this direction. Whether an inkling of Anna's circumstances reached the knowledge of Mrs. Harnham's husband or not cannot be said, but the girl was compelled, in spite of Edith's entreaties, to leave the house. By her own choice she decided to go back for a while to the cottage on the Plain. This arrangement led to a consultation as to how the correspondence should be carried on; and in the girl's inability to continue personally what had been begun in her name, and in the difficulty of their acting in concert as heretofore, she requested Mrs. Harnham – the only well-to-do-friend she had in the world – to receive the letters and reply to them off-hand, sending them on afterwards to herself on the Plain, where she might at least get some neighbour to read them to her, if a trustworthy one could be met with. Anna and her box then departed for the Plain.

Thus it befell that Edith Harnham found herself in the strange position of having to correspond, under no supervision by the real woman, with a man not her husband, in terms which were virtually those of a wife, concerning a corporeal condition that was not Edith's at all; the man being one for whom, mainly through the sympathies involved in playing this part, she secretly cherished a predilection, subtle and imaginative truly, but strong and absorbing. She opened each letter, read it as if intended for herself, and replied from the promptings of her own heart and no other.

Throughout this correspondence, carried on in the girl's absence, the high-strung Edith Harnham lived in the ecstasy of fancy; the vicarious intimacy engendered such a flow of passionateness as was never exceeded. For conscience's sake Edith at first sent on each of his letters to Anna, and even rough copies of her replies; but later on these so-called copies were much abridged, and many letters on both sides were not sent on at all.

Though sensuous, and, superficially at least, infested with the self-indulgent vices of artificial society, there was a substratum of honesty and fairness in Raye's character. He had really a tender regard for the country girl, and it grew more tender than ever when he found her apparently capable of expressing the deepest sensibilities in the simplest words. He meditated, he wavered; and finally resolved to consult his sister, a maiden lady much older than himself, of lively sympathies and good intent. In making this confidence he showed her some of the letters.

'She seems fairly educated,' Miss Raye observed, 'and bright in ideas. She expresses herself with a taste that must be innate.'

'Yes. She writes very prettily, doesn't she, thanks to these elementary schools?'

'One is drawn out towards her, in spite of one's self, poor thing.'

The upshot of the discussion was that though he had not been directly advised to do it, Raye wrote, in his real name, what he would never have decided to write on his own responsibility; namely that he could not live without her, and would come down in the spring and shelve her looming difficulty by marrying her.

This bold acceptance of the situation was made known to Anna by Mrs. Harnham driving out immediately to the cottage on the Plain. Anna jumped for joy like a little child. And poor, crude directions for answering appropriately were given to Edith Harnham, who on her return to the city carried them out with warm intensifications.

'O!' she groaned, as she threw down the pen. 'Anna – poor good little fool – hasn't intelligence enough to appreciate him! How should she? While I – don't bear his child!'

It was now February. The correspondence had continued altogether for four months; and the next letter from Raye contained incidentally a statement of his position and prospects. He said that in offering to wed her he had, at first, contemplated the step of retiring from a profession which hitherto had brought him very slight emolument, and which, to speak plainly, he had thought might be difficult of practice after his union with her. But the unexpected mines of brightness and warmth that her letters had disclosed to be lurking in her sweet nature had led him to abandon that somewhat sad prospect. He felt sure that, with her powers of development, after a little private training in the social forms of London, under his supervision, and a little help from a governess if necessary, she would make as good a professional man's wife as could be desired, even if he should rise to the woolsack. Many a Lord Chancellor's wife had been less intuitively a lady than she had shown herself to be in her lines to him.

'O – poor fellow, poor fellow!' mourned Edith Harnham.

Her distress now raged as high as her infatuation. It was she who had wrought him to this pitch – to a marriage which meant his ruin; yet she could not, in mercy to her maid, do anything to hinder his plan. Anna was coming to Melchester that week, but she could hardly show the girl this last reply from the young man; it told too much of the second individuality that had usurped the place of the first.

Anna came, and her mistress took her into her own room for privacy. Anna began by saying with some anxiety that she was glad the wedding was so near.

'O Anna!' replied Mrs. Harnham. 'I think we must tell him all – that I have been doing your writing for you? – lest he should not know it till after you become his wife, and it might lead to dissension and recriminations –'.

'O mis'ess, dear mis'ess – please don't tell him now!' cried Anna in distress. 'If you were to do it, perhaps he would not marry me; and what should I do then? It would be terrible what would come to me! And I am getting on with my writing, too. I have brought with me the copy-book you were so good as to give me, and I practise every day, and though it is so, so hard, I shall do it well at last, I believe, if I keep on trying.'

Edith looked at the copybook. The copies had been set by herself, and such progress as the girl had made was in the way of grotesque facsimile of her mistress's hand. But even if Edith's flowing calligraphy were re-produced the inspiration would be another thing.

'You do it so beautifully,' continued Anna, 'and say all that I want to say so much better than I could say it, that I do hope you won't leave me in the lurch just now!'

'Very well,' replied the other. 'But I – but I thought I ought not to go on!'

'Why?'

Her strong desire to confide her sentiments led Edith to answer truly: 'Because of its effect upon me.'

'But it *can't* have any!'

'Why, child?'

'Because you are married already!' said Anna with lucid simplicity.

'Of course it can't,' said her mistress hastily; yet glad, despite her con-science, that two or three outpourings still remained to her. 'But you must concentrate your attention on writing your name as I write it here.'

VI

SOON Raye wrote about the wedding. Having decided to make the best of what he feared was a piece of romantic folly, he had acquired more zest for the grand experiment. He wished the ceremony to be in London, for greater privacy. Edith Harnham would have preferred it at Melchester; Anna was passive. His reasoning prevailed, and Mrs. Harnham threw herself with mournful zeal into the preparations for Anna's departure. In a last desperate feeling that she must at every hazard be in at the death of her dream, and see once again the man who by a species of telepathy had exercised such an influence on her, she offered to go up with Anna and be with her through the ceremony – 'to see the end of her,' as her mistress put it with forced gaiety; an offer which the girl gratefully accepted; for she had no other friend capable of playing the part of companion and witness, in the presence of a gentlemanly bride-groom, in such a way as not to hasten an opinion that he had made an irremediable social blunder.

It was a muddy morning in March when Raye alighted from a four-wheel cab at the door of a registry-office in the S.W. district of London, and carefully handed down Anna and her companion Mrs. Harnham. Anna looked attractive in the somewhat fashionable clothes which Mrs. Harnham had helped her to buy, though not quite so attractive as, an innocent child, she had appeared in her country gown on the back of the wooden horse at Melchester Fair.

Mrs. Harnham had come up this morning by an early train, and a young man – a friend of Raye's – having met them at the door, all four entered the registry-office together. Till an hour before this time Raye had never known the wine-merchant's wife, except at that first casual encounter, and in the flutter of the performance before them he had little opportunity for more than a brief acquaintance. The contract of marriage at a registry is soon got through; but somehow, during its progress, Raye discovered a strange and secret gravitation between himself and Anna's friend.

The formalities of the wedding – or rather ratification of a previous union – being concluded, the four went in one cab to Raye's lodgings, newly taken in a new suburb in preference to a house, the rent of which he could ill afford just then. Here Anna cut the little cake which Raye had bought at a pastrycook's on his way home from Lincoln's Inn the night before. But she did not do much besides. Raye's friend was obliged to depart almost immediately, and when he had left the only ones virtually present were Edith and Raye, who exchanged ideas with much animation. The conversation was indeed theirs only, Anna being as a domestic animal who humbly heard but understood not. Raye seemed startled in awakening to this fact, and began to feel dissatisfied with her inadequacy.

At last, more disappointed than he cared to own, he said, 'Mrs. Harnham, my darling is so flurried that she doesn't know what she is doing or saying. I see that after this event a little quietude will be necessary before she gives tongue to that tender philosophy which she used to treat me to in her letters.'

They had planned to start early that afternoon for Knollsea, to spend the few opening days of their married life there, and as the hour for departure was drawing near Raye asked his wife if she would go to the writing-desk in the next room and scribble a little note to his sister, who had been unable to attend through indisposition, informing her that the ceremony was over, thanking her for her little present, and hoping to know her well now that she was the writer's sister as well as Charles's.

'Say it in the pretty poetical way you know so well how to adopt,' he added, 'for I want you particularly to win her, and both of you to be dear friends.'

Anna looked uneasy, but departed to her task, Raye remaining to talk to their guest. Anna was a long while absent, and her husband suddenly rose and went to her.

He found her still bending over the writing-table, with tears brimming up in her eyes; and he looked down upon the sheet of note-paper with some interest, to discover with what tact she had expressed her goodwill in the delicate circumstances. To his surprise she had progressed but a few lines, in the characters and spelling of a child of eight, and with the ideas of a goose.

'Anna,' he said, staring; 'what's this?'

'It only means – that I can't do it any better!' she answered, through her tears.

'Eh? Nonsense!'

'I can't!' she insisted, with miserable, sobbing hardihood. 'I – I – didn't write those letters, Charles! I only told *her* what to write! And not always that! But I am learning. O so fast, my dear, dear husband! And you'll forgive me, won't you, for not telling you before?' She slid to her knees, abjectly clasped his waist and laid her face against him.

He stood for a few moments, raised her, abruptly turned, and shut the door upon her, rejoining Edith in the drawing-room. She saw that something untoward had been discovered, and their eyes remained fixed on each other.

'Do I guess rightly?' he asked, with wan quietude. '*You* were her scribe through all this?'

'It was necessary,' said Edith.

'Did she dictate every word you ever wrote to me?'

'Not every word.'

'In fact, very little?'

Very little.'

'You wrote a great part of those pages every week from your own conceptions, though in her name!'

'Yes.'

'Perhaps you wrote many of the letters when you were alone, without communication with her?'

'I did.'

He turned to the bookcase, and leant with his hand over his face; and Edith, seeing his distress, became white as a sheet.

'You have deceived me – ruined me!' he murmured.

'O, don't say it!' she cried in her anguish, jumping up and putting her hand on his shoulder. 'I can't bear that!'

'Delighting me deceptively! Why did you do it – *why* did you!'

'I began doing it in kindness to her! How could I do otherwise than try to save such a simple girl from misery. But I admit that I continued it for pleasure to myself.'

Raye looked up. 'Why did it give you pleasure?' he asked.

'I must not tell,' said she.

He continued to regard her, and saw that her lips suddenly began to quiver under his scrutiny, and her eyes to fill and droop. She started aside, and said that she must go to the station to catch the return train: could a cab be called immediately?

But Raye went up to her, and took her unresisting hand. 'Well, to think of such a thing as this!' he said. 'Why, you and I are friends – lovers – devoted lovers – by correspondence!'

'Yes; I suppose.'

'More.'

'More?'

'Plainly more. It is no use blinking that. Legally I have married her – God help us both! – in soul and spirit I have married you, and no other woman in the world!'

'Hush!'

'But I will not hush! Why should you try to disguise the full truth, when you have already owned half of it? Yes, it is between you and me that the bond is – not between me and her! Now I'll say no more. But, O my cruel one, I think I have one claim upon you!'

She did not say what, and he drew her towards him and bent over her. 'If it was all pure invention in those letters,' he said emphatically, 'give me your cheek only. If you meant what you said, let it be lips. It is for the first and last time, remember!'

She put up her mouth, and he kissed her long. 'You forgive me?' she said, crying.

'Yes.'

'But you are ruined!'

'What matter!' he said, shrugging his shoulders. 'It serves me right!'

She withdrew, wiped her eyes, entered and bade good-bye to Anna, who had not expected her to go so soon, and was still wrestling with the letter. Raye followed Edith downstairs, and in three minutes she was in a hansom driving to the Waterloo station.

He went back to his wife. 'Never mind the letter, Anna, today,' he said gently. 'Put on your things. We, too, must be off shortly.'

The simple girl, upheld by the sense that she was indeed married, showed her delight at finding that he was as kind as ever after the disclosure. She did not know that before his eyes he beheld as it were a galley, in which he, the fastidious urban, was chained to work for the remainder of his life, with her, the unlettered peasant, chained to his side.

Edith travelled back to Melchester that day with a face that showed the very stupor of grief, her lips still tingling from the desperate pressure of his kiss. The end of her impassioned dream had come. When at dusk she reached the Melchester station her husband was there to meet her, but in his perfunctoriness and her preoccupation they did not see each other, and she went out of the station alone.

She walked mechanically homewards without calling a fly. Entering, she could not bear the silence of the house, and went up in the dark to where Anna had slept, where she remained thinking awhile. She then returned to the drawing-room, and not knowing what she did, crouched down upon the floor.

'I have ruined him!' she kept repeating. 'I have ruined him; because I would not deal treacherously towards her!'

In the course of half an hour a figure opened the door of the apartment.

'Ah – who's that?' she said, starting up, for it was dark.

'Your husband – who should it be?' said the worthy merchant.

'Ah – my husband! – I forgot I had a husband!' she whispered to herself.

'I missed you at the station,' he continued. 'Did you see Anna safely tied up? I hope so, for 'twas time.'

'Yes – Anna is married.'

Simultaneously with Edith's journey home Anna and her husband were sitting at the opposite windows of a second-class carriage which sped along to Knollsea. In his hand was a pocketbook full of creased sheets closely written over. Unfolding them one after another he read them in silence, and sighed.

'What are you doing, dear Charles?' she said timidly from the other window, and drew nearer to him as if he were a god.

'Reading over all those sweet letters to me signed "Anna",' he replied, with dreary resignation.

Discussion questions

Section I

- What do we learn about the backgrounds of Charles Raye and Anna, and their experience of the world?
- What is there about Anna that attracts Raye?
- How does he get to know her?

Section II

- What impressions do we get of the marital relationship of Edith Harnham and her husband from the dialogue between them?

- Look at the passage which begins: 'But this for the moment it was not easy to do' and ends: 'The thought that he was several years her junior produced a reasonless sigh'. Spend a few minutes considering the style of this passage, individually or in pairs, with this question in mind:

If you did not know that this passage was written slightly over a hundred years ago, how could you have guessed? Pick out phrases or sentences to back up your conclusions. You might look at:

the vocabulary

the general phrasing

the sentence-structure.

- What does the incident referred to above reveal about Raye and Mrs Harnham?
- What is the importance of this incident in the story's development?
- What effect has Raye had on Edith Harnham by the end of the section?

Section III

- How does Raye account for his conduct in winning Anna 'body and soul'? Does this justify his behaviour?
- Why does he decide to visit her again periodically?
- Why does he start writing to her regularly?

Section IV

- Why is Anna illiterate?
- Why does Edith Harnham agree to act as Anna's amanuensis?
- Why does Raye tell Anna to write every week?
- How, and why, is Edith Harnham affected by writing letters on Anna's behalf, and Raye's response to them?
- How does Raye react to the news of Anna's pregnancy?
- How does Edith Harnham save the situation for Anna?
- How does Edith Harnham feel about Raye by the end of the section?

Section V

- Why does Raye change his mind about deserting Anna?
- What is peculiar about the situation after Anna leaves her employment with the Harnhams?
- Why does Edith Harnham think, 'O – poor fellow, poor fellow!' when she reads of his belief that Anna 'would make as good a professional man's wife as could be desired'?

- Why does Mrs Harnham want to stop the pretence that Anna is writing the letters?

Section VI

- How does each of the central characters feel on the day of the wedding?
- How does Raye feel towards Mrs Harnham and Anna during the wedding ceremony?
- How does Anna behave when the truth is discovered?
- Is Raye exaggerating when he says to Edith Harnham: 'You have deceived me – ruined me!'
- Why does Raye kiss Edith Harnham?
- How does Raye view the prospect of married life with Anna? What is the meaning of the 'galley' image on the last page? Is Anna aware of how he feels?
- What are the feelings of each of the characters at the end of the story?

General

- How do you think the marital relationship between Raye and Anna will develop?
- Do you think Edith Harnham was wrong to begin and then maintain the deception?
- Do you feel sorry for any or all of the characters at the end?
- Who or what is to blame for the unfortunate marriage?

Wider reading programme

As part of the wider reading programme it is suggested that you read *Selected Stories of Thomas Hardy*, published by Macmillan. The last coursework suggestion is based on a reading of the whole short story collection.

Coursework suggestions

- Write an answer to the following question: Do you feel more sorry for Anna, Raye or Edith Harnham at the end of 'On the Western Circuit'? (You should answer this question with relation to all three characters.)
- Write either two or all three of the following letters from Edith Harnham, posing as Anna, to Charles Raye:

In answer to Raye's first letter (Sections III and IV).

After Raye has written to say that he cannot after all find time for the journey to see the pregnant Anna (Section IV).

In answer to Raye's letter to Anna saying he could not live without her, and would come down in the spring and marry her (Section V).

- Write an episode from the married life of Raye and Anna, twelve months into the marriage. It could, for instance, be during or after an important social occasion relating to Raye's work, at which Anna had to be present, or it could be after Raye has been forced to resign from his job because of the social stigma of being married to Anna. You should attempt to write in the style of Thomas Hardy, as far as you can.
- Write one or two entries from the diaries of Edith Harman, Charles Raye and Anna, either before or after the wedding.
- Write about the contrasting portrayal of love relationships in 'On the Western Circuit', Grace Nicholls' 'Loveact' (page 109) and Robert Graves 'Love Without Hope' (page 108).
- Choose your favourite story from *Selected Stories of Thomas Hardy* and write an analysis of it, showing why you enjoyed it. You should refer to particular details and episodes to back up your answer.

THOMAS HARDY

Punctuation: revision of inverted commas

Here is a section of 'On the Western Circuit' with the punctuation missing. Write it out, with all the necessary punctuation added, then find the original passage and check your punctuation against that of the printed story.

Anna he said staring what's this

It only means that I cant do it any better she answered through her tears

Eh Nonsense

I cant she insisted with miserable sobbing hardihood I-I-didn't write those letters Charles I only told her what to write

. . .

Do I guess rightly he asked with wan quietude You were her scribe through all this

It was necessary said Edith

SYLLABUS REQUIREMENTS COVERED

This unit covers the coursework requirements of all the syllabuses. Any of the coursework suggestions can be answered, except where indicated.

London: Work by an author published before 1900

MEG: Unit 2 (suggestions 2–4); Unit 3 (suggestion 1)

NEAB IIII: Wide reading (suggestion 5)

SEG: Pre-twentieth century prose

WJEC: Pre-twentieth century prose (further reading)

ADVERTISING

Questions on the language and presentation of advertisements are likely to feature on some of the GCSE boards' examanations, and can be set as media coursework writing assignments on others. This unit is devoted to the study of advertising.

Advertising is an enormously big business. No company can hope to succeed in popularising a product without employing all the tools of modern advertising. At least 50 per cent of the money spent by companies on advertising is devoted to ads in newspapers and magazines. By far the next highest proportion of their advertising budget goes on TV commercials (between 20 and 30 per cent). It is these two types of advertising that we shall focus on.

Essential to the advertising industry are the twin techniques of market research and motivational research. Market research involves exploring the nature of the potential market for a product. Motivational research is concerned with analysing people's motivation in order to sell products – in other words, finding ways of appealing to basic human drives and desires.

Appeals to drives and desires

There are several basic human desires and urges which advertising companies draw on when designing their advertisements:

identification with a fashionable élite   wealth, status and greed

glamour and sex appeal   health fears

domestic comfort and security   maternal feelings

fear of non-conformity and the urge for acceptance and popularity

Headlines, slogans and pictures

In order to make their appeals, newspaper and magazine ads invariably carry an eye-catching headline or slogan and a picture. These are the elements which attract the readers' attention, and persuade them to read the text which forms an additional part of most advertisements.

Look at the two advertisements for coffee on page 166. Working in pairs or groups of three of four, analyse the advertisements.

Advertising language

Some advertisements rely entirely on a catchy slogan and an arresting or enticing picture to create their effect. Most, however, use text as well, and often quite a substantial proportion of an advertisement is taken up with information and claims about the product.

There is a distinct language of advertising. These are some of its common features:

Imperatives: verbs commanding you to do things, like 'treat yourself', 'act now'.

Superlatives and exaggeration: words which claim that the product is the 'softest', 'best', etc., or which claim it is 'unique', 'a major breakthrough', etc.

Language making unprovable claims, like saying that the product 'costs less' or is 'a much better way' to do something, without saying *what* it costs less than or is better than.

Pseudo-scientific language, designed to sound impressive, like 'thanks to a unique ratifying complex'.

Repetition: key words are repeated to punch the message home.

Enticing words, like 'magic', 'beautiful', 'bargain', are used which are designed to make the product sound special.

Neologisms: words invented by advertisers, like 'tangy', 'flaky', 'crunchy'.

'Sound' words: literary devices like alliteration and assonance, or rhyme.

Language using humour and puns: word play and *'double entendre'* (sexual double meanings) are particularly popular in advertisements.

If it's Lavazza, all will be forgiven.

Rome 10 July, 4.45 pm. The light's perfect, but so is Maria's coffee.

Once you've sampled the aroma and flavour of Lavazza coffee, resistance is useless. Enjoy a moment of pleasure with the finest Italian espresso – no apologies necessary. Lavazza is suitable for all coffee makers.

LAVAZZA
The Italians' favourite coffee.

BRITAIN'S FAVOURITE AROMA SINCE 1904.

Lyons Gold. A new pure Arabica blend. For coffee lovers who appreciate a superior tasting coffee.

- What drives or desires is each advertisement appealing to?
- Consider the headline/main caption and the picture in each advertisement. Try to work out how they complement one another.
- Look at the pictures in detail. How effective do you think each is in attracting potential purchasers of the products advertised?

Analysing advertisements

Look at the advertisements which follow. Working in pairs or groups of three or four, discuss and make notes on these advertisements. You should comment on:

the visual impact; the drives and desires they are appealing to; the headlines and their connection with the pictures and text; the language used in the text; the layout of the advertisements, such as the relative positioning of the pictures, headlines and text; the overall effectiveness of the advertisement; the kinds of people the advertisements are appealing to.

Television commercials

To study TV commercials you will need a video of an evening's commercials for the class to study.

- Taking them one by one, discuss:

the visual effects

the drives and desires they are appealing to

the uses of language

the uses of music

the uses of humour

the overall effectiveness of each advertisement

the target audience at which they seem to be aimed.

Coursework suggestions

- Make a collection of about four advertisements from different sources: e.g. a Sunday broadsheet magazine section, a teenage magazine, a women's magazine, a tabloid newspaper. Write a detailed analysis of each advertisement, taking into account all the aspects of newspaper and magazine advertising discussed in this unit. A good way of doing this would be to choose three or four advertisements advertising the same sort of product, such as coffee or mobile phones, and compare the approaches of the different advertisements.
- Taking account of everything you have learned in this unit, design two advertisements for the same kind of product. Create headlines/slogans, pictures and text as realistically as you can.

Spelling test

Write out this passage, correcting all the spelling mistakes.

I was beggining to think I would never find a job, when I saw an advertisement in the local paper for a secetary at a solicitor's office in Newcastle. I begun writting a letter, and my father asked me what I was doing. He proberly thought I was planing to leave home, and he started an argument.

'I hope you no what your doing,' he said. 'Their isn't a lot of point in going to live miles away just for the sake of it.'

He must of thought I was tired of living with him. He was right. Their was know doubt that are relationship was becomming impossible.

I was thrilled when I recieved a letter offering me an interview. Soon I would be independant at last. I brought myself a new skirt to celebrate.

Punctuation: revision exercise

Write out the following text and punctuate it correctly.

I went to see shakespeares macbeth at taunton arts centre yesterday it was difficult to understand but it was pretty dramatic stuff macbeth who starts out as a hero turns into a villain after three witches have predicted that hell become king of scotland he kills the king whos called duncan to fulfil their prophecy and ends up becoming a tyrant
whats the point my girl-friend said afterwards of watching a play written hundreds of years ago

because its good I said

shes thick

SYLLABUS REQUIREMENTS COVERED

The work in this unit is likely to be of direct relevance as preparation for the examinations of the London, MEG, NEAB and WJEC boards.

The coursework suggestions relate to the coursework requirements of the syllabuses as follows:

NEAB: Media

WJEC: Best writing

NARRATIVE WRITING: THE ESSENTIALS

As a human activity, storytelling is as old as speech. All human beings tell stories. Every time we talk about something that happened to us in the past, we are telling a story. From the simplest verbal anecdote to the most sophisticated written fiction, there are common ingredients in all storytelling.

The main objective of this unit, Unit 14 and the first part of Unit 15, is to enable you to write a short story as well as you possibly can.

So what are the basic essentials of a story? They can be summarised thus:

characterisation

setting

plot (development → crisis → resolution)

point of view (first person/third person)

period (past/present).

Let us look at each.

Characterisation

Every story has to focus on some*body*, and his/her interactions with others. This is the essence of the story. The characters you create must be interesting to your readers.

It must be possible for your readers to imagine them in their mind's eye, hear them in their mind's ear, and identify with them in one way or another. It is therefore vital that you can imagine them clearly yourself and make them seem real.

Study the pictures below. Choose one of the pictures, then answer the questions, perhaps in groups of three or four.

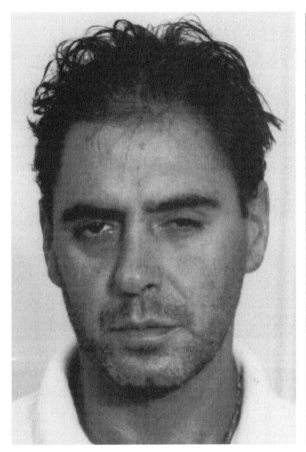 

- How would you describe the person's appearance?
- What impressions of his/her character can you get from his/her face?
- What do you think s/he might have been doing just before the picture was taken?
- What do you think s/he might have been planning to do in the next few weeks after the picture was taken?

Now study the picture above.

- How would you describe the mood and feelings of the people in the picture?
- Where are they?
- What has just happened?
- What is about to happen?
- What are they saying to one another?

As the last exercise may have shown, characterisation, setting and plot are inextricably linked, and one of the best ways of bringing an imaginary situation to life is through dialogue between characters.

Setting

Just as the readers of your story need to be able to picture your characters, they also need to be able to visualise the setting in which you place them. This is an important way of creating atmosphere in your story.

Look at the picture on the next page.

- Where do you think this scene might be? Why?
- How would you describe the setting?
- What impressions do you get of the two men?
- If this was a scene from a story, and they were planning something, what do you think it might be? Why?

Plot

A story stands or falls on its plot. The reader must be interested in your storyline, and must want to keep on reading to find out what happens at the end.

On the next page is a pictorial outline of a story. Working in pairs or small groups, plot the narrative outline of the story in words, with one person writing down the agreed version at each stage.

Compare versions when everyone has finished.

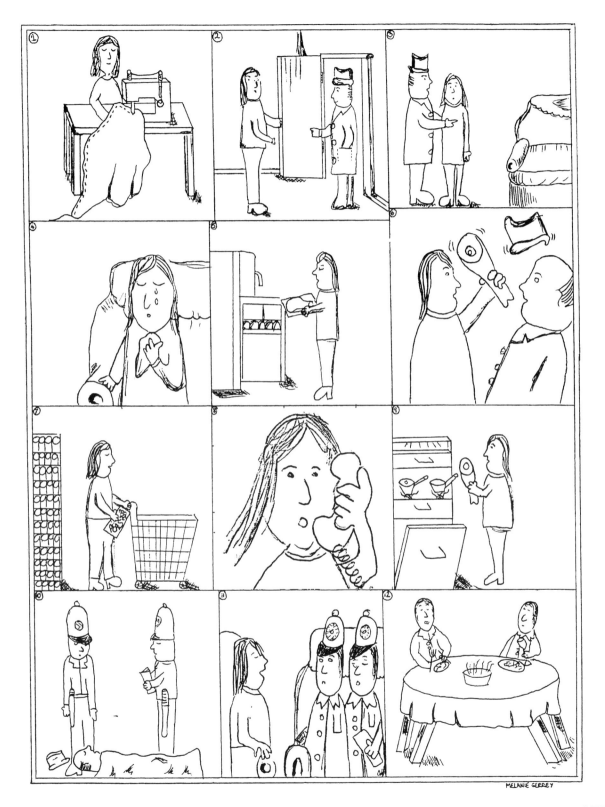

MELANIE GERREY

Point of view

When you are writing, or for that matter telling a story, you are a narrator. If you are narrating an anecdote about yourself, then you are telling the story in the first person (using the pronoun 'I'). A *written* story can also be told in the first person, whether you are telling a story about yourself or are creating a fictional narrator.

The alternative is to write a third person narrative, focusing on characters whom you refer to as 'he' or 'she'. The story can still be told from the point of view of one character, but the character will be referred to in the third person.

The stories which follow on pages 177 and 180 illustrate the use of both first and third person narrators.

Past or present

Most stories are written in the past tense, and it is generally less complicated to use this tense. What you absolutely must *not* do is switch from present tense to past and back again. Decide on the timescale of your story and stick to it.

Working on a storyline

You are given a narrative writing assignment with the title 'Silence'. Your task is to write a story in which silence plays a prominent part.

How are you going to fit the title word into your storyline? In groups of three or four, work out a storyline which fits the title and write it down for possible reading out to the class. Two or three students might then read out their storylines, for group discussion and further suggestions.

Here are some ideas:

The story could focus on someone who is permanently silent – an autistic child, for instance. It could lead up to the moment when (s)he feels impelled to break her/his silence for the first time.

The principal character could be someone in possession of secret information which other characters are determined to get her/him to reveal. (S)he could be forced to break her/his silence, with the consequences forming the climax of the story.

The central character could be someone who is placed in an eternally noisy setting, dreaming of silence, and finally achieving it, with unexpected consequences.

Now read the following story, which was written by a seventeen-year-old student called Jason West.

Silence

The bony little fist knocked three times against the brown door and awaited an answer. Its owner was a pale, skinny man, with a receding hairline, a beige cotton suit and a loud tie, holding a black briefcase. The door opened. Six foot eight of bulging muscles in a tuxedo stood in the doorway, looking down at the skinny little man.

'Get in! You're late!'

'Nice to see you, Rocco,' said the little man, walking in as the door was shut behind him.

Once inside, the little man walked straight over to a round table where a grossly fat man, with black, greased back hair, was already seated. He sat down, putting his briefcase on the table, and smiled.

'Good to see you, Mr Tate,' said the little man. 'You're looking good, in fact you're looking great. That diet is doing you wonders. What a wonderful day outside, isn't it! It's gorgeous out there.'

'Jimmy "The Mouth", you've come here to lose some more money,' said the fat man. A low, mirthless laugh escaped from his fleshy lips. The skinny man, known as 'The Mouth', opened the brief case to show piles upon piles of hundred dollar bills.

'I came to win today,' Jimmy said. 'I feel lucky today. You're gonna have to play well to beat me today, Mr Tate. I think it's my lucky day.'

'Then let's play cards,' said the fat man.

The hours went by, and the room filled with smoke as the fat man sucked on a large brown cigar. 'Three aces, I win again,' he said.

Jimmy looked down into his briefcase to see it empty, and then looked over to the fat man who had piles of hundred dollar bills in front of him. 'God!' said Jimmy. 'I knew it. I just knew I was gonna be unlucky today. It just felt like one of those days, you know what I mean? Unlucky!'

'You know your trouble, Jimmy "The Mouth"? You talk too much,' the fat man said. 'And because of it, you're a loser. You just talk and talk, and you don't stop. You know, I bet you couldn't stay quiet for ten minutes.'

'Really!' said Jimmy. 'You bet I couldn't keep quiet for ten minutes.

Huh! I'll tell you what – if the prize was big enough I could stay quiet forever. No problem! I can be quiet when I want to be, don't you worry about that!'

'If you can stay quiet for ten minutes, I'll give you your money back, but if not, you may lose more than just your money.'

'No problem,' Jimmy said. 'Ten minutes, piece of cake.'

'OK, then,' the fat man said. 'Your ten minutes starts now.'

Jimmy sat still in his chair, with his arms folded and not making a sound. He looked around the room, then at the fat man, and smiled.

'Remember,' the fat man said, 'not the slightest sound. You make just one sound and you'll lose.' Puffing on his cigar, he leaned across the table towards the silent Jimmy.

'I bet you don't even realise what a loser you are,' he said. 'You're such a skinny, pasty-faced loser,' said the fat man, blowing smoke into Jimmy's eyes. Jimmy clenched his fist, almost choking, desperately trying not to cough. He resisted the smoke well, and nodded his head, acknowledging Mr Tate's attempt to try and break him down. His lips stayed tight together, with the ends slowly turning up to give a wicked grin towards Mr Tate.

'Rocco,' Mr Tate said, 'get me the plank.' Jimmy suddenly stopped smiling and watched, horrified, as the giant handed the fat man a thick plank of wood.

'Just a sound,' said Mr Tate, 'one sound is all I want to hear.'

Jimmy shook his head.

'OK, then,' said the fat man. 'Let me help you.' He stood up and walked around the table to where Jimmy sat. Rocco grabbed Jimmy and pulled him up, holding him firmly around the waist while the fat man lifted the plank of wood. Jimmy closed his eyes. The fat man swung the plank of wood. It smashed into the little man's knee caps, hard. He gritted his teeth and his face went bright red. If it were possible, steam would have come out of his ears, but not a sound passed his lips. The fat man snarled and put the plank of wood down.

Slowly the pain began to drift away, and Jimmy's face resumed its natural pale colour. Opening his eyes, he became horrified at what faced him. The fat man stood in front of him placing a single bullet in the otherwise empty barrel of a shiny revolver. He twirled the barrel around, looking into Jimmy's eyes. Jimmy, though still silent, shook his head furiously with panic.

'All you got to do is say sorry,' the fat man laughed. 'Or say anything, I don't mind. Just say one word.' He paused to see the tears in Jimmy's eyes. 'Or I'll pull the trigger until we find out where the bullet is.' The fat man leaned forward, holding the gun just under Jimmy's chin, with his index finger tightly holding the trigger. Tears flowed from the little man's eyes and sweat rolled from his forehead down his cheeks. His whole body shook, but his mouth stayed firmly shut.

'Last chance,' said the fat man. The gun pressed tight against Jimmy's chin and the fat man suddenly clicked the trigger.

There was no report. 'Well!' said the fat man. 'That's the first real bit of luck you've ever had.' Lifting his hand, he looked at his watch.

Jimmy stared at him intensely. The fat man put the gun down and said, 'Well, I don't believe it. You've actually done it! Jimmy "The Mouth" has actually stayed quiet for ten minutes! You've won!'

Jimmy laughed. 'Ha, ha, I told you. Didn't I tell you. The king of silence, that's me!'

The fat man smiled, 'Not quite. I lied. You've only been silent for nine minutes, so I win.'

'No, no, you can't do that,' said Jimmy. 'That's not fair, you can't do that.'

'You lost the bet, now you must pay the price.'

Hours later, the brown door opened, with Rocco throwing Jimmy out.

'Bye, bye "Mouth",' the giant said. Jimmy lay in the hallway, not even trying to get up.

'Oh, and I do believe this is yours,' Rocco said, throwing Jimmy's briefcase at him. It struck Jimmy on the head and fell open in front of him. As it did so, a sudden rush of blood flowed out of the open briefcase, and in the middle of the red puddle lay a severed tongue. Jimmy tried to scream, but couldn't.

Jason West, 'Silence'

Discussion of 'Silence'

The first page of the story establishes the scene and the characters.

- At what point in the story do you realise the purpose of Jimmy's visit? Does it matter that it isn't made clear from the start?
- Can you picture the characters? Which words enable you to do this?
- How does the dialogue help to establish the characters?

The central episode of the story – the bet – is then set up.

- Is the reason for the bet convincing in terms of the characters and situation?

A clue is given that something gruesome might happen, by the words: 'you may lose more than just your money'.

- Did you guess at this point what was going to happen?

Jimmy's reactions to the attempts to break him down change as the story progresses.

- How are the changes indicated?
- How does the sentence-structure add to the build-up of drama in the paragraph beginning: ' "OK, then," said the fat man.'
- Does the heavy use of dialogue add to the effectiveness of this section of the story?

This is a story with a double twist. The first twist is the lie about Jimmy having won the bet. The second is the revelation that Jimmy has been permanently silenced.

- Do you think the first twist is convincing, or too far-fetched?
- Do you think the second twist is necessary to the success of the story? Do you think it is needlessly gruesome?

First person narrative

The assignment this time is to write a story in the first person, as follows:

Write a first person narrative explaining the consequences of a discovery that comes too late.

Spend about fifteen minutes thinking of a character, a setting and a storyline for this assignment. Then exchange and discuss one another's ideas, as a group.

Now read this story, which was written by a seventeen-year-old student called Louise Guppy.

The signs

Was it my fault? I think it was. I knew teenagers were difficult. I was told plenty of times. But I was out of my depth. I didn't even know what was going on, really. Oh, family? Yes, they have been kind and understanding. You know, the usual stuff: 'Oh, I'm sorry dear', and 'Fancy you not knowing!' I didn't know. There were no signs. Chris, my husband, says it would have happened even if we hadn't chucked him out of his home. I can't see that though. He must have been so alone and depressed.

I'll never forget the day we made him leave. He had been dismissed from college, lost his part-time job and had had a visit from the father of one of his ex-girlfriends, angrily telling him he was going to be a father too. I couldn't take any more. I was on medication from the doctor, and we were scraping the bottom of the barrel in order to keep him. We had given him advance warning and a little money. In fact it was all we had left. The bills we had to pay because of damage or theft he'd committed had taken a heavy toll.

That night, we didn't have to wait up for him. The house was quiet and lonely.

For the first time, I didn't have to take my sleeping tablets before going to bed. I slept soundly. When morning came, I woke to find the house had been turned upside down, and anything that was of value was gone. There was no forced entry and I knew who had done it! Some people said I should have shopped him. Chris nearly did. But that night, my son returned, and we saw the state that he was in and our hearts nearly broke.

Of course he denied the whole thing. We knew that by now the things he'd taken were in some pawn shop. But he had no money. He asked for more money, but Chris refused. I asked him to come back home. What else could I do? He was my son, for God's sake. I loved him! I know now that it was foolish and only made things worse, but at the time...

The final crunch came when I caught him breaking open our gas meter. I did nothing, just broke down and cried. It was Chris that blew his top. At one point, they nearly came to blows. I put myself in between them, to protect my son.

That was the last time I saw him. Funny really. I had longed for him to leave, but when he did I missed him so much. True, I gained a little health, but I had lost a son, who I loved even with his faults.

Two weeks later the police came to see us. We were expecting him to be in more trouble. We usually had a visit at least once a month. The curtains were twitching non-stop in our street. The neighbours loved it! The first question the police asked was, 'Did you know your son was taking drugs?' Like I said – no signs.

At the funeral, everyone was saying, 'What a shame!' and 'He was such a nice boy'. But I couldn't help feeling hatred towards the son I had loved so much that I would have died for him. He had left my husband and me in extreme poverty and debt, and all for an addiction. Could I have helped him? I know my husband feels bad about sending him away. If only we had known, we might have understood. It's the signs, you see, you have to know the signs...

Louise Guppy, 'The Signs'

Discussion of 'The Signs'

- Comment on the way the story is told. Do you think the narrative style works?
- The story contains a number of clichés (expressions and images which have lost all their freshness by constant use in speech and writing). Make a collection of the clichés in the story. Do they add to or detract from the effectiveness of the story?
- Do you think the mother's ignorance of her son's drug addiction is realistic?

Coursework suggestions

Choose one of the following as a coursework personal writing task to 'explore, imagine and entertain'.

- Write a story entitled 'Silence'.
- 'Too late!' Write a first person narrative explaining the consequences of a discovery that comes too late.
- Write a story featuring at least one of the characters and settings, and at least two of the sources of conflict and significant items listed below.

Characters	Setting
working mother	city suburb
rebellious teenager	coastal village
adopted child	waiting room
cinema usherette	beach

Sources of conflict	Significant items
divorce	letter
money	piece of jewellery
education	item of clothing
pregnancy	photograph
alcohol or drugs	hat
diet	animal
passion	old banger

- Write a first person story in which a misunderstanding is resolved.
- Write a comic or serious story about an obsession.

Individual orals

Individual speaking and listening assessment might be started in this unit. The general subject matter for individual oral presentations was introduced in Unit 8.

Each student who has agreed to make a presentation should talk for about five minutes about a work of literature that they have read and enjoyed since starting this course. The objective is to make the book sound as interesting as possible, so that the other members of the class will want to rush out and get it!

Ideally, you should select brief extracts to read out, to illustrate what is good about the way the book is written. What you must *not* do is simply summarise the story, without explaining *why* you think it is good. What you are trying to convey is *what you like about the book*, and *why other people might want to read it*.

The individual orals could be continued over the next few weeks, until everyone in the class has delivered one.

In addition, individual oral presentations can be assessed for 'speaking and listening' during the debate on capital punishment which is suggested at the end of Unit 16. For this activity to be successful *as* a debate, four students are required to prepare short speeches, two in favour of the debate motion and two against it.

The debate motion is: 'This house believes that capital punishment should be restored for first degree murder!' The four volunteer speakers should prepare their speeches – which should last about three minutes – after researching the arguments and evidence in a library. The debate procedure is explained on page 240, and extracts from speeches from a debate in Parliament, for and against the restoration of capital punishment, which appear at the end of Unit 17, can be read by the volunteer speakers in preparation for the debate.

SYLLABUS REQUIREMENTS COVERED

Analysis of short fiction is an examination requirement of the MEG, NEAB Post-16 and SEG syllabuses, and short story writing may feature in the MEG and WJEC examinations.

Imaginative writing is either a requirement or an option for coursework in all the syllabuses.

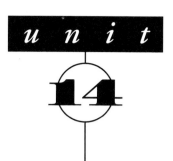
NARRATIVE WRITING TECHNIQUE: SOME HINTS

In this unit we shall go on to explore some of the techniques which are commonly used by writers to make their narratives lively and interesting. It is hoped that by looking at examples of how these techniques have been used by published writers, you may feel encouraged to try out some of them in your own writing. You should also find this unit valuable in extending your ability to analyse the various ways in which famous writers bring their ideas and imaginings to life by their uses of language. You will also get practice in writing dialogue and description, and you will revise sentence-structure variation and parts of speech.

We must be clear about one thing before we go any further, however. *There are no rules for short story writing.* While it is unquestionably true that the use of dialogue, brief physical descriptions and so on *can* help to bring a story to life, it is also true that stories can work perfectly well without them. The hints which follow, therefore, are not intended as some sort of prescription for writing a good story; they are merely offered as suggestions.

A lively opening

Somehow or other you need to capture your reader's interest from the very opening lines of your story. If you start a story in the obvious way, by *telling* the reader about a situation and characters, in a sort of summary, there is a danger that he or she will be bored by the end of the first paragraph. You *will* have to clarify the situation and explain who the characters are, of course, but there is no need to do so straightaway.

Beginning your story with an actual incident, *showing* your characters in action, is likely to capture the reader's interest from the start. Dialogue between the characters can be included straightaway. You can then use flashback to explain about the characters and situation. This is a favourite technique of short story writers.

Generally speaking, the reader is more likely to want to know about your characters once (s)he has seen them in action.

Here are three openings to short stories for exploration in terms of narrative technique.

Grace

Two gentlemen who were in the lavatory at the time tried to lift him up: but he was quite helpless. He lay curled up at the foot of the stairs down which he had fallen. They succeeded in turning him over. His hat had rolled a few yards away and his clothes were smeared with the filth and ooze of the floor on which he had lain, face downwards. His eyes were closed and he breathed with a grunting noise. A thin stream of blood trickled from the corner of his mouth.

James Joyce, 'Grace'

- What is Joyce trying to establish with this opening?
- What impressions do you get of the character and situation described here? Pick out the descriptive details/phrases which create the most vivid impression for you.
- What questions are you asking yourself by the time you've finished reading this opening passage?
- How do you think this opening section might be followed up?
- Do you think this is a good beginning to a story? Why?

The Comforts of Home

Thomas withdrew to the side of the window and with his head between the wall and the curtain he looked down the driveway where the car had stopped. His mother and the little slut were getting out of it. His mother emerged slowly, stolid and awkward, and then the little slut's long slightly bowed legs slid out, the dress pulled above the knees. With a shriek of laughter she ran to meet the dog, who bounded, overjoyed, shaking with pleasure to welcome her. Rage gathered throughout Thomas's large frame with a silent ominous intensity, like a mob assembling.

Flannery O'Connor, 'The Comforts of Home'

- Do you think this is a good opening to a story? Why/why not?
- From whose point of view is the situation being viewed? How do you know?
- What is the effect of the way the young woman is introduced to the reader?
- What questions are you asking yourself at the end of this opening paragraph?
- How do you think the story might develop?

The July Ghost

'I think I must move out of where I'm living,' he said. 'I have this problem with my landlady.'

He picked a long, bright hair off the back of her dress, so deftly that the act seemed simply considerate. He had been skilful at balancing glass, plate and cutlery too. He had a look of dignified misery, like a dejected hawk. She was interested.

'What sort of problem?'

A. S. Byatt, 'The July Ghost'

- Is this opening effective in arousing your interest? Why?
- Look at the descriptions of the man's (a) appearance and (b) behaviour.

What impressions do you get of him from each?

Pick out phrases which convey these impressions.

A strong ending

When a person reads a story, what keeps them reading, more than anything else, is the desire to know what is going to happen at the end. It is extremely important, therefore, that the ending of the story represents a natural development from what has happened before, and that it is powerful. It can be dramatic or funny, surprising or shocking, ironic or weird, but it *must* have punch. Nothing irritates a reader of a story so much as a weak ending. The major incident in a story, towards which everything else leads, is generally referred to as the climax. The great majority of short stories have a single climax, close to, if not right at, the end. One of the commonest failings of short stories written by students is that *too much* happens in the story. Too many incidents, too much drama, tends to weaken the climax. There is no need to write action-packed stories; very often a simple idea, interestingly developed, leading to an unexpected, poignant, etc., climax or revelation, makes the best story.

What is absolutely essential is to keep the reader *guessing* about what is going to happen in the end. You can, of course, lead the reader to *expect* a certain outcome, then provide an unexpected twist. But what you must *not* do is to provide the reader with clues which are so strong that they actually *do* guess the ending halfway through. This is likely to result in an **anticlimax**. If you *do* decide to give your story a twist ending, it is possible to leave it until the very last sentence, as is illustrated in the following climax of a story called 'The Coup de Grâce'. The story comes from a collection of American Civil War stories by the nineteenth-century American writer Ambrose Bierce.

Here is a summary of the plot, leading to the climax.

An American Civil War battle has ended. An officer, named Captain Downing Madwell, is walking back towards what is left of his regiment, and comes across a small group of bodies. In his regiment are two brothers, called Caffal and Creede Halcrow. Caffal is a sergeant and he and Captain Madwell are devoted friends. Creede is the major of the regiment, and between him and Captain Madwell there is a deadly animosity. Among the group of bodies is that of Caffal Halcrow, who is mortally injured, his body horribly lacerated, but still alive. After being shot, he had been gored by a herd of swine. Although he is unable to speak, the expression in his eyes conveys an unmistakable plea to be released from his agony. Madwell is irresolute. He strides away and puts a horse with a splintered foreleg out of its misery, with his revolver. Then he makes up his mind. He walks back to his friend. This is how the story ends:

The Coup de Grâce

He knelt upon one knee, cocked the weapon, placed the muzzle against the man's forehead, turned away his eyes and pulled the trigger. There was no report. He had used the last cartridge for the horse. The sufferer moaned and his lips moved convulsively. The froth that ran from them had a tinge of blood.

Captain Madwell rose to his feet and drew his sword from the scabbard. He passed the fingers of his left hand along the edge from hilt to point. He held it straight before him as if to test his nerves. There was no visible tremor of the blade; the ray of bleak skylight that it reflected

was steady and true. He stopped, and with his left hand tore away the dying man's shirt, rose, and placed the point of the sword just over the heart. This time he did not withdraw his eyes. Grasping the hilt with both hands, he thrust downward with all his strength and weight. The blade sank into the man's body – through his body into the earth; Captain Madwell came near falling forward upon his work. The dying man drew up his knees and at the same time, threw his right arm across his breast and grasped the steel so tightly that the knuckles of the hand visibly whitened. By a violent but vain effort to withdraw the blade, the wound was enlarged; a rill of blood escaped, running sinuously down into the deranged clothing. At that moment, three men stepped silently forward from behind the clump of young trees which had concealed their approach. Two were hospital attendants and carried a stretcher.

The third was Major Creede Halcrow.

Ambrose Bierce, 'The Coup de Grâce'

The use of descriptive detail

An interesting initial situation and a well-developed storyline leading up to a satisfying climax will go a long way towards making your stories successful. There are also other basic aspects of the narrator's art, which can add to the effectiveness of your writing.

The characters you create in your stories may be drawn partly from your experience of real people, or wholly from your imagination. Either way, it is necessary for your *reader* to be able to imagine them. It is thus a good idea to include a brief physical description of each character in your story. There are all sorts of ways of introducing them. Here are two examples.

… his face slowly re-emerged into light. It was an old man's face, very bony and hairy. The moist blue eyes blinked at the fire and the moist mouth fell open at times, munching once or twice mechanically when it closed.

James Joyce, 'Ivy Day in the Committee Room'

They stood side by side, shadowy, improbable figures. I was able to see them like that so often in the weeks to come – Mr Proudham, immensely tall and etiolated, with a thin head and unhealthy, yellowish skin: and Mr Sleight, perhaps five feet one or two, with a benevolent, rather stupid moon of a face. He was bald: Mr Proudham had dingy-white hair, worn rather long.

Susan Hill, 'Mr Proudham and Mr Sleight'

- Which of these descriptions appealed most to your imagination? Try to explain why.
- Introduce one or more of the following, with brief physical descriptions:

  a woman walking her dog

  a man stepping out of a lift

  a little girl lost in a crowd

  an elderly couple sitting opposite one another in a cafe

  two teenagers at a disco

  a drug dealer waiting for an appointment with a client.

- If they have appealed to your imagination, you could expand on the character and setting you have chosen, to write a complete short story.

The use of dialogue

A visual impression of the characters in a story is one way of making them seem real. Dialogue is another.

If you summarise a conversation between characters, you can cover a lot of ground quickly. If, on the other hand, you invent a conversation for them, in direct speech, although it will take longer, you can make your characters and situation come to life. The extra time and effort that it takes to invent dialogue rather than merely reporting it can be fully rewarded in the variety, conviction and sense of immediacy that it adds to the narrative.

The most commonly quoted principle in creative writing is 'showing not telling'. What this means is actually *creating* incidents and situations through *action*, rather than merely telling the reader about them or summarising what happened. Dialogue is an important aspect of 'showing not telling', as long as it is effectively and convincingly handled.

You should, if you can, try to imagine *how* each of your characters would speak. You can tell a great deal about a person from the way they speak. This necessitates being able to imagine the characters themselves before you start writing about them.

If you can invent a particular style or mode of speech for one or more of your characters, then they will be individualised still more. If, on the other hand, you make all your characters speak alike, much of the sense of immediacy and realism which dialogue creates will be lost.

Here is an example of the way in which action and dialogue can work together to create dramatic immediacy. It is taken from a story called 'An Outpost of Progress' by Joseph Conrad.

The story is set in the Belgian Congo in the nineteenth century. The two characters in the episode which follows are left in charge of a remote ivory trading station for six months, until the steamer, which brought them there, returns to relieve them. Kayerts is placed in overall authority, and Carlier, an ex-soldier, is his assistant.

The six months pass, during which the other permanent member of the trading company's staff, an African called Makola, gets the ten Africans who are working on fixed-term contracts drunk on palm wine, and trades them for ivory. The two whites are shocked by this 'slave-dealing', but as time passes their consciousness of the money that the ivory will bring them gradually overcomes their moral scruples. The men's health deteriorates, their veneer of civilised behaviour becomes increasingly stripped away and their provisions sink so low that they are forced to live on plain rice and coffee without sugar. Still the steamer fails to arrive. They get closer and closer to breaking point. The moment at which they crack is captured in this episode:

An Outpost of Progress

They waited. Rank grass began to sprout over the courtyard. The bell never rang now. Days passed, silent, exasperating and slow.

When the two men spoke, they snarled; and their silences were bitter, as if tinged by the bitterness of their thoughts.

One day, after a lunch of boiled rice, Carlier put down his cup untasted, and said, 'Hang it all! Let's have a decent cup of coffee for once. Bring out that sugar, Kayerts!'

'For the sick,' muttered Kayerts, without looking up.

'For the sick,' mocked Carlier. 'Bosh! . . . Well! I am sick.'

'You are no more sick than I am and I go without,' said Kayerts in a peaceful tone.

'Come, out with that sugar, you stingy old slave-dealer!'

Kayerts looked up quickly. Carlier was smiling with marked insolence. And suddenly it seemed to Kayerts that he had never seen that man before. Who was he? He knew nothing about him. What was he capable of? There was a surprising flash of violent emotion within him, as if in the presence of something undreamt-of, dangerous and final. But he managed to pronounce with composure –

'That joke is in very bad taste. Don't repeat it.'

'Joke!' said Carlier, hitching himself forward on his seat. 'I am hungry, I am sick, I don't joke! I hate hypocrites. You are a hypocrite. You are a slave-dealer. I am a slave-dealer. There's nothing but slave-dealers in this cursed country. I mean to have sugar in my coffee today, anyhow!'

'I forbid you to speak to me in that way,' said Kayerts with a fair show of resolution.

'You! What?' shouted Carlier, jumping up.

Kayerts stood up also. 'I am your chief,' he began, trying to master the shakiness of his voice.

'What?' yelled the other. 'Who's chief? There's no chief here. There's nothing here: there's nothing but you and I. Fetch the sugar you potbellied ass.'

'Hold your tongue. Go out of this room,' screamed Kayerts. 'I dismiss you, you scoundrel!'

Carlier swung a stool. All at once he looked dangerously in earnest. 'You flabby, good-for-nothing civilian, take that!' he howled.

Kayerts dropped under the table, and the stool struck the grass inner wall of the room. Then, as Carlier was trying to upset the table, Kayerts in desperation made a blind rush, head low, like a cornered pig would do, and over-turning his friend, bolted along the veranda and into his room. He locked the door, snatched his revolver, and stood panting. In less than a minute, Carlier was kicking at the door furiously, howling. 'If you don't bring out that sugar, I will shoot you at sight, like a dog. Now then, one, two, three. You won't? I will show you who's the master.'

Joseph Conrad, 'An Outpost of Progress'

- What impressions do you get of Carlier from what he says and the way he speaks?
- What impressions do you get of Kayerts?
- Look at the narrative passage between the two sections of dialogue ('Kayerts looked up quickly' etc.). What is the purpose and effect of this passage?
- Look at the way the dialogue is presented:

  - Is the speaker always named?
  - How many variations are there in the representations of *how* words are spoken, such as verbs of saying ('he said, he shouted', etc.). List them.
  - For what reasons does the writer begin a new paragraph?
  - How are actions by characters *within* sections of dialogue set out on the page?

As the above exercise will probably have shown, it is not always necessary to use a verb of saying at all. Quite often, several lines of dialogue can follow one another on the page without any indication of who is speaking. You should be careful, however, not to let this kind of unattributed dialogue go on so long that the reader loses track of which line is being spoken by whom. It is irritating and distracting for the reader to have to count back to the beginning of the dialogue to find out who is speaking.

A note of caution should also be sounded on the question of finding alternatives to 'he/she said'. The passage by Joseph Conrad which we have just looked at rings the changes on the verb of saying several times, as you will no doubt have noticed. But there is always a good reason for using verbs like 'howled' and 'shouted' instead of 'said'. The alternative verb of saying captures the exact tone or emotion in which a character is speaking.

Perhaps the best advice would be to try to think of alternatives to 'he/she said' only if there is a good reason for doing so, or else to dispense with the verb of saying altogether.

With regard to the matter of setting out dialogue on the page, there are various conventions of which you should be aware, as follows.

A new paragraph for a new speaker

The basic principle of layout is that you start a new paragraph every time the speaker changes. Any *action* by the character who has just spoken or is about to speak is written on the same line. Check back to the Conrad passage if you are still not quite sure how this works.

Single or double inverted commas

The only clear-cut convention about this is that you should distinguish between the words that your characters are actually saying, and other quotations. Thus, if you use single inverted commas for speech, you should use double inverted commas for everything else that needs them. For example:

'I know!' he said. 'Let's go to the "Crown and Anchor". It says in the "Advertiser" that it's got "the best range of real ales in town". How's that sound?'

Presenting thought rather than speech

This is another matter for which no rigid convention exists. Some writers use inverted commas for words which are both thought by a character and spoken out loud. However, this can cause confusion on the part of the reader. Perhaps the best advice here would be to use inverted commas for speech but *not* for thought, and to start the thought with a capital letter, perhaps prefacing it with a colon, thus:

He thought: She's lying. It wasn't like that at all. He looked into her eyes. They were as clear and innocent as a child's.

A couple of further points about the use of dialogue are worth making. You should only write dialogue if it adds something to the story. Rambling dialogue about nothing in particular detracts from the effectiveness of a story. It would be a good idea to read your dialogue out loud to yourself or someone else after you have written it. You need to get the rhythm of speech right, and the ear catches awkwardness of rhythm and stilted dialogue more easily than the eye.

Finally, you must try to punctuate your dialogue accurately. Dialogue is notoriously difficult to punctuate without making mistakes. If you are not entirely certain of the rules for punctuating dialogue, it would be worth revising the rules on pages 94–95, and attempting a practice exercise. It would be foolish to throw away marks for the faulty punctuation of an otherwise effective passage of conversation.

When you *do* use dialogue in a story, you might find it useful to check the rules to make sure that your punctuation is as accurate as you can get it.

You could now try writing some practice dialogues. Here are a few suggestions.

- Write a dialogue which takes place at midnight between a mother and her teenage daughter, who had promised to be home by eleven.
- Write a dialogue in which a boy confronts his girlfriend with his suspicions that she has secretly been seeing one of his friends.
- Add another ten to twenty or so lines to this extract:

'Since I've waited so long you could at least let me in,' she said.

'It's awfully late ...'

Miriam regarded her blankly. 'What difference does that make? Let me in. It's cold out here and I have on a silk dress.' Then, with a gentle gesture, she urged Mrs Miller aside and passed into the apartment. She dropped her coat and beret on a chair. She was indeed wearing a silk dress. White silk in February. The skirt was beautifully pleated and the sleeves long; it made a faint rustle as she strolled about the room. 'I like your place,' she said. 'I like the rug. Blue's my favourite colour.' She touched a paper rose in a vase on the coffee table. 'Imitation,' she commented warmly. 'How sad. Aren't imitations sad?' She seated herself on the sofa, daintily spreading her skirt.

'What do you want?' asked Mrs Miller.

'Sit down,' said Miriam. 'It makes me nervous to see people stand.'

Mrs Miller sank to a hassock. 'What do you want?' she repeated.

'You know, I don't think you're glad I came.'

Truman Capote, 'Miriam'

- You might now like to write a complete story, using the characters, situation and dialogue you have just created.

SYLLABUS REQUIREMENTS COVERED

Analysis of short fiction is an examination requirement of the MEG, NEAB Post-16 and SEG syllabuses, and short story writing may feature in the examinations of the MEG and WJEC syllabuses.

Imaginative writing is either a requirement or an option for coursework in all the syllabuses.

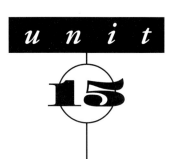

NARRATIVE AND DESCRIPTIVE WRITING

T he first two sections of this unit are a continuation of the hints on narrative writing begun in the previous unit. They are of equal relevance for descriptive writing.

Choosing the right words

Writing style is a personal matter. It is not something that can be taught. Any attempt to alter your natural style to comply with a model of supposedly 'good' writing is bound to take much of the enjoyment and naturalness out of the act of writing. The ideas which follow are not designed to make you abandon your personal writing style, but merely to encourage you to look at it in a slightly more critical light, and see if there are any ways in which you can make what you have written more lively and effective.

Let us begin with adjectives. They are the principal 'describing words', as probably most people will have been aware since early childhood. The adjective is also the most commonly over-used part of speech. Here is a suggestion: when you are reading through a piece of writing which you have completed in draft form, look out for unnecessary adjectives and adverbs, and see if there are any that you can remove. (If you are not sure of the distinction between these two types of 'describing words', look at Unit 2, page 11.)

Look at this piece of writing.

The strange young man was watching her with an eerily malevolent expression in his sinister eyes.

'What the hell are you staring at?' she yelled, angrily.

- Try reading and/or writing it out with all the adjectives and adverbs removed. Comment on the difference.
- Comment on the difference. Which of the describing words actually weaken the impact?

Well-chosen adjectives can, on the other hand, greatly enhance the effectiveness of your writing. It all depends on the words you choose. It is a good idea always to check through what you have written and to try to replace boring or obvious adjectives with more precise and interesting ones. In particular, you might try to think of more original alternatives for adjectives which are used so frequently with particular nouns that they have lost all force and effect. Here are some examples:

a bitter argument

a tragic accident

an ugly situation

a brutal assault

It is worth bearing in mind that adjectives and phrases which capture a precise sense impression are almost always more vivid and effective than abstract words. As a general principle, you could say that a word picture of a situation is always more effective than a statement about it. Look at these two versions of the same scene:

1 She entered the room, and was shocked at what she saw. It was a disgusting mess. It looked as if a bomb had hit it. There were old newspapers and clothes and dirty plates everywhere, and the revolting smell made her feel sick.

2 She entered the room, and was shocked at what she saw. Her immediate reaction was that the house had been burgled. Crumpled shirts and underpants and yellowing newspapers littered the floor, and dishes and plates, smeared with coagulated remnants of bacon and egg, or decomposing meat, lay under the sofa and on the sideboard. The room was filled with the sickly, fetid stench of decay.

- Which of these two versions is more effective? Why?

Here is another passage.

He could hear shouting coming from the lighted house, which made him more scared than ever. He plucked up courage and rang the bell. A fat man with rippling muscles under a dirty T-shirt opened the door and let him into the hall, which was full of junk, and smelt disgusting.

● Write an improved version.

A useful habit to develop would be to think about the relative strengths and weaknesses of *all* the important words you use, and not just the adjectives. Verbs and nouns also need to convey appearance, emotion, movement, sound and so on, as exactly as you can make them. Think about the words you use: try to make sure they're not clichéed, dull or vague, but precise and expressive.

The English language is uniquely rich in the range of its vocabulary, with words indicating the subtlest and most precise degrees and shades of meaning. You could try to draw on this richness. If some-one in a story you are writing is frightened, don't just plump for the obvious word. They might just be frightened, but a word indicating a stronger degree of fear may be called for: they could be terrified, horrified, paralysed with fear.

A **thesaurus** is an extremely useful tool in this respect. It will provide you with all possible alternative options for any word. You could have one handy whenever you are engaged in imaginative writing.

Another useful habit would be to read out loud the completed draft of a piece of writing, and ask yourself if the sentences run smoothly and easily. You can then make any changes which seem necessary and then read the whole piece out loud again to check how well it flows after your revisions.

Here are some passages taken from short stories.

Men are hunting deer up in the hills, and the noise of the shots volleys across the field with greater clarity because of the soundlessness created by the snow.

Again, on their way back, they pass the snarling dogs and they literally run down a hill and across a stubbled field to take a short cut home.

Edna O'Brien, 'Ways'

The boy sat quite still, staring at the bathers in the pool. Then he re-membered suddenly he hadn't lighted his cigarette. He put it between his lips, cupped his hands around the lighter and flipped the wheel.

The wick lighted and burned with a small, steady, yellow flame and the way he held his hands the wind didn't get to it at all.

Roald Dahl, 'Man from the South'

We looked around apprehensively. The professor was gone. A harassed guard threw open the front door from the outside to yell that the professor had escaped. He brandished his pistol in the direction of the gates, which hung open, limp and twisted.

In the distance, a speeding government wagon topped a ridge and dropped from sight into the valley beyond. The air was filled with choking smoke, for every vehicle on the grounds was ablaze. Pursuit was impossible.

'What in God's name got into him?' bellowed the general.

Mr Cuthnell, who had rushed out onto the front porch, now slouched back into the front room, reading a pencilled note as he came. He thrust the note into my hands.

Kurt Vonnegut Jr, 'Report on the Barnhouse Effect'

- Which word in the Edna O'Brian passage stands out for you as being the most expressive and effective in conveying atmosphere? Try to explain why.
- Write a description of a simple, everyday operation, such as lighting a cigarette in the open air, trying to make it as precise and vivid as Roald Dahl's description.
- On a copy of the Kurt Vonnegut Jr extract, underline all the verbs and adjectives. Discuss their effectiveness.
- Write a passage, no more than half a page long, capturing as vividly as you can the dramatic possibilities of one of the following situations:

an escape

the scene of a fire

a car smash and its immediate aftermath

a confrontation between a thief and a policeman

Varying your sentence-structure

Sentence-structure (or **syntax**, as it is also known) is an important element of writing style. To avoid monotony, it is a good idea to vary the lengths of your sentences. This applies particularly to moments of drama or heightened emotion in narratives. Short sentences stand out. A short sentence surrounded by longer sentences becomes a focus of the reader's attention. It is likely to be more dramatic than a longer sentence; to have more punch. It is therefore worth thinking of interspersing short and longer sentences, especially at moments of climax, special intensity or poignancy in your narrative writing. Let us look at a dramatic moment in a short story and see how the syntax helps to create dramatic impact. The story is by Daphne du Maurier and is called 'The Little Photographer'.

The female character in this extract has married into the French aristocracy and become a marquise. She has been conducting an extramarital affair with the little photographer of the title while on holiday at a seaside resort. He has fallen in love with her, and after they have had intercourse in their usual love nest, in bracken, near a cliff's edge, he declares his love. She spurns him contemptuously and in anger and despair the little photographer threatens to tell her husband, Edouard, everything. This is what happens next:

He reached for his coat, he reached for his hat, he slung his camera around his shoulder, and panic seized the Marquise, rose from her heart to her throat. He would do all that he threatened to do; he would wait there, in the hall of the hotel by the reception desk, he would wait for Edouard to come.

'Listen to me,' she began, 'we will think of something, we can perhaps come to some arrangement . . .'

But he ignored her. His face was set and pale. He stooped, by the opening at the cliff's edge, to pick up his stick and as he did so the terrible impulse was born in her and flooded her whole being and would not be denied. Leaning forward, her hands outstretched, she pushed his stooping body. He did not utter a single cry. He fell and was gone.

The Marquise sank back on her knees. She did not move. She waited. She felt the sweat trickle down her face, to her throat, to her body. Her hands were also wet. She waited there in the clearing, upon her knees, and presently, when she was cooler, she took her handkerchief and wiped away the sweat from her forehead, and her face, and her hands.

It seemed suddenly cold. She shivered. She stood up and her legs were firm; they did not give way, as she feared. She looked about her, over the bracken, and no one was in sight. As always, she was alone upon the headland. Five minutes passed and then she forced herself to the brink of the cliff and looked down. The tide was in. The sea was washing the base of the cliff below. It surged, and swept the rocks, and sank, and surged again. There was no sign of his body on the cliff face, nor could there be, because the cliff was sheer. No sign of his body in the water and had he fallen and floated it would have shown there, on the surface of the still blue sea. When he fell he must have sunk immediately.

Daphne du Maurier, 'The Little Photographer'

- On a copy of the passage, underline all the sentences which you would consider short.
- Can you work out any reasons why the writer might have chosen to make these particular sentences short?
- Read the extract from 'The Pearl' by John Steinbeck (on pages 55–56) again. Comment on the syntax in this extract.

Some final thoughts on narrative writing

A story is likely to have more impact if there is an original idea behind it, rather than reliance on an obvious situation with a hackneyed resolution.

Most effective stories end up revealing something interesting about human relationships; in other words, they leave the reader thinking about the situation and train of events that they have just been reading about.

Too many characters and incidents tend to destroy the impact of a story and weaken its climax. Stories tend to work best if they focus on one main character, and some conflict or dilemma with which s(he) is concerned.

One absolute essential is to make sure that the story you write is clearly related to the title. If the reader gets to the end of the story and is left wondering what it has to do with the title, then, in an essential respect, the story has failed. You would be well advised to think carefully about this before you start.

You should never end a story with the alarm clock beside the bed ringing and the discovery that it was all a dream! This ending is always an anticlimax for the reader.

On a basic, practical level, it would be a good idea to develop the habit of reading your narrative to yourself slowly when you have finished it and checking for mistakes of spelling, sentence-structure and punctuation, especially the punctuation of dialogue.

You might then read your story once more, out loud, preferably to someone else, and decide whether there is anything else that you need to change.

On the issue of *planning* a short narrative, no definite advice can be given. As a general rule, it is safest to map out your story-line before you begin writing. If you do not have a clear idea of how the story is going to develop, and what is going to happen in the climax, then you run the risk of writing a story that has little shape or coherence, and of the ending seeming contrived. Having said this, it should be borne in mind that, once begun, stories have a tendency to take on a life of their own. For many people the best advice, as far as planning is concerned, would be to start with a guiding idea, and to rely on their imagination and creativity to guide them towards the climax. For others, a clear idea of the story-line would be helpful. It is impossible to generalise about this.

In fact, as was said at the beginning of this section of the book, it is impossible to generalise about narrative writing in any respect. There are no absolute rules.

Formula stories are required by magazines, but if you are not constrained by the requirements of a magazine you should rely ultimately on your instincts and your originality. All that can be offered to you are hints.

Before finally leaving the art of writing short narrative, we shall look at two stories written by students, and then, later in the unit, we shall read a short episode from a novel, which is, in effect, a complete story.

To begin with, here are two stories written by different students in response to the same title: 'Paradise'. Although they both rely to a considerable extent on the creation of a distinctive and powerful atmosphere, the two responses to the title could hardly be more different, in almost every respect.

The first story was written by an eighteen-year-old student called Jeremy Thorp. His approach was to write his own version of the Judaeo-Christian story of Satan's expulsion from the heavenly Paradise and his appearance in the Garden of Eden, the earthly Paradise, just before he brought about the fall of mankind by tempting Adam and Eve to eat the forbidden fruit.[1]

The second story was written by a nineteen-year-old student called Spencer Wakeling.

---

[1] The story of the fall of Satan can be found in Revelations 12:7. 'And there was war in heaven. Michael and his angels fought against the dragon, and the dragon and his angels fought back. But he was not strong enough, and they lost their place in heaven. The great dragon was hurled down – that ancient serpent called the devil, or Satan, who leads the whole world astray. He was hurled to the earth, and his angels with him.' The story of Satan tempting Eve can be found in Genesis.

THE FALL OF LUCIFER,
DETAILS FROM THE
QUEEN MARY PSALTER, C. 1310

Paradise

The gates closed behind him with a sepulchral thud, echoing in the darkness all around him. He reached out to touch the smooth, unyielding surface; though he could not see, he knew his fingers could find no entrance. He was alone, utterly alone. Behind him the walls of Hell stretched on forever, and before him the void.

Far away, and above, he noticed a minute point of light like a dying star. His muscles tensed as an icy numbness spread from his stomach. He felt dizzy as the grip grew tighter. He began to shake. There was a vague floating sensation, then...

The void imploded into his skull, a supernova of colours streaming into infinity. His stomach changed into a cold, tight knot as he was catapulted into a vortex of noise and chaos.

The blood boiled in his ears, spasms of pain kicked through his body. His skin began to split, his nose began to bleed, and he screamed...

He came to as if from some half forgotten nightmare. The pain was all gone. He could hear birdsong, and the gentle rustling of leaves. The warm sun caressed his skin, and the heady fragrance of apple blossom filled his nostrils. He opened his eyes. He was lying in the tall grass on a low hill, overlooking a valley. Down its middle a river gushed and sparkled, forming a lake of shimmering gold. The air was full of drunken honeybees, buzzing from flower to flower. He stood up, his head swimming with new emotions. The simple beauty of every daisy at his feet made him want to weep.

He walked down to the water's edge, invigorated with the love of creation. Kneeling on the river bank, he leant forward to cup some water to his mouth. It was then that he saw his reflection. His skin was cracked and pitted, his lips a grisly scar across his face. But it was his eyes that made him cry out. Sunken deep into his skull were two pits of engulfing darkness. A single glimpse into those eyes brought flooding back all the pain, indignation, shame, anger and despair tearing through him. Images of an almighty battle – the clashing of steel, the hot stench of blood. And then the fall.

'You who have dared to question my Divine authority, you who have brought discontent and violence upon my people – you whom I thought loveliest amongst them – you are hereby condemned to exile with all your followers.'

Despite the mortal pain of his wounds, and the crushing weight of chains wrapped around him, he did not flinch, nor plead for mercy. Lifting his steady gaze into the eyes of his tormentor, he spoke.

'Love, what do you know of love? You have nothing but selfish cravings for power and control – you only love what you possess! These, my followers, and I, we are the chosen few, the first of what you call "sinners". You created us, you put us here in this place of eternal stagnation, where no babe is born, no flowers grow, because you could not bear to lose your precious throne!' He paused to survey his audience, and with the level tone of a condemned man he delivered his judgement upon them.

'I will not bow to you. Thou art a jealous God, and a hypocrite. You may vanquish us, but you will not destroy us. Outnumbered as we are, we have only our courage and our determination – you have robbed us of all else. But our time will come, you cannot escape the inevitable.'

And they fell, through a dizzy chaos of darkness and silence. On and on, through the interstellar gulf, until at last they landed on a burning lake of sulphur. There was no light, but still he could see the writhing shapes of his loved ones, their agonised faces melting in the ceaseless flames. Their screams were horrible – all around him as far as he could see, the bodies of his friends sizzling and popping, burning fat and steaming blood. He could smell his own flesh burning, his beautiful skin curling off, his flesh like paper, his hair a mass of fire, and his eyes boiling in their sockets.

He looked down at the scars and blisters covering his naked body. His wounds would soon heal, but he would never forget the hideous torment he had suffered. No matter, for now he was here, a heretic in Paradise. He stood up, smiling grimly, and surveyed the land before him. His gaze fell on an apple tree, whose fruits were beginning to ripen...

Jeremy Thorp, 'Paradise'

Discussion points

- Discuss the writer's individual *approach* to the original story. How has he altered the emphasis?
- Do you think this story can be said to have a plot, in the ordinary sense? If not, does it matter?
- Do you think the structure and time-sequence of the story work, or is it unnecessarily confusing?
- What do you notice about the prose style of the two speeches by God and Satan?

The vividness and intensity of the word pictures in this story are created by what might be described as a kind of 'poetic prose'.

- Go through a copy of the story, underlining as many examples as you can find of the 'figures of sound' (onomatopoeia, alliteration and assonance) analysed in Unit 6 on pages 51–52).
- Choose two or three phrases which make use of these devices, and say what you think makes them particularly vivid.
- Do you think the last sentence makes a good ending to the story. Why?

Paradise

The sun cast long shadows on the glass still water, as John sipped the last remaining drops of milk from the coconut and lay back, looking out towards the warm glow of the horizon.

It was almost a year ago that he had first landed on the white sands of the island, and lay exhausted and heavy in the heat of the burning sun, unable even to lift his head and thank God that he was alive. He lay quite still, his heart beating with just enough strength to carry oxygenated blood to his tired brain, and he slept. It was almost twenty four hours later that he managed to open his eyes and see the island that was to be his home for the next ten months: a blur of colour and shapes so vivid and exciting that even through his exhausted vision they seemed out of place away from the artist's canvas.

He stood on legs of rubber and stared into the wondrous scene, marvelling at the cascade of colour bombarding his retina. Palm trees thrust their hairy trunks skyward and opened their leaves towards the sun; in the shadow of the palms, smaller, vibrantly coloured flowers caught the morning dew, and everywhere was silent.

Standing on the warm sand, greeted by this scene of tranquillity, John almost forgot the horror he had escaped: the screams, the blood, the noise, the terror, the panicked scramble for the lifeboats, the desperation for survival as man trampled man (women and children first) in a bid for freedom from the mangled metal and twisted steel of the two ships.

He had reached the island, half swimming, half drifting, half conscious. Others must have survived, been rescued and flown home to their families. John had drifted. He had no family anyway. The reason he was on the tragic ship was to escape the memory of the previous six months, during which he had lost his family, in a road accident in his car, his pals and his girlfriend. He wanted to escape the hurt and pain, to 'get away from it all'. He smiled as he realised the chronic irony of the situation.

'Well, you can't get further away from it all than this,' he said to himself and smiled again. He thought of what his next move should be. Breathing in the warm air and scanning the beauty of the island, he could do nothing. His brain swam, a kaleidoscope of images: panic, blood, sea, sand, death, paradise. He should look for food, build shelter, for he never knew what horned beasts inhabited this strange and wonderful land or if the temperature plummeted to arctic levels at night or rose to bake him while he slept, but he could do nothing but smile and bask in the sun's rays. He was alive.

The night came and went with little change of temperature and without attack from wild creatures. In the light of a fresh day the island looked even more beautiful, but John was hungry. Not even here in Eden can you simply bask and relax all day; there was food to be found. It wasn't long before he discovered a fresh water pool. He drank thirstily and washed his blood and sweat encrusted face, suddenly realising how tired and filthy he had become, and so spent a long hour bathing in the crystal waters and forgetting his hunger as the beauty of the scenery again engulfed him.

'This is the life,' John told himself as he crawled from the revitalising pool and sat back against a palm tree, cracking a nearby coconut and lapping its cool milk and tasting its welcome flesh. 'I could stay here forever.'

Almost a year had passed now as John again found himself leaning back against a palm sipping milk from a coconut and looking towards the warm glow of the horizon. He sat. The sun shone. Behind him he could hear the whisper of the wind gently blowing through the tops of the tall palm trees and below them through the dense, uninhabited jungle of inedible vegetation. 'I ... I could stay here forever,' he stammered through cracked lips, and coughed violently, sending his thin and distorted, malnourished body into spasm. He closed his eyes to the warm glow of the horizon. The sun beat down. All was silent.

Spencer Wakeling, 'Paradise'

Discussion points

The structure

- Trace the changes of time sequence in this story.
- Try to work out why the writer chose to vary the time sequence in this way.

The style

This is a story which depends for its effectiveness partly on its evocation of atmosphere and its vividness of description.

- Choose three or four sentences or phrases which create a particularly vivid atmosphere or sense impression.
- Try to explain why you have chosen them.

The use of irony

- Try to find examples of the use of irony in the story.
- Try to explain how this adds to the effectiveness of the story.

The last paragraph

- Re-read the last paragraph of the story and comment on:

  - the sentence-structure

  - the repetition of phrases and ideas used earlier in the story

  - its effectiveness as an ending to the story.

Coursework story: final draft

If you have followed up any of the suggestions for short stories already offered in this unit, now is the time to write your final draft. Think about all the narrative writing hints which you have been looking at and decide on any alterations and improvements you might usefully make in the plot, structure, characterisation, expression, etc., of your story. Redraft it in final form.

Additional suggestions for narrative writing coursework

If you would prefer to write a completely new story, rather than rework the one you have already written, here are some further ideas for your narrative writing coursework.

- Write a personal story based on something that happened to you in your childhood, which has stayed in your mind.

- 'Blind date'.
- 'The river'.
- Write a story featuring revenge.
- Write a story which centres on the occurrence of something mysterious or inexplicable.
- Write a story, making full use of dialogue, in which a quarrel figures prominently.
- Write a story about enchantment.
- Write a story about something ludicrous or embarrassing which is told in the first person.
- Write a story which focuses on an act of betrayal.
- 'Paradise.'

Descriptive writing

Much of this unit and the previous one is of relevance to descriptive writing as well as narrative writing. As descriptive writing is an option for coursework and is also a possible examination exercise in some syllabuses, the final section of this unit is concerned specifically with description.

Here are two short passages of descriptive writing. The first is from a story called 'Spit Nolan' in the English writer Bill Naughton's collection *The Goalkeeper's Revenge*. It describes a race between two boys, Spit and Leslie, in their go-karts, named 'Egdam' and 'The British Queen', respectively. If you want to find out what happens next, you will have to read the entire story!

Spit Nolan

Spit was away like a shot. That vigorous toe-push sent him clean ahead of Leslie. A volley of shouts went up from his supporters, and groans from Leslie's. I saw Spit move straight to the middle of the road camber. Then I ran ahead to take up my position at the winning-post.

When I turned again I was surprised to see that Spit had not increased the lead. In fact, it seemed that Leslie had begun to gain on him. He had settled himself into a crouched position, and those perfect wheels combined with his extra weight were bringing him up with Spit. Not that it seemed possible he could ever catch him. For Spit, lying flat on his trolley, moving with a fine balance, gliding, as it were, over the rough patches, looked to me as though he were a bird that might suddenly open out its wings and fly clear into the air.

The runners along the side could no longer keep up with the trolleys.

And now, as they skimmed past the half-way mark, and came to the very steepest part, there was no doubt that Leslie was gaining. Spit had never ridden better; he coaxed 'Egdam' over the tricky parts, swayed with her, gave her head, and guided her. Yet Leslie, clinging grimly to the steering-rope of 'The British Queen', and riding the rougher parts of the road, was actually drawing level. Those beautiful ball-bearing wheels, engineer-made, encased in oil, were holding the road, and bringing Leslie along faster than spirit and skill could carry Spit.

Dead level they sped into the final stretch. Spit's slight figure was poised fearlessly on his trolley, drawing the extremes of speed from her. Thundering beside him, anxious but determined, came Leslie. He was actually drawing ahead – and forcing his way to the top of the camber. On they came like two charioteers – Spit delicately edging in the side, to gain inches by the extra downward momentum. I kept my eyes fastened clean across the road as they came belting past the winning-post.

First was the plate of 'The British Queen'. I saw that first. Then I saw the heavy rear wheel jog over a pothole and strike Spit's front wheel – sending him in a swerve across the road. Suddenly...

Bill Naughton, 'The Down-hill Trolley Race'

- Pick out all the words and phrases indicating action and movement in this passage. Discuss their effectiveness.
- Think of ten other words indicating movement, and try to explain the *kind* of movement they represent.
- How is the sense of drama and excitement created in the description?

The second extract evokes the extreme opposite pace to the first one. It is taken from a novel called *The Naked Lunch* by the American writer William Burroughs. It describes two people meeting in a café to arrange a drugs deal.

The Naked Lunch

He laughed, black insect laughter that seemed to serve some obscure function of orientation like a bat's squeak. The Sailor laughed three times. He stopped laughing and hung there motionless listening down into himself. He had picked up the silent frequency of junk. His face smoothed out like yellow wax over the high cheek-bones. He waited half a cigarette. The Sailor knew how to wait. But his eyes burned in a hideous dry hunger. He turned his face of controlled emergency in a slow half pivot to case the man who had just come on. 'Fats' Terminal sat there sweeping the café with blank, periscope eyes. When his eyes passed the Sailor he nodded minutely. Only the peeled nerves of junk sickness would have registered a movement.

The Sailor handed the boy a coin. He drifted over to Fats's table with his floating walk and sat down. They sat a long time in silence. The café was built into one side of a stone ramp at the bottom of a high white canyon of masonry. Faces of the City poured through silent as fish, stained with vile addictions and insect lusts. The lighted café was a diving bell, cable broken, settling into black depths.

William Burroughs, The Naked Lunch

- How are the slowness of movement and lack of animation captured in the choice of words and phrases?
- How does the imagery add to the atmosphere?
- How does the sentence-structure add to the atmosphere?

Coursework suggestions

Write an extended description of one of the following:

a party

a café

a fight

a race

Hallowe'en

mist on the river

footsteps

SYLLABUS REQUIREMENTS COVERED

The narrative writing coursework tasks in this unit fulfil the personal/original writing requirements of all the syllabuses, and the descriptive writing tasks match the requirements of all the syllabuses except SEG.

Narrative writing is a possible examination exercise for MEG and WJEC, and descriptive writing may feature in the NEAB and WJEC examinations.

RACE

In this unit we shall look at some further examples of twentieth-century poetry and prose, which will lead into a group speaking and listening coursework session on the issue of race, and some writing and reading coursework suggestions.

The poem which follows was written by the Nigerian playwright, poet and novelist Wole Soyinka who was born in 1934, and has spent most of his life in Nigeria. He wrote this poem while he was living in London in the late 1950s.

Telephone conversation

The price seemed reasonable, location
Indifferent. The landlady swore she lived
Off premises. Nothing remained
But self-confession. 'Madam,' I warned,
'I hate a wasted journey – I am African.'
Silence. Silenced transmission of
Pressurized good-breeding. Voice, when it came,
Lipstick coated, long gold-rolled
Cigarette-holder pipped. Caught I was, foully.
'HOW DARK?' . . . I had not misheard . . . 'ARE YOU LIGHT?
OR VERY DARK?' Button B. Button A. Stench
Of rancid breath of public hide-and-speak.
Red booth. Red pillar-box. Red double-tiered
Omnibus squelching tar. It was real! Shamed
By ill-mannered silence, surrender
Pushed dumbfounded to beg simplification.
Considerate she was, varying the emphasis –
'ARE YOU DARK? OR VERY LIGHT?' Revelation came.
'You mean – like plain or milk chocolate?'

Her assent was clinical, crushing in its light
Impersonality. Rapidly, wave-length adjusted,
I chose. 'West African sepia' – and as afterthought,
'Down in my passport.' Silence for spectroscopic
Flight of fancy, till truthfulness clanged her accent
Hard on the mouthpiece. 'WHAT'S THAT?' conceding
'DON'T KNOW WHAT THAT IS.' 'Like brunette.'
'THAT'S DARK, ISN'T IT?' 'Not altogether.
Facially, I am brunette, but madam, you should see
The rest of me. Palm of my hand, soles of my feet
Are a peroxide blonde. Friction, caused –
Foolishly madam – by sitting down, has turned
My bottom raven black – One moment madam.' – sensing
Her receiver resting on the thunderclap
About my ears – 'Madam,' I pleaded, 'wouldn't you rather
See for yourself?'

Wole Soyinka

- Why do you think the narrator admits 'I am African'?
- How does Soyinka convey the landlady's initial reaction?
- Why are her words capitalised?
- Why do you think she asks how dark he is?
- How are the narrator's immediate feelings conveyed after the land-lady has first revealed her prejudice?
- Why do you think the narrator finally responds to her question the way that he does?
- How would you describe the tone of his replies after she repeats 'ARE YOU DARK? OR VERY LIGHT?' and then asks for clarification of the term 'sepia'.
- What is Soyinka trying to show in this poem?
- Do you think it is an effective poem?

Kath Walker, who wrote the second poem, is an Aboriginal Australian. She was born in 1931, at a time when Aboriginal people, who had inhabited Australia for 40,000 years, were barred from entering many places which were reserved for whites only. This is what the 'colour bar' of the title refers to.

The poem is followed by an autobiographical piece in which Kath Walker analyses her feelings about the treatment of her people by the dominant white society of her childhood.

Colour bar

When vile men jeer because my skin is brown,
This I live down.

But when a taunted child comes home in tears,
Fierce anger sears.

The colour bar! It shows the meaner mind
Of moron kind.

Men are but medieval yet, as long
As lives this wrong.

Could he but see, the colour-baiting clod
Is blaming God

Who made us all, and all His children He
Loves equally.

As long as brothers banned from brotherhood
You still exclude

The Christianity you hold so high
Is but a lie,

Justice a cant of hypocrites, content
With precedent.

Kath Walker

I was brought up in a mixture of black and white children, and from the time I was born, from the time I could make sense of myself, I realised that as far as whites were concerned, I was supposed to occupy an inferior place in society. We've never been without that feeling, but there was certainly never a time when I wished I was white. Good God, no! I was always ashamed of what the white people did. I didn't want to be white, and I still don't want to be white. I'd hate to be white, which is the racist coming out in me now, because I couldn't have on my conscience what the whites have to live with and I'm glad I'm black for that reason. You'd have to be a damned strong, unfeeling person to be a white person.

As a child I felt that in the white-dominated society we were the tailenders in everything. We weren't allowed to go to dances. The dance floors were for whites only. Blacks were not admitted. When we went swimming at our own lake there was a place put aside for whites and we had to go right away so that we wouldn't look upon the bodies of the white people while we were swimming. There had to be a lot of distance between us, and we were the second-class citizens. I didn't *feel* I was a second-class citizen, but I was put into that position.

Kath Walker

- 'Colour Bar' expresses anger in a different way from 'Telephone Conversation.' How would you explain the difference?
- Find examples of strongly emotive language in 'Colour Bar'. Is the language of the poem effective?
- What kind of racism is the author talking about in the first two verses? What causes her to feel particularly angry about this kind of racism?
- What does she mean by the use of the word 'medieval' in the fourth verse?
- What does she mean by saying 'the colour-baiting clod/Is blaming God'?
- What do you think the last verse means?
- Comment on the use of alliteration in the poem.
- Comment on the verse-form. Do you think it is effective?
- In the autobiographical extract Kath Walker uses the word 'racist' of herself. Do you think she is racist? Can you understand her attitude towards white Australians?
- Both the poem and the prose extract deal with the issue of institutionalised racism. Do you think the poem expresses it more powerfully than the prose extract, or vice versa?

In an essay written for the magazine *New Statesman and Society*, in 1989, the novelist Haneif Kureishi, who was born in London in 1954, analyses his feelings about being British and of Pakistani ancestry. On the next page are two extracts from the essay. Read them and then answer the questions below

- Do you agree with Kureishi's explanation of racism?
- Why do you think Kureishi looked forward to getting back to England after visiting Pakistan?
- Can you understand the attitude of Pakistanis and Indians in England who feel they 'belong' in the land of their ancestors? Why does Kureishi think they would be disappointed if they went 'home'? Why does he put 'home' in inverted commas?
- How do you think Kureishi himself feels about being British?

England their England

Racism goes hand in hand with class inequality. Among other things, racism is a kind of snobbery, a desire to see oneself as superior culturally and economically, and a desire actively to experience and enjoy that superiority by hostility or violence. And when that superiority of class and culture is unsure or not acknowledged by the Other – as it would be acknowledged by the servant and master in class-stable Pakistan – but is in doubt, as with the British working class and Pakistanis in England, then it has to be demonstrated physically.

Some of the middle class of Pakistan, who also used the familiar vocabulary of contempt about their own poor (and, incidentally, about the British poor) couldn't understand when I explained that British racists weren't discriminating in their racial discrimination: they loathed all Pakistanis and kicked whoever was nearest. To the English all Pakistanis were the same; racists didn't ask whether you had a chauffeur, TV and private education before they set fire to your house. But for some Pakistanis, it was their own poor who had brought this upon them.

Coming back to England was harder than going. I had culture shock in reverse. Images of plenty yelled at me. England seemed to be overflowing with … things. Things from all over the world. Things and information. Information, though, which couldn't bite through the profound insularity and indifference.

*   *   *

When I considered staying in Pakistan to regain more of my past and complete myself with it, I had to think that that was impossible. Didn't I already miss too much of England? And wasn't I too impatient with the illiberalism and lack of possibility in Pakistan?

So there was always going to be the necessary return to England. I came home … to my country.

This is difficult to say. 'My country' isn't a notion that comes easily. It is still difficult to answer the question, where do you come from?

It is strange to go away to the land of your ancestors, to find out how much you have in common with people there, yet at the same time to realise how British you are. You look forward to getting back; you think often of England and what it means to you – and you think often of what it means to be British.

Two days after my return I took my washing to a launderette and gave it to the attendant, only to be told she didn't touch the clothes of foreigners: she didn't want me anywhere near her launderette. More seriously, I read in the paper that a Pakistani family in the East End had been fire-bombed. A child was killed. This, of course, happens frequently. It is the pig's head through the window, the spit in the face, the children with the initials of racist organisations tattooed into their skin with razor blades, as well as the more polite forms of hatred.

I was in a rage. I thought: who wants to be British anyway? Or as a black American writer said: who wants to be integrated into a burning house anyway?

And indeed I know Pakistanis and Indians born and brought up here who consider their position to be the result of a diaspora: they are in exile, awaiting return to a better place, where they belong. And there this 'belonging' will be total. This will be home, and peace.

It is not difficult to see how much illusion and falsity there is in this view. How much disappointment might be involved in going 'home' only to see the extent to which you have been formed by England and the depth of attachment you feel to the place, despite everything.

It isn't surprising that some people believe in this idea of 'home'. The alternative to believing it is more conflict here; it is more self-hatred; it is the continual struggle against racism; it is the continual adjustment to life in Britain. And blacks in Britain know they have made more than enough adjustments.

Haneif Kureishi, *New Statesman and Society*, 1989

In a book called *'Race' in Britain*, published in 1982, edited by Charles Husband, a young British man of West Indian origin talks about his life in Britain from earliest childhood. This is his autobiographical account.

'Race' in Britain

Ever since I can remember, and this is going way back, early 1960s, from being very small I was always aware of being dark – black – and for a six-year-old it wasn't very pleasant being called 'darkie' and 'monkey'. Because if you're dark then you're stupid – a fool – and I wasn't stupid, I wasn't a fool, but I was quiet and different. I remember wanting to be white when I grew up because being black was something bad and awful, and in all my dreams I was white and I'd go round in space from planet to planet in my spaceship doing good deeds and rescuing people. Then we moved to Leeds and Leeds was a big frightening place...

I remember the first day I went to school in Leeds. I don't know why – perhaps it was because I spoke differently or looked different, but this white kid came up and started to pick on me. All the resentment, all the fear and frustration of coming to Leeds just came out and I found myself attacking him. I'd never done anything before like that in my life and I haven't since, but I had to be dragged away. Since then nobody ever picked on me, which was surprising because there were kids who were stronger than me who got picked on and cowed. I still wanted to be white and most of my friends were white, I suppose, and then we moved to junior school which was just across the playground. There I had to be much more aware of black kids because we all seemed to be lumped together in the same class, and I suppose because we were all black we just got on – it wasn't a question of making friendships but I still went around with my white friends. I felt I didn't belong to either group – white or black, I was in a sort of limbo of my own...

The weird thing was that, although I had this attitude in me that I wasn't going to be a 'blackie' no matter what, the people I used to go round with used to come out with 'nigger' jokes. It was okay because I was supposed not to mind. 'It's all right, he doesn't take offence.' I was part of their group so I had to accept it. I did mind, but I didn't say, because it was something apart from me. I wasn't what they were talking about – I was almost like them. It was a really strange attitude when I look back on it now – I don't understand it – but at the same time I wasn't going to conform to what other people wanted me to be. I wasn't going to be a 'happy nigger' or an athlete, or a footballer. I wanted to be something that everyone else was – everyone white that is. As far as I could see there were no black guys doing A Levels and writing essays, they were all playing football – and I wanted to be somebody...

Racism doesn't exactly help you feel secure as a person; I've been followed by the police and I don't look your sort of heavy dread guy. I've had the police follow me in a car all the way up Roundhay Road at ten o'clock at night, just cruising by the side of me not saying a word. It was really eerie and I just carried on walking, because I knew that if I stopped or jumped over a wall or something they'd have got me and there'd have been no witnesses. And I've had people in the middle of town trying to run me over and other people don't believe it. Patti and I have suffered abuse from people – it happens all the time, and when we tell people they're so amazed. Drivers have made U-turns to come back at me, shouting 'you wog, you bastard, you nigger', and people just walk on – I just walk on, I mean I'm so hardened to it now. I've been attacked in Safeways in Headingley and nobody did a thing – and that was when I was out with one of the children from the home where I work. You can't go into a shop without being the focus of attention because people expect you to steal something. If you go into a restaurant for a meal then you are shunted off into a corner where you won't offend the other all-white clientele.

Being a mixed couple we tend to move in racially mixed circles when we can, except where we have to move in all-white ones because of work or colour reasons. This means that for a lot of the time we are with a lot of white people and we stand out. We have to fight continuously against people's stereotyped ideas about us as a racially mixed couple. When you are out, you are always aware of people because they are always aware of you. They are always staring and making comments and you learn to sum people up in one go, because you have to for your own survival, otherwise you could be walking straight into trouble. You learn to read body language – you immediately know if someone is being friendly or not, then you have to decide how to deal with it... For the majority of white people who see us in the streets, we just fulfil their idea of the sexual stereotype – white girls who go with black men must be of 'loose morals', just looking for sexual excitement.

I'm a lot more secure now in my black identity than I have ever been, but it took a long time getting there, through a lot of stages. It was easier to get along without any hassle by conforming to a stereotype because you were being what people expected of you, whereas it was harder and more threatening if you were something that was close to them. If you wear a woolly hat and spend your time building a sound system, then you also conform to the stereotype, but if you aspire to be something else, a substitute white, an imitation white as they see it, wanting to study and do well, then you are threatening because you have the ability to take people's jobs away and be in a position of telling other people – especially white people – what to do. But in doing that you don't feel comfortable on either side of the fence because you're not black and you're not white...

Most of the things I've been talking about are psychological – how people see themselves and how they see other people. Black people in Britain in my opinion are still slaves, but the chains are not on their bodies but on their minds, and black kids especially need someone to help them break out of these chains, because otherwise they've got no future, they've got nothing. They've got to learn, but more important, white people have got to learn to accept them for themselves, then perhaps we can learn to accept each other.

Race in Britain, ed. Charles Husband

- Why do you think the young man in *'Race' in Britain* was always white in his childhood dreams?
- Why do you think he felt he was 'in a sort of limbo' when he moved to junior school?
- How do you explain his attitude to 'nigger' jokes when he was at school?
- Do you think the kind of racism which he describes in the paragraph beginning 'Racism doesn't exactly make you feel secure as a person' is still going on nowadays? Do you know of anyone who has had similar experiences to the ones described?
- Do you think the kind of sexual stereotyping which he describes in the paragraph beginning 'Being a mixed couple' is still prevalent?
- In the paragraph beginning 'I'm a lot more secure in my black identity', he claims that most white people prefer blacks to conform to the stereotype, rather than 'wanting to study and do well'. Why do you think this is? Do you think the attitude is becoming less common? Do you understand the attitude of whites, as he describes it?
- What do you think he means by saying 'black people in Britain ... are still slaves'?
- Do you think his hope, expressed in the final sentence, is gradually being fulfilled?

The final extract deals with racial problems in the United States in the 1950s. It is taken from James Baldwin's novel, *Go Tell It On the Mountain,* which was published in 1953, and reads as a self-contained short story.

James Baldwin is a black American writer, born in 1924 in the Harlem district of New York, where *Go Tell It On the Mountain* is set.

Go Tell It On the Mountain

She lived quite a long way from Richard – four subway stops; and when it was time for her to go home, he always took the subway uptown with her and walked her to the door. On a Saturday when they had forgotten the time and stayed together later than usual, he left her at her door at two o'clock in the morning. They said goodnight hurriedly, for she was afraid of trouble when she got upstairs – though, in fact, Madame Williams seemed astonishingly indifferent to the hours Elizabeth kept – and he wanted to hurry back home and go to bed. Yet, as he hurried off down the dark, murmuring street, she had a sudden impulse to call him back, to ask him to take her with him and never let her go again. She hurried up the steps, smiling a little at this fancy: it was because he looked so young and defenceless as he walked away, and yet so jaunty and strong.

He was to come the next evening at suppertime, to make at last, at Elizabeth's urging, the acquaintance of Madame Williams. But he did not come. She drove Madame Williams wild with her sudden sensitivity to footsteps on the stairs. Having told Madame Williams that a gentleman was coming to visit her, she did not dare, of course, to leave the house and go out looking for him, thus giving Madame Williams the impression that she dragged men in off the streets. At ten o'clock, having eaten no supper, a detail unnoticed by her hostess, she went to bed, her head aching and her heart sick with fear; fear over what had happened to Richard, who had never kept her waiting before; and fear involving all that was beginning to happen in her body.

And on Monday morning he was not at work. She left during the lunch hour to go to his room. He was not there. His landlady said that he had not been there all weekend. While Elizabeth stood trembling and indecisive in the hall, two white policemen entered.

She knew the moment she saw them, and before they mentioned his name, that something terrible had happened to Richard. Her heart, as on that bright summer day when he had first spoken to her, gave a terrible bound and then was still, with an awful, wounded stillness. She put out one hand to touch the wall in order to keep standing.

'This here young lady was just looking for him,' she heard the land-lady say.

They all looked at her.

'You his girl?' one of the policemen asked.

She looked up at his sweating face, on which a lascivious smile had im-mediately appeared, and straightened, trying to control her trembling.

'Yes,' she said. 'Where is he?'

'He's in jail, honey,' the other policeman said.

'What for?'

'For robbing a white man's store, black girl. That's what for.'

She found, and thanked Heaven for it, that a cold stony rage had en-tered her. She would, otherwise, certainly have fallen down, or begun to weep. She looked at the smiling policeman.

'Richard ain't robbed no store,' she said. 'Tell me where he is.'

'And I tell you,' he said, not smiling, 'that your boyfriend robbed a store and he's in jail for it. He's going to stay there, too – now, what you got to say to that?'

'And he probably did it for you, too,' the other policeman said. 'You look like a girl a man could rob a store for.'

She said nothing; she was thinking how to get to see him, how to get him out. One of them, the smiler, turned to the landlady and said: 'Let's have the key to his room. How long's he been living here?'

'About a year,' the landlady said. She looked unhappily at Elizabeth. 'He seemed like a real nice boy.'

'Ah, yes,' he said, mounting the steps, 'they all seem like real nice boys when they pay their rent.'

'You going to take me to see him?' she asked of the remaining police-man. She found herself fascinated by the gun in his holster, the club at his side. She wanted to take that pistol and empty it into his round, red face; to take that club and strike with all her strength against the base of his skull where his cap ended, until the ugly, silky, white man's hair was mat-ted with blood and brains.

'Sure, girl,' he said, 'you're coming right along with us. The man at the station house wants to ask you some questions.'

The smiling policeman came down again. 'Ain't nothing up there,' he said. 'Let's go.'

She moved between them, out into the sun. She knew that there was nothing to be gained by talking to them any more. She was entirely in their power; she would have to think faster than they could think; she would have to contain her fear and her hatred, and find out what could be done. Not for anything short of Richard's life, and not, possibly, even for that, would she have wept before them, or asked of them a kindness.

A small crowd, children and curious passers-by, followed them as they walked the long, dusty, sunlit street. She hoped only that they would not pass anyone she knew; she kept her head high, looking straight ahead, and felt the skin settle over her bones as though she were wearing a mask.

And at the station she somehow got past their brutal laughter. (*What was he doing with you, girl, until two o'clock in the morning? – Next time you feel like that girl, you come by here and talk to* me.) She felt that she was about to burst, or vomit, or die. Though the sweat stood out cruelly, like needles on her brow, and she felt herself, from every side, being covered with stink and filth, she found out, in her own good time, what she wanted to know: he was being held in a prison downtown called the Tombs (the name made her heart turn over), and she could see him to-morrow. The state, or the prison, or someone, had already assigned him a lawyer; he would be brought to trial next week.

But the next day, when she saw him, she wept. He had been beaten, he whispered to her, and he could hardly walk. His body, she later dis-covered, bore almost no bruises, but was full of strange, painful swellings, and there was a welt above one eye.

He had not, of course, robbed the store, but, when he left her that Saturday night, had gone down into the subway station to wait for his train. It was late, and trains were slow; he was all alone on the platform, only half awake, thinking, he said, of her.

Then, from the far end of the platform, he heard a sound of running; and, looking up, he saw two coloured boys come running down the steps. Their clothes were torn, and they were frightened; they came up the platform and stood near him, breathing hard. He was about to ask them what the trouble was when, running across the tracks toward them, and followed by a white man, he saw another coloured boy; and at the same instant another white man came running down the subway steps.

Then he came full awake, in panic; he knew that whatever the trouble was, it was now his trouble also; for these white men would make no dis-tinction between him and the three boys they were after. They were all coloured, they were about the same age, and here they stood together on the subway platform. And they were all, with no questions asked, herded upstairs, and into the wagon and to the station house.

At the station Richard gave his name and address and age and occu-pation. Then for the first time he stated that he was not involved, and asked one of the other boys to corroborate his testimony. This they rather despairingly did. They might, Elizabeth felt, have done it sooner, but they probably also felt that it would be useless to speak. And they were not believed: the owner of the store was being brought there to make the identification. And Richard tried to relax: the man could not say that he had been there if he had never seen him before.

But when the owner came, a short man with a bloody shirt – for they had knifed him – in the company of yet another policeman, he looked at the four boys before him and said: 'Yeah, that's them, all right.'

Then Richard shouted: 'But *I* wasn't there! Look at me, goddammit – I wasn't *there!*'

'You black bastards,' the man said, looking at him, 'you're all the same.'

Then there was silence in the station, the eyes of the white men all watching. And Richard said, but quietly, knowing that he was lost: 'But all the same, mister, I wasn't there.' And he looked at the white man's bloody shirt and thought, he told Elizabeth, at the bottom of his heart: 'I wish to God they'd killed you.'

Then the questioning began. The three boys signed a confession at once, but Richard would not sign. He said at last that he would die before he signed a confession to something he hadn't done.

'Well then,' said one of them, hitting him suddenly across the head, 'maybe you *will* die, you black son-of-a-bitch.' And the beating began. He would not, then, talk to her about it; she found that, before the dread and the hatred that filled her mind, her imagination faltered and held its peace.

'What we going to do?' she asked at last. He smiled a vicious smile – she had never seen such a smile on his face before.

'Maybe you ought to pray to that Jesus of yours and get Him to come down and tell these white men something.' He looked at her a long, dying moment. 'Because I don't know nothing else to do,' he said.

She suggested: 'Richard, what about another lawyer?'

And he smiled again. 'I declare,' he said, 'Little-bit's been holding out on me. She got a fortune tied up in a sock, and she ain't never told me nothing about it.'

She had been trying to save money for a whole year, but she had only thirty dollars. She sat before him, going over in her mind all the things she might do to raise money, even to going on the streets. Then, for very helplessness, she began to shake with sobbing. At this, his face became Richard's face again. He said in a shaking voice: 'Now, look here, Little-bit, don't you be like that. We going to work this out all right.' But she could not stop sobbing. 'Elizabeth,' he whispered. 'Elizabeth, Elizabeth.' Then the man came and said it was time for her to go. And she rose. She had brought two packs of cigarettes for him, and they were still in her bag. Wholly ignorant of prison regulations, she did not dare to give them to him under the man's eyes. And, somehow, her failure to remember to give him the cigarettes, when she knew how much he smoked, made her weep the harder. She tried – and failed – to smile at him, and she was slowly led to the door. The sun nearly blinded her, and she heard him whisper behind her: 'So long, baby. Be good.'

In the streets she did not know what to do. She stood awhile before the dreadful gates, and then she walked and walked until she came to a coffee shop where taxi drivers and the people who worked in nearby offices hurried in and out all day. Usually she was afraid to go into downtown establishments, where only white people were, but today she did not care. She felt that if anyone said anything to her she would turn and curse him like the lowest bitch on the streets. If anyone touched her, she would do her best to send his soul to Hell.

But no one touched her; no one spoke. She drank her coffee, sitting in the strong sun that fell through the window. Now it came to her how alone, how frightened she was; she had never been so frightened in her life before. She knew that she was pregnant – knew it, as the old folks said, in her bones; and if Richard should be sent away, what, under Heaven, could she do? Two years, three years – she had no idea how long he might be sent away for – what would she do? And how could she keep her aunt from knowing? And if her aunt should find out, then her father would know, too. The tears welled up, and she drank her cold, tasteless coffee. And what would they do with Richard? And if they sent him away, what would he be like, then, when he returned? She looked into the quiet, sunny streets, and for the first time in her life, she hated it all – the white city, the white world. She could not, that day, think of one decent white person in the whole world. She sat there, and she hoped that one day God, with tortures inconceivable, would grind them utterly into humility, and make them know that black boys and black girls, whom they treated with such condescension, such disdain, and such good humour, had hearts like human beings, too, more human hearts than theirs.

But Richard was not sent away. Against the testimony of the three robbers, and her own testimony, and, under oath, the storekeeper's indecision, there was no evidence on which to convict him. The courtroom seemed to feel, with some complacency and some disappointment, that it was his great good luck to be let off so easily. They went immediately to his room. And there – she was never all her life long to forget it – he threw himself, face downward, on his bed and wept.

She had only seen one other man weep before – her father – and it had not been like this. She touched him, but he did not stop. His own tears fell on his dirty, uncombed hair. She tried to hold him, but for a long time he would not be held. His body was like iron; she could find no softness in it. She sat curled like a frightened child on the edge of the bed, her hand on his back, waiting for the storm to pass over. It was then that she decided not to tell him yet about the child.

By and by he called her name. And then he turned, and she held him against her breast, while he sighed and shook. He fell asleep at last, clinging to her as though he were going down into the water for the last time.

And it was the last time. That night he cut his wrists with his razor and he was found in the morning by his landlady, his eyes staring upward with no light, dead among the scarlet sheets.

James Baldwin, *Go Tell It On the Mountain*

- Do you think this is a good story? Try to work out what makes the story powerful.
- Why do you think Richard committed suicide at the end of the story?
- Can you understand why Elizabeth has her murderous fantasy about the policeman?
- Why do you think she is so determined not to weep in front of the policeman?
- Why did she finally weep when she saw Richard in prison?
- How does she feel when she leaves the prison? Why?
- How do you explain her feelings towards white people as she sits in the café?
- What do you think the story has to say about race relations in America in the 1950s? Do you think the racial situation in Britain is in any way similar?

Discussion

You could now go on to discuss any issues relating to race which interest you. Here are some suggestions which might guide the discussion.

- What was the political connection between Britain and most African countries, the Indian subcontinent and other parts of Asia, and the West Indies, until the early 1960s?
- Why was there a substantial influx of immigrants to Britain in the 1960s?
- Do you think immigration controls in Britain should be tightened?
- How do you respond to the following commonly heard complaints of white Britons against blacks and vice-versa, quoted in a book called *Learning to be Prejudiced* by Alfred Davy, published in 1953.

Whites about blacks:

'They don't fit in.'
'They take the houses needed by the whites.'
'They won't learn the language.'

'They don't like us, they just tolerate us because they have to live here; they should ship them back.'

'They don't mix; they pretend to be tolerant but they're not.'

'There's too many of them.'

'They do their toilet in the street, they take houses and turn them into slums.'

Blacks about whites:

'Blacks seem to be synonymous with barbarians.'

'Too many black kids are relegated to ESN schools; they see us as inferior.'

'Parliament pays lip-service to equality; we are dominated by whites; they treat us like second-class people.'

'They say we take their jobs; they think only of themselves.'

'We're picked on by the police.'

● Do you think that as black and Asian people become second, third and fourth generation immigrants in this country, racial problems will decline?

Coursework suggestions

1 Write an essay about race relations in Britain. (You might leave this until after the next unit, on essay writing.)

2 Write a comparative study of 'Telephone Conversation' by Wole Soyinka and 'Colour Bar' by Kath Walker, showing the different ways in which they bring out the nature and effects of racism.

3 You are an investigative journalist employed by the *New York Times*. You decide to do a feature article on the surprising suicide of a young black man called Richard after his acquittal on a charge of robbery and grievous bodily harm. Note down all the relevant details of the James Baldwin story, and then write your article.

You will have attended the court case, and interviewed individuals involved, such as Elizabeth, her landlady, the arresting officers and the victim of the attack. Your article should include details of the court case, the quoted views of Elizabeth and anyone else you want to quote, and possibly your own conclusions and recommendations. You will need to invent surnames for the characters, and also place names.

SYLLABUS REQUIREMENTS COVERED

Two of the core aspects of speaking and listening coursework ('explain, describe, narrate' and 'discuss, argue, persuade') are covered by the oral work in this unit.

The coursework suggestions relate to the coursework requirements of the different syllabuses as follows:

Suggestion 1:

NEAB: Original writing

SEG: Personal writing – non-fiction

WJEC: Best writing

Suggestion 2:

London: Unit 2

Suggestion 3:

MEG: Unit 2

NEAB: Original writing

SEG: Personal writing – fiction

WJEC: Best writing

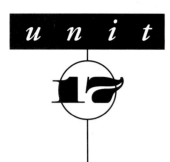

ESSAY WRITING AND CAPITAL PUNISHMENT

The essay is the standard form of academic writing. Almost anyone who has gone through secondary education will have written essays. It is likely that one of the examination requirements of GCSE English will be to write an essay, and you may well write one as a coursework piece. Essay writing is the main focus of study in this unit.

An essay is a specific genre of writing, with its own rules. You must be aware of these rules, and how to structure an essay according to them. We shall start with the basics.

- What is an essay?
- What is a paragraph?

There is, as you may have concluded, a formal pattern which any essay on any topic must follow. There are three components:

introduction

main paragraphs

conclusion

We shall look at each of these in a generalised way, and then study two short essays of different kinds to back up the general analysis.

Essay structure

The introduction

- Why is it necessary to write an introduction to an essay?

If you start straight into exploring the subject of the essay without introducing the question and the approach you are going to take to it, then you are leaving the reader to work this out for him/herself. The main purpose of the introduction, therefore, is to explain the focus of your essay.

The introduction does not need to be long. A concise statement in two or three sentences is all that is usually necessary.

The main paragraphs

These form the body of the essay. Each paragraph must concentrate on one aspect of the subject. This aspect must be **developed**. This means that a paragraph must consist of several sentences.

- What is wrong with a one-sentence paragraph?
- How long should a main paragraph be?

Just to make it clear what the **theme** of a paragraph is going to be will take a sentence. The term for an opening sentence of a paragraph which states the topic of the paragraph is a **topic sentence**.

You will obviously need more than one further sentence to *develop* the topic. It would be almost impossible to develop a topic at all fully in less than a third of a page. Something like half a page may well be needed. It should be obvious, then, that very short paragraphs of one or two sentences are unsatisfactory. All you can do in a sentence or two is to *state* an idea. You cannot develop it in such a short space.

The main paragraphs, therefore, must develop a series of perhaps three or four topics/themes/aspects of the question, at reasonable length. In an argument/discussion essay it is a good idea to establish a link between one paragraph and the next, to create a sense of a developing argument.

The conclusion

The object of the concluding paragraph is to round off the essay in a satisfactory way, so that it is not left hanging.

One way of doing this is to summarise what you have said in the essay. This is not, however, a particularly good way to end an essay. If the points you have made in the essay are clear, they should not need restating at the end.

Perhaps the best way to round off an essay is to think of an idea which ties in with the subject of the essay as a whole, and end with a sentence which sums up the whole argument or experience which you have been writing about.

Planning an essay

As it is essential to structure an essay into a series of related paragraphs, it is important to *think the structure through* before you begin writing. Unless you decide on the *topic* of each paragraph before you write an essay, you are likely to end up with an unstructured essay with undeveloped or single-sentence paragraphs. It is therefore a good idea to *write a plan first*.

The few minutes you spend thinking of ideas for your essay, and arranging them into a paragraph plan, is time well spent, whether or not you are writing the essay within the time limit of an exam. It is certainly not time wasted, because if you have not thought it out before you start, you will have to keep stopping to think about the structure of your essay while you are writing it.

A good way of planning an essay is to start by just thinking of ideas and jotting them down at random. You can then arrange them into a paragraph plan when you have got enough ideas.

Here is an example. You are asked to write an argument/discussion essay in answer to this question:

● Many people claim that the global environment is under threat. Do you support the environmentalists or do you think they are exaggerating the dangers?

Here is a set of random notes, with numbers, written in after the final plan has been decided on, indicating which paragraph each point goes in: this is a quick way of checking that you've included all the points relating to the paragraph you are working on.

introduction – the state of the environment over the years (1)

problems caused by man (2)

CFCs (3)

rainforest destruction (3)

ways to solve the problems (4)

recycling (4)

public transport/bikes (4)

birth control (4)

conservation: how important is it? (3)

plans for the future (5)

what could happen if the environment is not protected? (2)

methods of conservation (4)

Here is a paragraph plan based on these notes:

1 introduction: background information
2 environmental problems
3 importance of conservation
4 ways to solve the problems
5 the future: sum up

This could be written in the form of a *spider diagram*, like this:

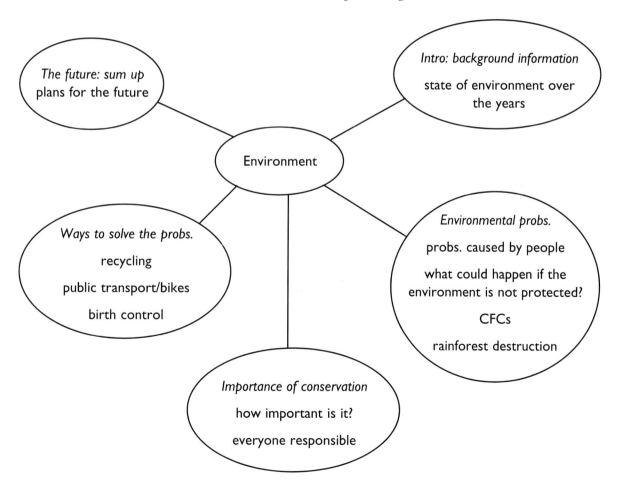

An argument essay

Here is an essay written by a sixteen-year-old college student called Hannah Hawkins. The plan above was written by her also.

'Many people claim that the global environment is under threat. Do you support the environmentalists or do you think they are exaggerating the problems?'

Over the years, man has gradually been destroying the environment. Nowadays it is no surprise to hear of world-wide problems on the news, from the destruction of rainforests to pollution of the seas. It is somewhat ironic when we realise that we are the cause of these problems.

With our growing need for technology and expansion, we are destroying the world in which we live. CFCs used in aerosol cans and carbon dioxide from coal and cars add to the greenhouse effect – resulting in harmful rays from the sun reaching the earth. This results in what is known as 'global warming', which is melting the ice caps and thus raising the sea level. Coastal regions are said to be at risk over the next 40 to 60 years. The destruction of the rainforests also adds to the greenhouse effect. Rainforests are known as 'the lungs of the earth', by taking in carbon dioxide and producing large amounts of vital oxygen. Burning the forests releases vast quantities of CO_2 into the atmosphere. Over the past 50 years, nearly half of the world's rainforests have been destroyed. This has led to over 50 species of animals and plants becoming extinct every day. Then there is over-fishing, pollution, over-population and, of course, poverty. With so many environmental problems in the world, it all seems impossible to cope with. So is it already too late?

In my opinion, conservation of our environment is very important and is not overstated at all – our world is facing a crisis and not many people seem to take the matter seriously. We need to take action now, before it does become too late. The population of the world is rising, and this creates more strain on the earth. I think people should be properly aware of the consequences all these problems could have, and if everyone did their bit to help the environment then maybe there's still hope for our world. So what can we do?

To start with, simple things like buying CFC-free products can be done, as well as taking plastic and glass bottles, aluminium cans and newspapers to recycling bins. Then there's transport. People use their cars all the time now, even if their destination is within walking distance. This can be solved by using public transport whenever possible, or even bicycles. Failing this, lead-free petrol can fuel people's cars as an alternative method. Recycled paper can be bought to reduce the amount of trees being cut down too. The population could be kept down by issuing methods of birth control within third world countries, although this would need quite a lot of work due to poverty and illiteracy. Over-population also occurs in developed countries, so this problem would need to be looked into further. Some of these methods may be only little things, but they can be effective. However, to solve bigger problems such as pollution we need the help of governments and other countries.

So, as you can see, these growing environmental problems aren't so easy to solve. It needs the help of lots of people – not just individuals. I think that it is very important to try to conserve our environment. If something is done now, then the future generations will have a better chance of survival. Of course, conservation involves many different parts of the environment: pollution, rainforest destruction, global warming, over-population, over-fishing and poverty. All of these problems are very serious matters and action needs to be taken now if we want to solve them. The world is a precious place after all, and no one knows what the future will be like.

Hannah Hawkins

Obviously, a lot of research has gone into this essay, and the points are backed up with precise explanations of what the environmental problems are (in paragraph 2) and ways in which they can be solved (in paragraph 4). Paragraph 3 acts as a bridge between these two heavily informative paragraphs. The brief introduction establishes the overall viewpoint of the essay, and the brief conclusion acts as a definitive final statement.

There is, then, a clear sense of development between the paragraphs. Notice how paragraphs 2 and 3 end. How does the use of questions help to enhance the sense of development between one paragraph and the next?

A descriptive essay

The points made about discussion essay writing apply to other kinds of essays also.

Here is a descriptive essay, together with a plan. The task, this time, is of the 'silk purse out of sow's ear' variety: to produce an interesting essay out of a dry essay title.

'Describe the scene at a busy railway station'

Random notes

escalator

barrier with arrivals and deps. board

queues at ticket windows

magazine stall

bar – 4 drunks shouting and singing

crowd of football supporters pile down escalator

platform – people milling about

          – tramp lying on bench

train arrives – couple caress

Plan

Intro: personal introduction

                 station entrance

                 crowds of people

Para. 2: electric arr. and dep. board

                 magazine stall

                 tea bar

Para. 3: bar

Para. 4: platform: tramp

                           arrival of 1st train

Para. 5: my train arrives

It is six o'clock on a Saturday evening in mid-October, and I have just got out of my uncle's car on the forecourt of New Street Station, Birmingham. I allow the escalator slowly to draw me down into the station itself. I am in no hurry; my train does not leave for forty-five minutes. I have time to relax and observe.

As the escalator descends, a man rushes by, brushing my knee with the suitcase in his left hand. A woman in a fur coat also scurries past, a startled-looking poodle under her arm and an exasperated expression on her face. At the bottom she totters awkwardly towards the barrier, her poodle yapping and struggling in her grasp. Other people step past purposefully, while others again, like me, allow the machinery to usurp the function of their legs. I step off, onto the huge open area housing all the many amenities of a major modern railway station: bar, restaurant, coffee stall, book stall, telephone booths, ticket office, information office and platform entrances.

The first feature to attract my attention, however, is the massive electric arrivals and departures board. I stand watching it in fascination for a couple of minutes as it clicks up its messages: '11.05 from Edinburgh 40 minutes late', then '14.52 from Reading at platform 5'. A bell jingles over the tannoy and a metallic voice pronounces semi-audibly about 'the train now standing on platform 5'. I saunter over to the books, magazines and sweets counter and stand in line to purchase a means to while away the hours ahead. Then I wander over to the far side of the station entrance to buy some coffee. A couple of children are flicking orange juice at one another and shrieking with delight. At the counter an old lady in a dirty, shapeless brown coat is haggling over the price of coffee with the woman behind the counter, who is saying, in a tone of weary irritation, 'Look, I don't decide on the price. You don't have to have it.' Here, everything is plastic: the cups, cutlery, sauce bottles, sandwich wrappers; even the contents look as if they are made of the same ubiquitous material. The coffee is tasteless. I feel a sudden urge for a proper drink.

The bar is crowded. At a table over the far side sit four men. They are already drunk. They sing lugubrious snatches of song, and one of them shouts an incoherent remark at the girl who moves around the tables collecting glasses, while the others laugh raucously. She ignores them. I stand next to a group of pin-stripe suited men who swap jokes in fruity accents. The beer is as tasteless as the coffee. I tire of the crush and the din in the bar.

Moving through the milling throng, I queue to buy my ticket. A young woman wearing jeans and anorak pushes to the front. She looks distraught. 'Do you mind if I get my ticket first? My train leaves in two minutes,' she says to a little balding man at the front of the queue. He grudgingly steps back for her and a woman in front of me mutters irritably to her husband, who says nothing. It is now ten minutes before my train is due and as I walk towards the barrier I hear a commotion on the escalator. A couple of dozen youths in blue and white scarves, one of them blowing a whistle and all of them shouting, are clanging down the escalator, jostling the other passengers, who cower against the rail. They break into a discordant song, repeatedly inviting certain unnamed 'bums' to 'go home'. People scuttle out of their way as they go marauding aimlessly around.

I queue at the barrier and the ticket collector cheerily tells me to go to platform seven. On the platform there are scores of people. My eyes light on a youngish man, his dark suit in tatters, who lies asleep on a bench, a wine bottle beneath him. A train arrives. It disgorges its passengers and amongst the throngs who hustle with anxious expressions to get a window seat a girl wearing a bobble hat steps down and stares around her. She suddenly darts forward and into the arms of a young man. She grabs off her hat and shakes out her long, auburn hair, and my heart warms at the look of rapture on her face.

Soon my own train arrives and no sooner am I settled in than the train is swallowed into a tunnel and leaving New Street Station and its multifarious cross-section of humanity behind. I am not sorry to depart.

As with the discussion essay on the environment, each of the paragraphs covers a distinct aspect of the question. In some of the paragraphs, as with the other essay, links are established between one paragraph and the next. How are the paragraphs linked in this essay?

You may have noticed that the essay contains seven paragraphs, two more than the plan indicates. What happened was that some aspects of the description needed fuller treatment than was anticipated at the planning stage, and other ideas surfaced while writing, so that the plan was, to some extent, abandoned. There is nothing wrong with this. The purpose of writing a plan is to develop an overall structure for your essay. There is no need to stick to it rigidly.

- Read the essay paragraph by paragraph, and pick out a sentence from each paragraph which you think captures the atmosphere of a scene or incident particularly effectively. Discuss your choice.

The description is not, needless to say, a reconstruction of the actual events of a single visit to Birmingham New Street Station. Memories from several visits were dredged up at the random note making stage and, in the case of the description of the drunks and the waitress in the bar in paragraph 4, this was actually a recollection of a scene in Swindon Railway Station. The sleeping 'wino' in paragraph 6 was borrowed from a London tube station!

Perhaps the greatest essay writer in the English language, or at any rate the most lucid, is George Orwell. We will conclude our look at essay writing by reading and discussing an essay in which he describes a disturbing experience which he had while serving as a member of the British Imperial Police in Burma in the 1920s.

George
Orwell

'A Hanging' by George Orwell

It was in Burma, a sodden morning of the rains. A sickly light, like yellow tinfoil, was slanting over the high walls into the jail yard. We were waiting outside the condemned cells, a row of sheds fronted with double bars, like small animal cages. Each cell measured about ten feet by ten and was quite bare within except for a plank bed and a pot for drinking water. In some of them brown, silent men were squatting at the inner bars, with their blankets draped round them. These were the condemned men, due to be hanged within the next week or two.

One prisoner had been brought out of his cell. His was a Hindu, a puny wisp of a man, with a shaven head and vague liquid eyes. He had a thick, sprouting moustache, absurdly too big for his body, rather like the moustache of a comic man on the films. Six tall Indian warders were guarding him and getting him ready for the gallows. Two of them stood by with rifles and fixed bayonets, while the others handcuffed him, passed a chain through his handcuffs and fixed it about their belts, and lashed his arms tight to his sides. They crowded very close about him, with their hands always on him in a careful, caressing grip, as though all the while feeling him to make sure he was there. It was like men handling a fish which is still alive and may jump back into the water. But he stood quite unresisting, yielding his arms limply to the ropes, as though he hardly noticed what was happening.

Eight o'clock struck and a bugle call, desolately thin in the wet air, floated from the distant barracks. The superintendent of the jail, who was standing apart from the rest of us, moodily prodding the gravel with his stick, raised his head at the sound. He was an army doctor, with a grey tooth-brush moustache and a gruff voice. 'For God's sake hurry up, Francis,' he said irritably. 'The man ought to have been dead by this time. Aren't you ready yet?'

Francis, the head jailer, a fat Dravidian in a white drill suit and gold spectacles, waved his black hand. 'Yes sir, yes sir,' he bubbled. 'All iss satisfactorily prepared. The hanging iss waiting. We shall proceed.'

'Well, quick march, then. The prisoners can't get their breakfast till this job's over.'

We set out for the gallows. Two warders marched on either side of the prisoner, with their rifles at the slope; two others marched close against him, gripping him by arm and shoulder, as though at once pushing and supporting him. The rest of us, magistrates and the like, followed behind. Suddenly, when we had gone ten yards, the procession stopped short without any order or warning. A dreadful thing had happened – a dog, come goodness knows whence, had appeared in the yard. It came bounding among us with a loud volley of barks and leapt round us wagging its whole body, wild with glee at finding so many human beings together. It was a large woolly dog, half Airedale, half pariah. For a moment it pranced round us, and then, before anyone could stop it, it had made a dash for the prisoner, and jumping up tried to lick his face. Everybody stood aghast, too taken aback even to grab the dog.

'Who let that bloody brute in here?' said the superintendent angrily. 'Catch it, someone!'

A warder, detached from the escort, charged clumsily after the dog, but it danced and gambolled just out of his reach, taking everything as part of the game. A young Eurasian jailer picked up a handful of gravel and tried to stone the dog away, but it dodged the stones and came after us again. Its yaps echoed from the jail walls. The prisoner, in the grasp of the two warders, looked on incuriously, as though this was another formality of the hanging. It was several minutes before someone managed to catch the dog. Then we put my handkerchief through its collar and moved off once more, with the dog still straining and whimpering.

It was about forty yards to the gallows. I watched the bare brown back of the prisoner marching in front of me. He walked clumsily with his bound arms, but quite steadily, with that bobbing gait of the Indian who never straightens his knees. At each step his muscles slid neatly into place, the lock of hair on his scalp danced up and down, his feet printed themselves on the wet gravel. And once, in spite of the men who gripped him by each shoulder, he stepped slightly aside to avoid a puddle on the path.

It is curious, but till that moment I had never realised what it means to destroy a healthy, conscious man. When I saw the prisoner step aside to avoid the puddle I saw the mystery, the unspeakable wrongness of cutting a life short when it is in full tide. This man was not dying, he was alive just as we are alive. All the organs of his body were working – bowels digesting food, skin renewing itself, nails growing, tissues forming – all toiling away in solemn foolery. His nails would still be growing when he stood on the drop, when he was falling through the air with a tenth of a second to live. His eyes saw the yellow gravel and the grey walls, and his brain still remembered, foresaw, reasoned – even about puddles. He and we were a party of men walking together, seeing, hearing, feeling, understanding the same world; and in two minutes, with a sudden snap, one of us would be gone – one mind less, one world less.

The gallows stood in a small yard, separate from the main grounds of the prison, and overgrown with tall prickly weeds. It was a brick erection like three sides of a shed, with planking on top, and above that two beams and a crossbar with the rope dangling. The hangman, a grey-haired convict in the white uniform of the prison, was waiting beside his machine. He greeted us with a servile crouch as we entered. At a word from Francis the two warders, gripping the prisoner more closely than ever, half led, half pushed him to the gallows and helped him clumsily up the ladder. Then the hangman climbed up and fixed the rope round the prisoner's neck.

We stood waiting, five yards away. The warders had formed a rough circle round the gallows. And then, when the noose was fixed, the prisoner began crying to his god. It was a high, reiterated cry of 'Ram! Ram! Ram! Ram!' not urgent and fearful like a prayer or cry for help, but steady, rhythmical, almost like the tolling of a bell.

The dog answered the sound with a whine. The hangman, still standing on the gallows, produced a small cotton bag like a flour sack and drew it down over the prisoner's face. But the sound, muffled by the cloth, still persisted, over and over again: 'Ram! Ram! Ram! Ram! Ram!'

The hangman climbed down and stood ready, holding the lever. Minutes seemed to pass. The steady, muffled crying from the prisoner went on and on, 'Ram! Ram! Ram!', never faltering for an instant. The superintendent, his head on his chest, was slowly poking the ground with his stick; perhaps he was counting the cries, allowing the prisoner a fixed number – fifty, perhaps, or a hundred. Everyone had changed colour. The Indians had gone grey like bad coffee, and one or two of the bayonets were wavering. We looked at the lashed, hooded man on the drop, and listened to his cries – each cry another second of life; the same thought was in all our minds: Oh, kill him quickly, get it over, stop that abominable noise!

Suddenly the superintendent made up his mind. Throwing up his head he made a swift motion with his stick. 'Chalo!' he shouted almost fiercely.

There was a clanking noise, and then dead silence. The prisoner had vanished, and the rope was twisting on itself. I let go of the dog, and it galloped immediately to the back of the gallows; but when it got there it stopped short, barked, and then retreated into a corner of the yard, where it stood among the weeds, looking timorously out at us. We went round the gallows to inspect the prisoner's body. He was dangling with his toes pointed straight downwards, very slowly revolving, as dead as a stone.

The superintendent reached out with his stick and poked the bare brown body; it oscillated slightly. 'He's all right,' said the superintendent. He backed out from under the gallows, and blew out a deep breath. The moody look had gone out of his face quite suddenly. He glanced at his wristwatch. 'Eight minutes past eight. Well, that's all for this morning, thank God.'

The warders unfixed bayonets and marched away. The dog, sobered and conscious of having misbehaved itself, slipped after them. We walked out of the gallows yard, past the condemned cells with their waiting prisoners, into the big central yard of the prison. The convicts, under the command of warders armed with lathis, were already receiving their breakfast. They squatted in long rows, each man holding a tin pannikin, while two warders with buckets marched round ladling out rice; it seemed quite a homely, jolly scene, after the hanging. An enormous relief had come upon us now that the job was done. One felt an impulse to sing, to break into a run, to snigger. All at once everyone began chattering gaily.

The Eurasian boy walking beside me nodded towards the way we had come, with a knowing smile: 'Do you know, sir, our friend (he meant the dead man) when he heard his appeal had been dismissed, he pissed on the floor of his cell. From fright. Kindly take one of my cigarettes, sir. Do you not admire my new silver case, sir? From the box wallah, two rupees eight annas. Classy European style.'

Several people laughed – at what, nobody seemed certain.

Francis was walking by the superintendent, talking garrulously: 'Well, sir, all has passed off with the utmost satisfactoriness. It was all finished – flick! like that. It iss not always so – oah, no! I have known cases where the doctor wass obliged to go beneath the gallows and pull the prisoner's legs to ensure decease. Most disagreeable!'

'Wriggling about eh? That's bad,' said the superintendent.

'Ach, sir, it iss worse when they become refractory! One man, I recall, clung to the bars of hiss cage when we went to take him out. You will scarcely credit, sir, that it took six warders to dislodge him, three pulling at each leg. We reasoned with him. "My dear fellow," we said, "think of all the pain and trouble you are causing us!" But no, he would not listen! Ach, he wass very troublesome!'

I found that I was laughing quite loudly. Everyone was laughing. Even the superintendent grinned in a tolerant way. 'You'd better all come out and have a drink,' he said quite genially. 'I've got a bottle of whisky in the car. We could do with it.'

We went through the big double gates of the prison into the road. 'Pulling at his legs!' exclaimed a Burmese magistrate suddenly, and burst into a loud chuckling. We all began laughing again. At that moment Francis' anecdote seemed extraordinarily funny. We all had a drink together, native and European alike, quite amicably. The dead man was a hundred yards away.

George Orwell, 'A Hanging'

- What atmosphere is created in the first paragraph? Pick out phrases which are particularly effective in creating atmosphere?
- How effective is the 'fish' simile in the second paragraph?
- Which do you think is the most expressive sentence in the third paragraph? Why?
- Why does Orwell refer to the dog's arrival as 'dreadful' in the paragraph beginning 'We set out for the gallows'?
- Pick out phrases which capture a sense impression of the dog and of the prisoner in the section from 'We set out' to 'a puddle on the path'. Discuss them.
- How does the prisoner's action in stepping aside to avoid a puddle affect Orwell?
- Why do you think the condemned man started chanting when the noose was placed round his neck?
- What is the effect of the reintroduction of the dog in the paragraph beginning: 'There was a clanking noise...'?
- How do you explain the reactions of Orwell and the other warders immediately after the execution?
- How do you explain Orwell's reaction to Francis's story? Do you think it shows that he is insensitive?
- What is the effect of the final sentence?

Coursework suggestions

- Write a personal essay describing a particularly disturbing experience.
- Write an essay giving your views on capital punishment.
- Write an essay entitled 'Christmas'.

- Write a descriptive essay about a rock concert or a festival.
- Write a personal essay about a family occasion.
- Write a personal essay about junior school, middle school or secondary school.
- Write an essay about the paranormal.
- Write an essay entitled 'The end of term'.

AN ELECTRIC CHAIR,
USED TO EXECUTE PEOPLE
IN ATLANTA, AMERICA

Debate: capital punishment

This part of the unit relies on students having agreed to prepare speeches for and against the motion: 'This house believes that capital punishment should be restored for first degree murder', as suggested at the end of Unit 13 (page 183).

Before beginning the debate it might be a good idea if everyone in the class read and, in pairs, briefly discussed the ideas expressed in the following extracts from speeches made by MPs during a parliamentary debate on capital punishment in 1983.

The four volunteer speakers can then give their speeches, for individual speaking and listening assessment, in the following order: the proposer of the motion, the opposer of the motion, the seconder of the motion, the seconder of the opposition to the motion. The chairperson should introduce the debate motion, ask for a vote on it, then introduce each of the debate speakers before they give their speeches.

He or she should then throw the motion open for public debate (and group speaking and listening assessment), and take a second vote at the end, to see who won the debate.

Here are the extracts from speeches made in the House of Commons on 13 July 1983.

... Even if the deterrent claim can be justified, its effect on the murder rate in Britain will be negligible ... Time after time the hanging lobby repeats the old remedies and the venerable prejudices that capital punishment deters. I tell the hanging lobby what every informed person knows – that there is absolutely no evidence to support the view that capital punishment is in itself a deterrent.

If we compare abolitionist and retentionist countries and countries before and after abolition, we find that there is no evidence to prove that execution reduces the murder rate or reduces crimes of violence...

If the deterrent case is to be accepted, if we are to vote for capital punishment as a deterrent, we ought at least to be sure that it deters. ... Unless there is some positive proof that hanging deters, the case for hanging cannot be made even by its most sophisticated proponents.

They cannot provide that case. I must provide for them the other statistic, of which we are certain. Had hanging not been abolished in 1964, at least five innocent men would be dead today. That seems to me ... the only statistic about which we can be sure in this entire debate...

I conclude as I began. Were all the practical or pragmatic arguments against capital punishment not to apply, I should still resist its introduction. Supporters of capital punishment insist on comparing crime rates before and after abolition, as though abolition itself had created a more violent society. The truth is something different. Violence has grown within our society during the past 25 years for many reasons. To legalise violence in the way proposed would make Britain not a more peaceful nation, but one in which violence had become accepted and institutionalised ... By killing murderers we become like the murderers themselves. The whole community is lowered to their standards. For that reason I shall vote against the motion.

Roy Hattersley (MP for Birmingham, Sparkbrook)

... I was in the House when we abolished the capital sentence. We did so largely in the belief that life imprisonment would be an effective deterrent in its place. It has not worked out that way. On the contrary, violence and murder have increased rapidly...

When the capital sentence was abolished, the Police Federation warned the House that it would lead to a dramatic increase in the carrying and using of firearms. That is exactly what has happened. In the year before abolition, the number of guns used in crimes in London was 43; last year the number was close to 2,000. That is a 25-fold increase. Before abolition, when a professional gang planned a job the elder members frisked the younger members to ensure that they were not carrying guns. ... It is no longer that way. Today, it is the norm and not the exception for criminals to carry guns when they commit robberies. They do so for the simple reason that they know that their lives are not at risk.

There is also a new balance of risk for the police officer. When a policeman confronts a criminal with a gun, the odds are tilted against him. In that split second when the armed robber must decide whether to pull the trigger and shoot the policeman, the robber knows that if he surrenders he will go to prison for, perhaps, five to seven years for armed robbery. But if he shoots the policeman, he eliminates the witness and greatly improves his chances of getting away with the loot. And even if he is caught and convicted of murder the worst that can happen to him is life imprisonment. With remission that can mean little more than ten and a half years ... I do not accept, and I doubt if the House would accept, that the difference between five to seven years for armed robbery and only ten years for murder is worth the life of a police officer.

There is a further consequence. Whereas, before abolition, unarmed police officers would not hesitate to tackle armed criminals because they knew, or they believed, that they were protected by the invisible bullet-proof waistcoat of the capital sentence, today even the bravest of policemen hesitates. He often sends for a gun.

What the Police Federation and I predicted when the House abolished the capital sentence has come to pass. We have put an end to the once-proud tradition of our unarmed police force. We therefore face the risk ... that we have not succeeded in abolishing the capital sentence. On the contrary, it will be administered more and more not by due process of law and by courts, but by armed criminals and, on occasion, by armed police officers defending themselves and the public.

Eldon Griffiths (MP for Bury St Edmunds)

SYLLABUS REQUIREMENTS COVERED

The oral work in this unit can fulfil the requirements for individual and group speaking and listening in all the syllabuses.

Essay writing is a feature of the examination in the SEG syllabus, and a written piece arguing a case is a likely question in the NEAB examination. Descriptive writing may be set in the NEAB and WJEC examinations.

An essay can be presented as a writing coursework piece for all the syllabuses.

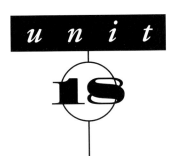
WORLD POVERTY AND THE ENVIRONMENT

In this unit we are concentrating on two interrelated global issues: the living conditions of the poor in countries in which the safety net of a Social Security system does not exist, and the condition of the global environment.

The work will focus on group speaking and listening assessment, and on pamphlet writing, with essay writing as another writing course-work option.

Global poverty

To give a sense of the scale of the problem, the following passages should give you something to think about.

While you are reading these words, four people will have died of starvation, most of them children.

(From the front cover of Paul Ehrlich's book, *The Population Bomb*)

The wealth of the world's 358 billionaires exceeds the combined annual incomes of countries with nearly half the global population. The gap between rich and poor countries is growing. Since 1980, 100 countries have had stagnant or declining incomes, reducing living standards for a quarter of the world's population – or 1.6 billion people.

The losers fall into four main regional groups: sub-Saharan Africa, where decline mostly began in the late Seventies; Latin America and the Caribbean, although several here began to recover in the late Eighties; many Arab countries, which suffered from declining oil prices in the Eighties; and Eastern Europe and the countries of the former Soviet Union, where per capital income has fallen on average by a third since the mid-Eighties.

The dilemma facing sub-Saharan Africa, Latin America and the Arab countries is how to end the cycle of decline. The biggest questions of all surround Africa. It is not difficult to explain the continent's lack of success: rising population, a delicate agrarian eco-system, poor and corrupt government, immense disparities of wealth and low levels of literacy.

Martin Jacques, the Observer, July 1996

Britain's 0.2 per cent annual population growth rate adds 116,000 people per year to its population. By contrast, Bangladesh, with a 2.4 per cent growth rate, adds 2.7 million. But every person in Britain uses more than 80 times as much fossil fuels as a Bangladeshi, so Britain's population growth effectively contributes 3.5 times as much carbon dioxide to the global atmosphere as Bangladesh's.

Sanjay Kumar, New Scientist, 6 November 1993

- Discuss your reactions to the facts and issues brought out in each of these extracts.

A poor family in Brazil

To get some sense of what it must be like to be born to a poor family in a Third World country, here is a description of a family which the English journalist and writer, Paul Harrison, met in Brazil. The extract comes from his book, *Inside the Third World*.

Francisco's mother Fatima is small for her age. She is visibly weak, distant, yet easily irritated by the children. Years of pregnancy and menstruation, along with an iron-poor diet of maize, have made her chronically anaemic. Her husband Jaime is a landless labourer, with a low, erratic income barely enough to keep them all alive and clothed. No-one eats enough, and when there's not enough to go round, Fatima goes without, even when she's pregnant. And that is frequently, as the couple use no form of contraception. They have had ten children, six of whom survived to adulthood.

Fatima went through several periods of under-nourishment while Francisco was in her womb. There were times when Jaime could not get regular work and everyone went hungry. Fatima also had several attacks of stress and anxiety when Jaime beat her. Francisco probably suffered his first bout of growth retardation, both mental and physical, before he even saw the light of day.

He was born underweight, and his brain was already smaller than normal size. For the first few months he was breast-fed and suffered few infections, as he was partly protected by the anti-bodies in his mother's milk. Then he was weaned onto thin gruels and soups, taken off the breast and put onto tinned evaporated milk, thinned down with polluted water from the well. His diet, in itself, was inadequate. Then he started to get more and more infections, fever, bronchitis, measles and regular bouts of gastro-enteritis. With well-fed children these pass within a few days, but in his case, they went on for weeks and sometimes a month or more. In these periods he could tolerate no milk and few solids, and so was given weak broths, tea or sugar water. By now he was 25 per cent underweight. Because of poor nutrition, he was even more susceptible to infection, and each time he was ill, he lost his appetite and ate even less. Then he got bronchitis which developed into pneumonia. But Fatima borrowed money off a relative, went to town and got antibiotics for him. So he survived. But malnutrition made him withdrawn and apathetic. His mother got no reward for playing with him, so he received little of the stimulation his brain needed to develop properly. As he grew older, infections grew less frequent, but by the time he went to school, aged eight, he was already a year behind normal physical development and two years behind mentally. The school, in any case, was a poor one, with only three classes, no equipment, and a poorly qualified teacher.

As Francisco was continually worried about whether and what he was going to eat that day, he was distracted, unable to concentrate, and seemed to show little interest in schoolwork. The teacher confirmed that he was a slow learner, and could not seem to get the hang of maths or reading and writing. As the family was poor, they did not want to keep him on at school. He was doing so badly anyway that there seemed no point. He did a year, then was away for three years helping an uncle who had a farm, then did another year, then left for good, barely able to read or write more than a few letters. He soon forgot what little he had learned. So, like his father, he began tramping round the local ranches asking for work. Without any educational qualifications or skills, that was all he could ever hope for. And because so many were in the same boat, pay was low. When he was twenty-two he married a local girl, Graciela, aged only fifteen. She too had been under-nourished and was illiterate. She soon became pregnant and had to feed another organism inside her before she herself had fully developed. Graciela had heard about family planning from a friend, but Francisco would not let her use it and anyway she was not sure she wanted to. So by the age of only twenty-five, Graciela already had five children and had lost two. The children had every prospect of growing up much as Francisco and Graciela did, over-populating, underfed, in poor health and illiterate.

Paul Harrison, *Inside the Third World*

Summary note-making

Summarise in note form the reasons for poverty and backwardness in the Third World, which are highlighted by the story of Francisco's life. Use these headings:

health problems   malnutrition   illiteracy   poverty

You might underline the key words and phrases in the text in pencil before you start.

Discussion

- What do you imagine happens to Third World families when the breadwinner has no regular paid employment?

- Why do you think the birth rate tends to be higher in Third World countries than in developed countries?
- Why are the literacy levels so much lower in most Third World countries than in developed countries?
- Why do you think that wage rates are so much lower in Third World countries than in developed countries?
- Do you think that major world fund-raising efforts like the Live Aid, Sport Aid and Comic Relief campaigns have any significant effect on relieving hunger in the Third World?
- Do you think that the development projects of charities like Oxfam and Christian Aid are helpful?
- Do you think governments in the developed world should offer more aid to help development in the Third World?

The global environment

The greatest threat to the long-term survival of the human race is almost certainly that of global warming. A major cause of this potentially catastrophic development is what is happening to the world's rainforests.

In an article contained in a report published in September 1996 in the *Observer*, in conjunction with the World Wide Fund for Nature (WWF), David Bellamy explains the dangers of uncontrolled tree felling, and suggests a solution. Here is an extract from the article.

Act now, or pay later

'THREE BILLION TREES WILL BE REQUIRED EACH YEAR JUST TO WIPE THE BOTTOMS OF THE WORLD'

Your lifestyle is cocooned in products of the forest world – a lifestyle which, by the time your children or grandchildren have grown up, will be the dream of at least ten billion people. In this nightmare scenario, three billion trees will be required each year just to wipe the bottoms of the world. And that's pulp fact, not fiction. Forests are of immense importance to life, and that includes us. Not only are they places of great beauty, changing with the seasons, but they provide habitats for more than 70 per cent of all land-living plants and animals. They also play an important role in keeping the planet in working order.

Forests make humus-rich soil, their tree roots holding it safe from erosion; water is stored and minerals are recycled, maintaining water and soil in good heart. That was the way of five billion hectares 8,000 years ago. Since that dim and not-so-distant time, more than half of those forests have been destroyed to make way for crops, concrete and degraded land. The rate of forest destruction continues unabated, and recently acid rain has taken an increasing toll. Deserts are on the march, engulfing 27 million hectares of crop and range land every year, while catastrophic floods bankrupt communities or their insurers.

The time has come to put people and their forests back together.

We need a world-wide moratorium on the felling of what is left of our 'old growth' forests. It could be rapidly phased in by turning to timber produced in well-designed and well-managed plantations. There are already ample that are either on-stream or coming on-stream, and the sooner independent assessment of such plantations is up and running the better.

David Bellamy, the Observer, 29 September 1996

In the same *Observer*/WWF report, Martin Wright describes a project in Mexico which highlights the importance of the preservation of the rainforests in simple human terms.

Development without the destruction

In the cloud forests of the Sierra Norte in southern Mexico, a living relic of pre-Ice Age landscapes, jaguars, panthers, salamanders and spider monkeys share their home with a number of Indian tribes, including the Mixe, Mixtec, Chinantec and the Zapatec, who make use of more than 1,000 of the forest's plant species for food, medicine and other needs. Many are unknown to Western science, and have only local names. Under a project run by WWF, in partnership with Britain's Overseas Development Administration (ODA), the Mixe have launched their own programme of identifying, collecting and marketing medicinal plants. Children of this remote part of Oaxaca state are being taught skills that would otherwise be lost. As a result, the communities have come to value the forest more as a living resource than as something that can only be of value when destroyed.

Foreign aid has often meant forest destruction: international money has cut roads across the Amazon and planted vast dams in Asia, as well as directly funding destructive logging. But there is another, less well-known side to the story. Sensitively applied, and working with, rather than in spite of, local people, foreign aid can save forests. Successful projects range from major schemes aimed at redefining a nation's forest strategy, to smaller programmes whose goal is to help local communities make a living from a living forest on their doorstep.

Martin Wright, *Observer*, September 1996

Global warming is not only caused by rainforest destruction. In the extracts which follow, from a book by the Canadian environmentalists, Anita Gordon and David Suzuki, called *It's a Matter of Survival*, published in 1990, the threat of global warming is explored in full, and solutions suggested.

The danger

The 'Big Warming' we expect is the result of human activity. We release heat-trapping molecules of such gases as carbon dioxide and methane as the by-products of our civilisation; carbon dioxide from burning coal and oil, driving our cars, and heating our homes, and from the destruction of forests; methane from cattle herds, and from rice paddies...

We also add heat-trapping gases like CFCs from the consumer products we have made part of our lives: spray cans, air conditioners, and refrigerators. Like a pane of glass in a greenhouse, all these molecules let lots of sunlight in but prevent a large amount of heat from escaping the earth's atmosphere into outer space...

With global warming will come a rise in sea level of as much as 1.5 metres (5 ft) ... Something in the order of a third of the world's population and more than a third of the world's economic infrastructure are concentrated in coastal regions with altitudes below 1.5 metres (5 ft). All that is at risk over the next 40 to 60 years. Whole nations are at risk ... The temperature of the planet is higher than it's been since record-keeping began...

Food scarcity is emerging as the most profound and immediate consequence of global environmental degradation. It is already affecting the welfare of hundreds of millions of people ... Every day around the world 40,000 people die of hunger. That's 28 human beings every minute, and three out of four of them are children under the age of five. And that is the toll in times of relative plenty...

Perhaps a billion or more of the world's people already spend 70 per cent of their income on food. For many in this group, a dramatic rise in the cost of grain is life-threatening...

The spectre of Ethiopia is abroad. The television images are haunting: an 18-year-old Eritrean, driven out of her homeland because of starvation, stands and gives birth to an emaciated infant. Do we want that quality of human life?

The principal causes

The disappearance of the rainforest would be nothing less than an incalculable disaster for the whole planet. The rainforests are, in effect, 'the lungs of the planet', helping to regulate the exchange of oxygen and carbon dioxide, just as our own lungs do ... As trees are cut or burned, they release their carbon into the air as carbon dioxide, exacerbating the greenhouse effect.

Perhaps the hardest question of all that we must face is whether, given the state of the world, there can be a future for the automobile ... The automobile is proving itself to be incompatible with human survival and the well-being of the planet. It destroys our quality of life, the air we breathe, our crops and our trees with toxic emissions. It destroys the ozone layer. It is responsible for the paving over of our cropland and wilderness. Every time we climb into a car and put our foot on the gas, we're jeopardising our family's future ...

More than 400 million vehicles clog the world's streets today, and the production and use of fuels for automobiles accounts for an estimated 17 per cent of all carbon dioxide released from fossil fuels ...

China and India together account for 38 per cent of the world's population, and at this point, they own scarcely 0.5 per cent of its automobiles ... Imagine one billion Chinese deciding they all want to have a car. It could happen ...

The heart of the dilemma is energy, the world's reliance on fossil fuel ... The industrial countries' fossil-fuel emissions are going to heat the atmosphere for the whole world ... And the route the Third World takes to industrialisation could determine the future for the whole planet ...

One North American does 20 to 100 times more damage to the planet than one person in the Third World, and one rich North American causes 1,000 times more destruction.

The profligacy of the United States has already put us in grave peril; if the Third World follows out example, it will finish us off.

What needs to be done

Twenty per cent of the world is living an orgy of mindless consumption, and the rest struggle to survive by destroying the life-support systems of the planet. Each one of us is responsible for the carnage of the rainforests as surely as if we were to take an axe or a match to the forests ourselves ... The goal of development, for rich and poor, must be to create conserver societies; that basically means the rich must live more simply so the poor may simply live ... There is no quick fix for the environmental crisis; however, each of us has the power to make a crucial difference to the mounting odds against survival ... In the world of garbage management, recycling is one of the three Rs – recycle, reuse and reduce. Glass bottles, aluminium beverage cans and newspapers can be ground up and re-processed and then recycled, at a real energy saving...

If recycling glass bottles to be ground up and remade uses 25 per cent less energy than creating a bottle from virgin material, imagine the energy saving, not to mention the pollution that isn't being created or the resources that aren't being used up, if those same glass bottles are simply washed out and reused for pop or milk. Standardising glass containers for food would go a long way toward creating that kind of saving...

Reuse is heading in the right direction, but the journey is futile without restraint: the most efficient way to avert the looming garbage crisis is to avoid producing garbage at all...

Starting with Berkeley, California, in 1987, a number of municipalities have joined the rush to ban plastics and packaging ... [However] for survival's sake, we must add a fourth R to the garbage-management primer – *rethink* – and that, in the end, is what will save us ... What we've got to rethink is our consumer society.

As the car overruns us, more and more people are becoming convinced that the true solution is much more brutal than fuel efficiency and alternative funds. We must restrict our driving...

Stockholm may become the first European capital to charge for road use, with the money collected devoted to improving public transport ... The major policy of the Western world has to be to virtually eliminate dependence on fossil fuels overall, as fast as is humanly possible to achieve ... Not only are we going to have to cut carbon emissions by as much as 80 per cent, we're going to have to do it in this decade if we want to avoid a hothouse future.

Now that we are faced with this greenhouse apocalypse, it is extraordinary to discover that there are – researched, developed and ready to go – technologies that could clean up the First World's mess and provide the Third World with an alternative route to development. We must tell our legislators at every level that they must lead us into this new world, with hope and with vision, and we must speak with one voice:

- If our leaders must legislate us into a new era of renewable energy, then do it.
- If they must redistribute the pie to help Third World countries so we all survive, then do it.
- If we must be legislated out of our cars, then do it.
- If industry must be legislated in order to become environmentally responsible, then do it...

Our own cheap road to prosperity is leading to the end of global civilisation; there is no future via that route. Even if a fraction of the remaining 80 per cent of the planet headed down the same highway, the ecological chaos could bring all our civilisations tumbling down ... 'Don't we need to think about those who come after us?' says US Senator Al Gore. That's really the bottom line, isn't it? How do we get up in the morning and look our children in the eye and tell them that we spent their future?' ...

This is the test for humanity. Will we degenerate into territorial creatures struggling for power, land and survival, or will we emerge with a new collective image of ourselves as a species integrated into the natural world?

In times of crisis, people have pulled together and forgotten their mistrust and petty rivalries. They've sacrificed and worked to change their lives. There has never been a bigger crisis than the one we now face. And we are the last generation that can pull us out of it. We must act because this is the only home we have. It is a matter of survival.

Anita Gordon and David Suzuki, *It's a Matter of Survival*

Discussion

- Why are the rainforests so important to individuals and to the human race as a whole?
- Why are the rainforests being destroyed?
- Do you think there is any hope that the rainforests will survive?
- What do you imagine will happen if the sea level rises by 1.5 metres or more?
- Why is the car regarded as such an important contributor to global warming?
- In the section headed 'What needs to be done?' in the series of extracts from 'It's a Matter of Survival', the writers suggest four things that 'we must tell our legislators at every level to do'. What is your opinion of the four suggestions?
- Do you think the human race will pull together before it is too late?

Writing a leaflet

Leaflet writing is a possible examination exercise. It can also provide a writing coursework assignment.

Here is an example of a leaflet produced by the environmental pressure group Friends of the Earth in October 1996 for their forest preservation campaign. It is printed on both sides, and folds up so that only the cover (headed 'WILD WOODS!') is displayed. It then opens out as shown here.

FRIENDS OF THE EARTH IS CAMPAIGNING FOR:

- a halt to logging in old-growth forests in Scandinavia

- a 65 per cent reduction in the UK's wood use from 1990 levels by the year 2010

- new wood to be produced sustainably, with as little damage to forests and wildlife as possible

WHAT YOU CAN DO

- Write to the Finnish and Swedish governments (addresses below), urging that they protect all their old-growth forest. Say you can't buy wood and paper from their countries with a clear conscience until they have done so.

Mr Kalevi Hemilä
Minister of Agriculture and Forestry
P.O. Box 232
00171 Helsinki
Finland

Mr Göran Persson
Minister of State
Statsrådsberedningen
10333 Stockholm
Sweden

- Save wood - reduce, reuse and recycle.
- If you need wood products, buy secondhand or reclaimed wood. Always buy recycled paper.
- Urge your council or employer to set up recycling schemes for wood and paper.
- Support Friends of the Earth's *Wild Woods!* campaign.

FRIENDS OF THE EARTH

- is the largest international network of environmental groups in the world

- is one of the UK's most influential national environmental pressure groups

- is a unique network of campaigning local groups, working in 250 communities in England, Wales and Northern Ireland

Friends of the Earth exists to protect the environment, now and for the future.

Friends of the Earth launched the world's first campaign to save the tropical rainforests in 1985. We have saved rainforests in Brazil and Belize from logging schemes, and persuaded major DIY stores to stop selling mahogany. UK mahogany imports have dropped by 80 per cent in response to our campaign.

Join us and help save the forests.

To become a national supporter or give a donation to our campaign, please phone 01582 482297.

To read more about this issue, order your copy of Friends of the Earth's booklet Paper, Wood and the World's Forests, 50p from Friends of the Earth Publications Despatch, 56-58 Alma Street, Luton LU1 2PH

FRIENDS *of the* earth
for the planet for people
October 1996 © Friends of the Earth Limited
Published by Friends of the Earth Limited Cover photo: Laurie Campbell
Printed on paper made from 100% post-consumer waste
Friends of the Earth, 26-28 Underwood Street, London N1 7JQ
Telephone: 0171 490 1555 Fax: 0171 490 0881 Email: info@foe.co.uk
URL: http://www.foe.co.uk

WILD WOODS!

SAVE THE WORLD'S FORESTS - USE LESS PAPER AND WOOD

FRIENDS *of the* earth

THE GREAT TIMBER RUSH

Natural forest, Finland

Massive global demand for wood and paper is driving destruction of the world's natural forests. Dozens of plant and animal species go extinct each day, while the way of life of millions of forest people is threatened.

Global wood and paper consumption in 1990 was 1.7 billion cubic metres. This is predicted to increase by almost 60 per cent by the year 2010! All over the world, forests are being cut down or converted to intensive plantations to meet the demand for newspapers, writing paper, window frames, doors and a host of other everyday items.

The world's forests can produce wood and paper *and* support wildlife and forest people. But first, overall use of wood and paper must be reduced. Consumers, governments and companies all have a part to play.

LESS WOOD AND PAPER, MORE FORESTS

If there is to be much real forest in the future, less paper and wood must be used - especially in developed countries like the UK. Using metal or plastic instead isn't the answer, as these have their own environmental costs.

The way forward is to reduce, reuse and recycle paper and wood products, for example, by:

- Reducing paper use in offices and cutting out unnecessary packaging
- Making wood products more efficiently, and designing them to last longer
- Recycling much of the 5 million tonnes of paper currently sent to landfill sites each year
- Reclaiming and reusing the thousands of tonnes of timber thrown away by the wood trade each year

Grey Wolf - inhabitant of natural forest

SCANDINAVIAN SCANDAL

White-backed Woodpecker - endangered by modern forestry

More than a third of the UK's paper and over 20 per cent of our wood comes from forests in Scandinavia, especially Finland and Sweden. Heavy exploitation has left just 5 per cent of the natural old-growth forest in these countries - the rest has been converted to intensively managed plantations.

Incredibly, these last, valuable fragments of old-growth forest in Scandinavia are being cut down to satisfy our enormous demand for timber and paper.

The old, natural forests were home to a rich variety of plants, animals and fungi. Only a fraction of these can live in the new intensive 'factory forests'. Hundreds of species, including the white-backed woodpecker and the flying squirrel, are nationally endangered, while the traditional way of life of the Saami people in Lapland is threatened by logging in the forests where their reindeer graze.

Note the use of headings for the sections; pictures; bulleted points for the suggestions for action by the readers, and for the campaigns list.

Coursework suggestions

- Write a leaflet with the title 'How to Save the World'. You should include explanations of how and why the world is threatened, and suggestions for action. You need to decide which organisation the leaflet is to be issued by, and find or create pictures or illustrations. You can, of course, draw on information and ideas from anywhere in the unit or from your own research. You must, however, select your points with care, because space is limited. You will probably need to produce two drafts. You should decide what kind of audience the leaflet is aimed at, and use a style of writing which will suit your audience. Whichever audience you choose, your leaflet must be punchy and attractive to the eye.
- Write an essay in answer to this question: 'Should Britain provide more aid to help tackle famine and poverty in the Third World?'
- Write an essay with this title: 'What is the major environmental problem at the turn of the twenty-first century, and what suggestions do you have to solve it?'

NB: If you are considering writing an essay, it would be a good idea to look again at Unit 16, which contains an essay on the environment.

SYLLABUS REQUIREMENTS COVERED

The oral work in this unit can be assessed for speaking and listening in the categories 'explore, analyse, imagine' and 'discuss, argue, persuade'.

The coursework suggestions are of potential relevance as practice for examinations of NEAB (leaflet writing) and SEG (essay writing).

The coursework suggestions are relevant to the coursework requirements of the syllabuses as follows:

MEG: Unit 1

NEAB: Unit 4: original writing

SEG: Personal writing – non-fiction

WJEC: Best writing

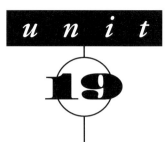
SHAKESPEARE'S *MACBETH* (1)

B oth this unit and the next one are given over to the study of Shakespeare's *Macbeth*. All students of GCSE English are now required to study a complete Shakespeare play and to write about it as coursework. The onus will be on you to read the play in your own time. If you can get hold of a performance of the play on audiocassette, and listen to it while you are reading the play, this will help.

The best way to bring the play to life *as* a play is to see it in performance. If this is not possible, the next best way is to watch a good film version of it. This is the approach taken in this unit.

A SCENE FROM POLANSKI'S *MACBETH*

Perhaps the most atmospheric film version of the play is Roman Polanski's *Macbeth*, made in 1971, and issued on Columbia Tristar video, number CVR 20668. This can be watched in various ways:

straight through, without interruptions

scene by scene, pausing for discussion

watching selected scenes, using the scene summary which follows both as an aid to your understanding of the action and as a way of filling in the scenes missed out on the video.

First, let us say a few words about the play. It was written in 1606 and is a tragedy. Like all Shakespeare's major tragedies (such as *Hamlet*, *Othello* and *King Lear*), it centres on a nobleman who is in many respects an admirable person, but who finds himself in a situation which tests his strength and virtue beyond its limits. Macbeth is a leading nobleman in the land of Scotland at the time when it was a self-governing country, ruled by its own kings. He is a fearless military leader, and is so highly regarded by the King of Scotland that he is rewarded, in the second scene of the play, with the title Thane of Cawdor, after the owner of that title is found guilty of treason and sent to be executed. Just before receiving the news of his elevation to this exalted title, Macbeth has encountered three witches who possess prophetic powers and who prophesy that not only will he become Thane of Cawdor, but also King. When the first prophecy is immediately fulfilled, and King Duncan then announces that he will spend the next night at Macbeth's castle, the temptation to ensure the speedy completion of the witches' predictions is born. It is from this that the tragedy grows.

Here is a summary of the plot.

Act I, Scene 1

Three witches meet on a heath, and an atmosphere of malevolence is created. They speak of meeting with Macbeth on the heath.

Act I, Scene 2

News is brought to King Duncan of the battle between the Scottish King's army, led by Macbeth and Banquo, and an invading force from Norway. The Norwegian army has been defeated, and Macbeth's bravery has played a major part in the Scottish victory. As a result of this, King Duncan announces that Macbeth will be rewarded with the title Thane of Cawdor, after the arrest of the current Thane, who had treacherously sided with Norway.

Act I, Scene 3

The three evil witches confront Macbeth and Banquo as they return from the battle, and prophesy Macbeth's elevation to the titles of Thane of Cawdor and then King, but also say that it will be Banquo's heirs who will be kings after Macbeth. Macbeth is startled by this.

The first part of the witches' prophecy to Macbeth is immediately fulfilled, and Macbeth begins to fear his own ambitious nature once the possibility of ultimate power is suddenly within his grasp.

Act I, Scene 4

King Duncan informs Macbeth, now formally recognised as Thane of Cawdor, that Malcolm, the King's eldest son, will inherit the throne. Malcolm thus stands in the way of the fulfilment of the witches' prophecy, and Macbeth's 'black and deep desires'.

Act I, Scene 5

Lady Macbeth, receiving her husband's news by letter, fears that Macbeth lacks the necessary ruthlessness to gain the throne by foul means. Further news, that the King will be spending the night at Macbeth's castle, excites her murderous ambitions. When Macbeth arrives, she begins to tempt him to murder the King.

Act I, Scene 6

Duncan arrives and is greeted warmly by Lady Macbeth. He is surprised by Macbeth's absence.

Act I, Scene 7

Macbeth, alone, contemplates the assassination of the King. His 'vaulting ambition' is weighed against the practical and moral arguments against murdering Duncan. He expresses his doubts to his wife, who mocks his unmanly cowardice and unfolds a plan to get Duncan's guards drunk, steal into the King's chamber and stab him, and accuse the guards of the murder. Macbeth is persuaded.

Act II, Scene 1

Macbeth, in restless agitation, imagines that he sees a bloody dagger in the air above his head, leading him towards the King's chamber.

Act II, Scene 2

Having carried out Lady Macbeth's plan, and stabbed Duncan and the guards, Macbeth is riddled with guilt, imagining a voice saying, 'Macbeth shall sleep no more'. Lady Macbeth tells him to wash his hands, attempting to reassure him that: 'A little water clears us of this deed'. In his panic Macbeth came away from the chamber with bloody daggers in his hands, which she has to take back because Macbeth is too horrified by what he has done to return to the chamber of death. Someone is knocking at the door.

Act II, Scene 3

The tension is briefly relaxed as a drunken porter takes his time to open the door, offering comic reflections on human frailty. Macduff and Lennox, two other leading noblemen, are at the door. Macduff is greeted by Macbeth, and then makes the discovery of the murder of Duncan. Macbeth puts on a convincing performance of shocked ignorance, rushes into the chamber, and claims, when he comes back out, to have killed Duncan's guards, assuming they were the murderers. Malcolm and Donaldbain, the dead King's sons, decide to flee the country, in fear of meeting the same fate as their father if they stay.

Act II, Scene 4

Malcolm and Donaldbain's flight has aroused suspicion that they were behind the murder of Duncan. Macbeth has been named as King.

Act III, Scene 1

Banquo privately suspects Macbeth of the murder. Macbeth requests Banquo's presence that night at supper, and mentions rumours that Malcolm and Donaldbain are in England and Ireland, openly making accusations against Macbeth.

Macbeth, in soliloquy, speaks of his fears about Banquo and the witches' prophecy that it would be Banquo's rather than his sons who would form a dynasty. He secures the services of two bitter and desperate men to murder Banquo and Fleance, Banquo's son, while they are out riding that afternoon.

Act III, Scene 2

Macbeth speaks darkly to his wife of his fears and the mental torture induced by guilt over the murder of Duncan. He speaks mysteriously of a deed of darkness which will be performed before nightfall. Despite his feelings of guilt and self-disgust, he is now taking the initiatives to safeguard his position, and is sinking deeper into evil.

Act III, Scene 3

Banquo is killed by the hired murderers, but Fleance escapes.

Act III, Scene 4

Macbeth hears from one of the hired killers of the murder of Banquo, but the news of Fleance's escape only increases his anguish.

The guests are all seated at table for the evening's banquet. Macbeth is invited to take the last empty seat. He cannot find one, however, and suddenly realises, to his stark horror, that the seat he has been offered is filled with the gashed and bloody figure of Banquo. His seemingly insane ramblings, addressed to Banquo's ghost which only he can see, are explained away by Lady Macbeth as a childhood infirmity which will soon pass. The ghost fades, and Macbeth seems to recover, but then it returns, and the banquet is called off by Lady Macbeth.

The ghost again disappears, but Macbeth is convinced that 'blood will have blood'. The absence of Macduff at the banquet is a further worry. Macbeth decides to return to the 'weird sisters', for another glimpse into the future.

Act III, Scene 5

The witches meet again, and speak of Macbeth's imminent visit to 'meet his destiny'.

Act III, Scene 6

Suspicions of Macbeth are now rife, and are voiced by Lennox, another leading nobleman. Malcolm, Duncan's son, now in England, is plotting a civil war to overthrow Macbeth, who is now openly being called a 'tyrant'. Macbeth is also making preparations for war, and Macduff, in secret consultation with Macbeth's enemies, has refused to join on Macbeth's side.

Act IV, Scene 1

The witches are preparing for the visit of Macbeth by casting spells over a cauldron. Macbeth arrives, and a series of prophetic apparitions appear before him. The first warns him to 'beware Macduff', but the second and third seem reassuring: he cannot be killed by anyone 'of woman born', and he will not be defeated until Birnam Wood moves to the hill of Dunsinane. The final vision is of a procession of eight kings, with Banquo appearing last with a mocking smile.

News is brought of Macduff's flight to England. Macbeth's heart hardens at the news, and he resolves to have Macduff's wife and babies murdered, to wipe out his line, as he had failed to wipe out Banquo's.

Act IV, Scene 2

Lady Macduff is angry and distraught at her husband's abandonment of his family. Lady Macduff's eldest son bravely and wittily stands up for his father in the face of his mother's bitterness. The hired killers arrive, stab the child, and chase the fleeing Lady Macduff.

Act IV, Scene 3

Macduff and Malcolm, the dead King Duncan's son, now at the King of England's palace, talk of the tyranny set in train by Macbeth, as 'Each new morn/New widows howl, new orphans cry'. Malcolm longs to 'tread upon the tyrant's head'. He then pretends that he would become an even more evil tyrant than Macbeth if he were to become king; in the process he describes the qualities of an ideal ruler, which he claims to lack. The King of England, Edward the Confessor, is described, presenting a portrait of the noble and virtuous ruler.

Ross, another Scottish nobleman, brings news of the full extent of the tyranny which reigns in Scotland, where 'sighs and groans and shrieks' daily rend the air. He speaks of rumours of an impending civil war in Scotland to overthrow 'the tyrant' Macbeth, and asks Malcolm and Macduff to return to Scotland to join the rebel army. He then informs Macduff of the murder of his wife and children. Macduff vows revenge.

Act V, Scene 1

Lady Macbeth has gone mad, and wanders round the castle talking to herself and rubbing her hands constantly, trying to clear imaginary blood from them. She hints at the cause of her obsession – her involvement in the murders of Duncan, Banquo and Macduff's wife.

Act V, Scene 2

The rebel forces, led by Malcolm, Macduff and Malcolm's Uncle Siward, are massed near Dunsinane Castle, which Macbeth is fortifying to withstand a siege. Macbeth's control over his own forces is growing steadily weaker.

Act V, Scene 3

Macbeth remains defiant, emboldened by the recollection of the witches' promises that he could be killed only when Birnam Wood comes to the castle where he now is, and by a man not born of woman. News of an enemy army of ten thousand approaching causes Macbeth merely to give the order: 'Hang those that talk of fear'. His inner feelings are bordering on despair, however: he knows that he is hated by everyone, and his life has lost all meaning. The doctor brings news of his wife's mental illness, and he longs that not only she but the country could be cured of its sickness.

Act V, Scene 4

Malcolm gives the order that boughs be cut from the trees in Birnam Wood, which the rebel army has now reached, so that his troops can carry them to conceal their numbers.

Act V, Scene 5

Macbeth remains confident that Dunsinane can withstand a siege. The cry of women is heard, and Macbeth reveals that he has become completely insensitive to 'horrors'. He is told that Lady Macbeth is dead, and the news provokes an outburst of the deepest despair: he feels now that human life is worthless and meaningless. News is brought that Birnam Wood is on the move. Macbeth's confidence is shaken; all that is left to him now is to die bravely.

Act V, Scene 6

Final preparations are made by Malcolm for the imminent battle.

Act V, Scene 7

The battle is raging, and Macbeth is confronted by Young Siward, whom he kills, again feeling invulnerable because of the witches' prediction that he cannot be killed by 'man that's of a woman born'. Macduff appears, bent on personal revenge for the murder of his wife. Siward reveals that the castle has been breached, and victory for the rebels is now close.

Act V, Scene 8

Macduff confronts Macbeth, who defiantly tells him of the 'charmed life' the witches' prophecy promises him. Macduff reveals that he was 'ripped' from his mother's body by a Caesarean operation, and therefore not 'born' in the natural way. Macbeth's last hope is gone but he has sufficient pride left to fight to the death rather than surrender.

Act V, Scene 9

Macduff brings in the head of Macbeth, and Malcolm is hailed as the new King of Scotland. Malcolm pronounces that everyone who fled the tyranny of Macbeth's rule should be welcomed home to Scotland, and all the agents of Macbeth should be punished. Everyone is invited to attend the coronation of the new King.

Performing a scene

When you have watched the film and discussed the issues it raises, you might attempt a performance of one of the scenes. A good one to act out is Act V, scene 5, as it is particularly dramatic and emotionally charged.

The person playing Macbeth will need to study his speeches carefully, and work out how to convey the different feelings expressed in the scene.

Reading the play

In preparation for the next unit, you should read the play at home, so that you have a full enough understanding of it to be able to explore sections of it in depth, with an awareness of how the sections chosen for detailed study fit into the development of the play as a whole.

Shakespeare's language

Perhaps the major stumbling block to the appreciation of Shakespeare is the difficulty of actually understanding the words he uses. The language used by the characters in Shakespeare's plays seems so different from the language spoken today that people often refer to it as 'old English'.

In fact, it isn't. There *is* a form of English which language experts refer to as 'Old English', but this was spoken 800 years before Shakespeare. It was also known as Anglo-Saxon English, and pre-dates the Norman Conquest of 1066.

Here is a passage from the anonymous poem 'Beowulf', which was probably written in the eighth century, to show what *real* Old English looks like:

> Forþan biþ andgit æghwær selest,
> Ferhþes foreþanc. Fela sceal gebidan
> Leofes ond laþes se þe longe her
> On þyssum windagum worolde bruceþ.

- Can you recognise any similarities with modern English?

After the Norman Conquest, French words and formations began filtering into the old Anglo-Saxon language, and a new form of English developed, which came to be known as Middle English. This is the language of the poet Chaucer, whose most famous work, *The Canterbury Tales*, was written in the late fourteenth century. Here is a passage taken from 'The Wife of Bath's Tale', which is one of the *Canterbury Tales*:

> For God so wys be my savacioun,
> I ne loved nevere by no discrecioun,
> But evere falwede myn appetit,
> Al were he short, or long, or blak, or whit;
> I took no kep, so that he liked me,
> How poor he was, ne eek of what degree.

- How many of the words can you recognise?
- What seems to you to be the main difference between the English of Chaucer and our own time?

Compared even with Middle English, let alone Old English, Shakespeare's language is *comparatively* easy to understand, once you have got used to it. Here is a brief extract from *Macbeth*:

> If thou speaks't false,
> Upon the next tree shalt thou hang alive,
> Till famine cling thee. If thy speech be sooth,
> I care not if thou dost for me as much.

There are 31 words in this extract.

- How many of them are modern words?
- Underline all the words that are not modern.
- What do you notice about these words?

As you will no doubt have recognised, one of the archaic words is 'thou' (used three times), another is 'thee', and another is 'thy'. Two of the 'thous' are followed by words that are not quite modern. This is, in fact, one of the main reasons why Shakespeare's English seems so different from modern English, and why people think of it as 'old English'. In fact, the language of Shakespeare is referred to by linguists as Modern English, *as distinct* from Old English and Middle English. Once you've got to grips with the 'thees', 'thous' and 'thys' (which are simply archaic forms of 'you' and 'your'), and the verb forms which go with them – thous speaks't' (instead of 'you speak'), 'thou dost' (instead of 'you do'), etc., etc. – then it really isn't very different from modern English.

The other main differences are also illustrated in this extract. A comparatively small proportion of Shakespeare's words have disappeared from the English language over the intervening four centuries ('sooth' in this extract, for example), and others have gradually changed their meaning over the centuries (like 'cling'). Such words, should be explained in the notes in your text. Most of the words, however, have retained their spelling and meaning, unlike Chaucer's words from two centuries before Shakespeare.

Shakespeare's verse

Another of the difficulties which people experience with Shakespeare is that his plays are written in verse (or poetry). This makes them seem all the more remote, in comparison with a modern play.

Writing plays in verse form was a convention of Shakespeare's time. It makes the language seem much grander and, of course, poetic, which people in Shakespeare's day thought fitting for plays about kings and queens and the nobility.

There is a form and rhythmic pattern to Shakespeare's verse. It is called **iambic pentameter** verse. If we look at a line from *Macbeth* we can see how it works:

Till famine cling thee. If thy speech be sooth.

- How many separate syllables are there in this line?
- Which of the syllables receive stress when you speak them out loud?

You may have decided that the stressed syllables are the second ('fa-' of 'famine'), the fourth ('cling'), the eighth ('speech') and the tenth ('sooth'). This illustrates the basic pattern. The lines are generally of ten syllables, and there is a pattern of stresses: generally an unstressed syllable followed by a stressed syllable, repeated five times. The rhythmic (or metrical) pattern of unstressed syllable followed by stressed syllable is called an **iamb**, hence the name **iambic pentameter**, meaning a metre of five iambs ('pent' meaning 'five'). Shakespeare does not stick rigidly to this pattern, which would quickly make it seem unduly artificial and wooden, but it provides an overall rhythmic flow to the language, which is part of its power.

SYLLABUS REQUIREMENTS COVERED

A coursework piece on a complete play by Shakespeare is a requirement in all the syllabuses.

SHAKESPEARE'S *MACBETH* (2)

In this unit, we shall focus on the central theme of *Macbeth*. In the previous unit, it was pointed out that *Macbeth* is an example of the genre of drama called 'tragedy'. All Shakespeare's major tragedies have aspects in common. In all of them, the character after whom the play is named is a man of noble birth who is confronted with a situation which tests him to the limits and ultimately brings about his destruction and that of those nearest to him.

- What do you think *is* the central theme of *Macbeth*?
- What causes Macbeth to contemplate murdering the king to achieve ultimate power?
- What causes him to lose all moral scruples and become a tyrant?
- Do you think that *Macbeth*, which was written at the turn of the seventeenth century, has any relevance to the world at the turn of the twenty-first century?

The coursework suggestions at the end of this unit will focus on these issues.

We shall now look in more detail at ten key passages, tracing Macbeth's descent into tyranny and despair, and attempt to analyse the way Shakespeare captures the growth of his ambition and the emotions which accompany it.

1 Macbeth, having heard the witches' prophecies in Act I, Scene 3, has just been informed of the fulfilment of the first of them. He expresses his private reactions to the news.

(*Aside*) This supernatural soliciting
Cannot be ill; cannot be good: – if ill,
Why hath it given me earnest of success,
Commencing in a truth? I am Thane of Cawdor.
If good, why do I yield to that suggestion
Whose horrid image doth unfix my hair,
And make my seated heart knock at my ribs
Against the use of nature? Present fears
Are less than horrible imaginings.
My thought, whose murder yet is but fantastical,
Shakes so my single state of man, that function
Is smothered in surmise, and nothing is,
But what is not.

- How would you describe Macbeth's reaction?
- How is it conveyed through Shakespeare's choice of language?

2 Goaded by his wife to follow his own darkest impulses and murder Duncan and therefore achieve absolute power, Macbeth, in
Act I, Scene 7, agonises over the temptation to commit the ultimate act of betrayal.

He's here in double trust:
First, as I am his kinsman and his subject,
Strong both against the deed; then, as his host,
Who should against his murderer shut the door,
Not bear the knife myself. Besides, this Duncan
Hath borne his faculties so meek, hath been
So clear in his great office, that his virtues
Will plead like angels, trumpet-tongued, against
The deep damnation of his taking-off;
And pity, like a naked new-born babe,
Striding the blast, or heaven's cherubin, horsed
Upon the sightless couriers of the air,
Shall blow the horrid deed in every eye,
That tears shall drown the wind. I have no spur
To prick the sides of my intent, but only
Vaulting ambition, which o'erleaps itself
And falls on th' other.

- What does this soliloquy show us about Macbeth's character?
- Try to explain how the similes ('angels', 'new-born babe',
'Heaven's cherubim') help to convey Macbeth's emotions.

3 Lady Macbeth confronts her husband, in the same scene, with the

imminent prospect of carrying out the plan to murder Duncan.
He tells her: 'We will proceed no further in this business', and she
becomes angry and scornful.

MACBETH

Pr'ythee, peace.
I dare do all that may become a man;
Who dares do more is none.

LADY MACBETH

What beast was 't then
That made you break this enterprise to me?
When you durst do it, then you were a man;
And, to be more than what you were, you would
Be so much more the man. Nor time nor place
Did then adhere, and yet you would make both:
They have made themselves, and that their fitness now
Does unmake you. I have given suck, and know
How tender 't is to love the babe that milks me:
I would, while it was smiling in my face,
Have plucked my nipple from his boneless gums,
And dash'd the brains out, had I so sworn as you
Have done to this.

MACBETH

If we should fail –

LADY MACBETH

We fail?
But screw your courage to the sticking-place
And we'll not fail.

- Do you find Lady Macbeth's appeal to Macbeth persuasive? What
  is powerful about the way she expresses it?

4 Having murdered Duncan, Macbeth, in Act II, Scene 2, is filled
  with a sense of horror at what he has done, and Lady Macbeth attempts to reassure him.

Knocking within

MACBETH

Whence is that knocking?
How is 't with me, when every noise appals me?
What hands are here? Ha! they pluck out mine eyes.
Will all great Neptune's ocean wash this blood
Clean from my hand? No, this my hand will rather
The multitudinous seas incarnadine,

Making the green one red.

Re-enter LADY MACBETH.

LADY MACBETH

My hands are of your colour; but I shame
To wear a heart so white. (*Knock*) I hear a knocking
At the south entry: retire we to our chamber.
A little water clears us of this deed:
How easy is it then! Your constancy
Hath left you unattended. (*Knock*) Hark! more knocking,
Get on your night-gown, lest occasion call us,
And show us to be watchers. Be not lost
So poorly in your thoughts.

MACBETH

To know my deed, 't were best not know myself.

Knock

Wake Duncan with thy knocking: I would thou couldst!

CHERYL CAMPBELL AND DEREK JACOBI IN *MACBETH,* RSC BARBICAN 1993

● How is the difference between Macbeth's and Lady Macbeth's reactions to the murder of Duncan highlighted by what they say
about washing hands? What is ironic about this in the light of
what happens later in the play?

5 Macbeth is established as king, but is not at peace in his mind. In this soliloquy in Act III, Scene 1, he expresses his anxiety about Banquo.

> To be thus is nothing,
> But to be safely thus. – Our fears in Banquo
> Stick deep, and in his royalty of nature
> Reigns that which would be feared. 'T is much he dares,
> And, to that dauntless temper of his mind,
> He hath a wisdom that doth guide his valour
> To act in safety. There is none but he
> Whose being I do fear; and under him
> My genius is rebuked, as, it is said,
> Mark Antony's was by Caesar. He chid the sisters
> When first they put the name of King upon me,
> And bade them speak to him; then, prophet-like,
> They hailed him father to a line of kings.
> Upon my head they placed a fruitless crown,
> And put a barren sceptre in my gripe,
> Thence to be wrenched with an unlineal hand,
> No son of mine succeeding. If 't be so,
> For Banquo's issue have I filed my mind;
> For them the gracious Duncan have I murdered;
> Put rancours in the vessel of my peace
> Only for them; and mine eternal jewel
> Given to the common enemy of man,
> To make them kings, the seed of Banquo kings!
> Rather than so, come, Fate, into the list,
> And champion me to th' utterance! – Who's there? –

- Why does Macbeth wish to see Banquo dead?
- What does he feel he has done to himself by murdering Duncan?

6 Having hired murderers to kill Banquo and Fleance, in Act III, Scene 2, Macbeth speaks ominously and mysteriously to his wife.

MACBETH
> O! full of scorpions is my mind, dear wife!
> Thou know'st that Banquo and his Fleance lives.

LADY MACBETH
> But in them nature's copy's not eterne.

MACBETH
> There's comfort yet; they are assailable:
> Then be thou jocund. Ere the bat hath flown
> His cloistered flight; ere to black Hecate's summons

> The shard-borne beetle, with his drowsy hums,
> Hath run night's yawning peal, there shall be done
> A deed of dreadful note.

LADY MACBETH

> What's to be done?

MACBETH

> Be innocent of the knowledge, dearest chuck,
> Till thou applaud the deed. Come, seeling Night,
> Scarf up the tender eye of pitiful day,
> And, with thy bloody and invisible hand,
> Cancel, and tear to pieces, that great bond
> Which keeps me pale! Light thickens; and the crow
> Makes wing to the rooky wood;
> Good things of day begin to droop and drowse,
> Whiles night's black agents to their preys do rouse.
> Thou marvellest at my words; but hold thee still,
> Things bad begun make strong themselves by ill.
> So, prithee, go with me.

- How does Shakespeare capture the sense of a mind increasingly in the grip of evil thoughts and deeds in the language which Macbeth uses?
- What change do you notice in the way Macbeth speaks to Lady Macbeth?

7 The ghost of the murdered Banquo has appeared to Macbeth at the banquet in Act III, Scene 4, and the guests have been told to depart. Macbeth and Lady Macbeth are left alone.

MACBETH

> It will have blood, they say, blood will have blood:
> Stones have been known to move, and trees to speak;
> Augurs, and understood relations, have
> By maggot-pies and choughs, and rooks, brought forth
> The secret'st man of blood. What is the night?

LADY MACBETH

> Almost at odds with morning, which is which.

MACBETH

> How say'st thou, that Macduff denies his person
> At our great bidding?

LADY MACBETH

> Did you send to him, Sir?

MACBETH

> I hear it by the way; but I will send.

> There's not a one of them, but in his house
> I keep a servant fee'd. I will tomorrow
> (And betimes I will) to the weird sisters:
> More shall they speak; for now I am bent to know,
> By the worst means, the worst. For mine own good
> All causes shall give way: I am in blood
> Stepped in so far, that, should I wade no more,
> Returning were as tedious as go o'er.
> Strange things I have in head, that will to hand,
> Which must be acted, ere they may be scanned.

LADY MACBETH

> You lack the season of all natures, sleep.

MACBETH

> Come, we'll to sleep. My strange and self–abuse
> Is the initiate fear, that wants hard use:
> We are yet but young in deed.

- How do you explain Macbeth's reactions to the ghostly apparition?
- How is he keeping a check on what the leading noblemen are thinking?
- How would you imagine he was going to behave from now on?

8 Macbeth has just met with the witches again, in Act IV, Scene 1, and been warned to 'beware Macduff'. He is now informed by Lennox of Macduff's flight to England. His thoughts are revealed in this aside.

MACBETH

> (*Aside*) Time, thou anticipat'st my dread exploits:
> The flighty purpose never is o'ertook,
> Unless the deed go with it. From this moment
> The very firstlings of my heart shall be
> The firstlings of my hand. And even now,
> To crown my thoughts with acts, be it thought and done:
> The castle of Macduff I will surprise,
> Seize upon Fife; give to th' edge o' th' sword
> His wife, his babes, and all unfortunate souls
> That trace him in his line. No boasting, like a fool;
> This deed I'll do, before this purpose cool.

- How does Macbeth intend to act in future to ensure the maintenance of his power?

9 The plans for a civil war to overthrow Macbeth are well advanced.

Malcolm and Macduff discuss the justification for such drastic action in Act IV, Scene 3.

> Each new morn,
> New widows howl, new orphans cry; new sorrows
> Strike heaven on the face, that it resounds
> As if it felt with Scotland, and yelled out
> Like syllable of dolour.

MALCOLM

> What I believe, I'll wail;
> What know, believe; and what I can redress,
> As I shall find the time to friend, I will.
> What you have spoke, it may be so, perchance.
> This tyrant, whose sole name blisters our tongues,
> Was once thought honest: you have loved him well;
> He hath not touched you yet.

● What method is Macbeth using now to hang on to his power?

10 Macbeth and his followers are preparing for the siege of Dunsinane, in Act V, Scene 3. A servant comes in with disturbing news of the strength of the army from England, which is advancing on the castle.

Enter a SERVANT

MACBETH

> The devil damn thee black, thou cream-faced loon!
> Where gott'st thou that goose look?

SERVANT

> There is ten thousand –

MACBETH

> Geese, villain?

SERVANT

> Soldiers, sir.

MACBETH

> Go, prick thy face, and over-red thy fear,
> Thou lily-livered boy. What soldiers, patch?
> Death of thy soul! Those linen cheeks of thine
> Are counsellors to fear. What soldiers, whey-face?

SERVANT

> The English force, so please you.

MACBETH

> Take thy face hence. (*Exit* SERVANT) – Seyton! – I am sick at heart,
> When I behold – Seyton I say! – This push
> Will cheer me ever, or disseat me now.

I have lived long enough: my way of life
Is fall'n into the sere, the yellow leaf;
And that which should accompany old age,
As honour, love, obedience, troops of friends,
I must not look to have; but, in their stead,
Curses, not loud but deep, mouth-honour, breath,
Which the poor heart would fain deny, and dare not.

● How would you describe Macbeth's mood, and the way he talks
to the servant? How does the language he uses reveal his mood?

Act V, Scene 5

The final section chosen for detailed discussion is a complete scene,
Act V, Scene 5. This is a scene of changing moods, with Macbeth
again the focus. It would be a good scene to present in performance
if anyone is willing to take the part of Macbeth and do a little advance work on his speeches. Here is the scene.

Scene five
Dunsinane. Within the castle.
Enter, with drum and colours, MACBETH, SEYTON, *and* SOLDIERS.
MACBETH
    Hang out our banners on the outward walls;
    The cry is still, 'They come!' Our castle's strength
    Will laugh a siege to scorn; here let them lie,
    Till famine and the ague eat them up.
    Were they not forc'd with those that should be ours,
    We might have met them dareful, beard to beard,
    And beat them backward home. (*A cry within, of women*) What is that
        noise?
SEYTON
    It is the cry of women, my good lord.

                                                    Exit

MACBETH
    I have almost forgot the taste of fears.
    The time has been, my senses would have cooled
    To hear a night-shriek, and my fell of hair
    Would, at a dismal treatise, rouse and stir,
    As life were in 't. I have supped full with horrors;
    Direness, familiar to my slaughterous thoughts,
    Cannot once start me.
Re-enter SEYTON.

Wherefore was that cry?

SEYTON

The queen, my lord, is dead.

MACBETH

She should have died hereafter:

There would have been a time for such a word.

Tomorrow, and tomorrow, and tomorrow,

Creeps in this petty pace from day to day,

To the last syllable of recorded time;

And all our yesterdays have lighted fools

The way to dusty death. Out, out, brief candle!

Life's but a walking shadow, a poor player

That struts and frets his hour upon the stage,

And then is heard no more; it is a tale

Told by an idiot, full of sound and fury,

Signifying nothing.

Enter a MESSENGER

Thou com'st to use thy tongue; thy story quickly.

MESSENGER

Gracious my lord,

I should report that which I say I saw,

But know not how to do 't.

MACBETH

Well, say, sir.

MESSENGER

As I did stand my watch upon the hill,

I looked toward Birnam, and anon, methought,

The wood began to move.

MACBETH

Liar and slave!

MESSENGER

Let me endure your wrath, if 't be not so.

Within this three mile may you see it coming;

I say, a moving grove.

MACBETH

If thou speak'st false,

Upon the next tree shalt thou hang alive,

Till famine cling thee: if thy speech be sooth,

I care not if thou dost for me as much.

I pull in resolution, and begin

To doubt th' equivocation of the fiend,

That lies like truth: 'Fear not, till Birnam wood

Do come to Dunsinane'; and now a wood

Comes toward Dunsinane. Arm, arm, and out!
If this which he avouches does appear,
There is nor flying hence, nor tarrying here.
I 'gin to be aweary of the sun,
And wish th' estate o' th' world were now undone.
Ring the alarum bell! – Blow, wind! come, wrack!
At least we'll die with harness on our back.

Exeunt

- What is Macbeth's mood in the first 15 lines? Pick out a quotation which particularly expresses this mood.
- How does Macbeth's mood change at the news of his wife's death? Discuss the effectiveness of the images in conveying his feelings about life.
- How does he react to the messenger's news? Pick out phrases which express his feelings particularly strongly.

Writing an essay on Macbeth

If you decide to write an essay for your Shakespeare coursework, there are certain guidelines which you should bear in mind.

There are formal requirements which govern the writing of an essay on any subject and these are explained in Unit 17. The structure of your essay must follow this pattern:

a general introduction to the essay topic

a series of paragraphs developing different aspects or sections of the topic

a final general concluding paragraph.

In an essay on a literary work, it is necessary to develop an argument by means of a series of points, backed up by references to the text. The purpose of these textual references is to provide evidence for the points you are making – to prove them. They can take the form of either references to incidents or speeches from the text, expressed in your own words, or direct quotations from the text. You may then need to add some further comment on the textual evidence.

Here is an example. You are tracing the growth of Macbeth's descent into tyranny and are discussing his decision to wipe out Macduff and his whole family, in Act IV, Scene 1. This is an illustration of how to make a point and back it up by indirect reference to the text rather than by direct quotation.

The news of Macduff's flight to England stings Macbeth into even greater ruthlessness, as he abandons any moral considerations whatever, and decides to arrange the slaughter of Macduff's wife and children and all his lineage, without allowing time for any scruples to deflect his murderous purpose.

Here is another example, this time using direct quotations from the text. You are discussing the moment in Act III, Scene 4 when, having already killed Banquo, Macbeth decides that there is no going back on his murderous course.

When the ghostly figure of Banquo fades away, Macbeth realises that he has come to a point of no return in his course of violence:

> ... for mine own good,
> All causes shall give way; I am in blood,
> Steeped in so far, that, should I wade no more,
> Returning were as tedious as go o'er.

The image of wading across a river of blood suggests that from now on his only consideration will be to hang on to his power, regardless of the bloody consequences.

Notice that the remarks which follow the quotation offer a *comment on it*, not just a *paraphrase of it*. There is no point in simply *rewriting* the quotation in your own words.

Notice also that the quotation is set out in lines of verse, as in the text. This is the correct way to set out quotations, unless you are quoting a single line or less. In this case you can just fit the quotation in as part of the sentence, like this:

Macbeth feels it is only 'vaulting ambition' which is spurring him to contemplate the murder of Duncan.

Whenever you quote directly from the text, you must always make sure that you make the **context** of the quotation clear: explain who speaks to whom and in what situation.

Here is an exercise to test your understanding of how to use quotations. Turn to Act V, Scene 3, and make a statement about the effects on Macbeth's own mental state of his ruthless pursuit of ambition, using this quotation:

I have lived long enough: my way of life
Is fall'n into the sere, the yellow leaf. (V, 3, lines 22–3.)

Coursework suggestions

- Write an essay on the effects of the ruthless pursuit of ambition, as shown in *Macbeth*.
- Write an essay on Act V, Scene 5 of *Macbeth*, analysing the effectiveness of the language and imagery of the scene in capturing mood and feeling. You must make sure that you discuss the scene in terms of *types* of language and imagery and their *effects*.
- Write a critique of Roman Polanski's film version of *Macbeth*. You might focus on scenes which were particularly well presented, with reference to the written text. You might also discuss sections of the film which you found less effective, in terms of the written text.
- Write a series of entries from Macbeth's diary, written at various stages in his progress from respected general to despairing tyrant. It would be best to write the diary entries in modern English.
- Write a magazine article on the dangers of the lust for absolute power, using *Macbeth* as the main illustration, and relating the play to research into the lives of historical figures such as Hitler and Stalin.

SYLLABUS REQUIREMENTS COVERED

A coursework piece on a complete play by Shakespeare is a requirement in all the syllabuses.

PERSUASIVE WRITING

A nalysing persuasive writing in the mass media, or applying knowledge of techniques of persuasion, is a core element of GCSE work across the boards. In this unit you will be offered a range of texts, reflecting different ways of presenting viewpoints persuasively, in a range of media. By studying these texts you will develop skills of analysis which will help you with the examinations, and perhaps also provide you with further coursework options.

Before looking at the actual texts, it would be useful to consider some of the techniques used by writers to make their writing persuasive. These techniques can be divided into two main categories: *methods* of presenting a case, and *style* and language use.

Techniques of persuasion

Methods

providing evidence to support the case

making reference to recognised authorities to back up the case

creating a sense of a structured argument

making a reference to counter-arguments, and refuting them

providing comparative examples and illustrations to make the argument seem more real

setting the issue under discussion in a historical framework

offering personal anecdotes, to which the reader can relate

offering inside knowledge, to make the writer sound authoritative

creating the impression that any sane person would agree with what is being said using humour, so that the reader is *laughing* with the writer

using irony (saying the opposite of what is actually meant, in order to mock an opposed viewpoint by pretending to support it)

Style and language

creating a sense of personal 'voice', so that the reader can relate to the argument on a human level

forceful and/or emotive language, to appeal to the reader's feelings and emotions

everyday, colloquial language, to bring the argument 'down to earth'

expressive, colourful language, including literary devices like alliteration and simile, to charm the reader

manipulation of tone, such as a mocking, scornful, sarcastic, angry or bitter tone, to add 'bite' to the argument

loaded questions, creating the impression that the reader is being invited to think for him/herself

rhetorical questions, enforcing agreement

short sentences, adding force and 'punch' to the writing

rhetorical repetition, hammering a point home

Many of these techniques of persuasion are also ways of making an argument biased. Some others *can* be, depending on how they are used, such as presenting a single piece of evidence, and falsely drawing a general conclusion from it. (This is known as arguing from the particular to the general.) A similar use of bias would be to offer *irrelevant* personal anecdotes to back up an argument.

If you are asked to write an analysis of persuasive writing in the examination, the text on which the question is set is likely to be a newspaper or magazine article. Three of the texts offered for analysis in the following pages are newspaper articles. There are, of course, other forums for presenting arguments and viewpoints. Speeches are an important means by which public figures air their views. The text on page 282–83 is a speech. Even poems can argue a case and the first text offered for study is a poem.

- Using the checklist of techniques of persuasion above as a guide, attempt to analyse the methods used by each of the writers, in the extracts which follow, to make their case persuasive.

- Then go on to assess how effectively and convincingly you think each of the writers has presented his/her case.
- Finally, on the evidence of the ideas and attitudes expressed, and of the style and language used, draw what conclusions you can about the kind of audience for which each piece was intended.

The first text is a poem by the seventeenth-century English poet Andrew Marvell. He is presenting a proposition to his 'mistress' (in this case a currently platonic girlfriend).

To His Coy Mistress

Had we but world enough and time,
This coyness, lady, were no crime.
We would sit down and think which way
To walk, and pass our long love's day.
Thou by the Indian Ganges' side
Shouldst rubies find: I by the tide
Of Humber would complain. I would
Love you ten years before the Flood,
And you should, if you please, refuse
Till the conversion of the Jews.
My vegetable love should grow
Vaster than empires and more slow.
An hundred years should go to praise
Thine eyes, and on thy forehead gaze;
Two hundred to adore each breast,
But thirty thousand to the rest;
An age at least to every part,
And the last age should show your heart.
For, lady, you deserve this state,
Nor would I love at lower rate.
   But at my back I always hear
Time's winged chariot hurrying near,
And yonder all before us lie
Deserts of vast eternity.
Thy beauty shall no more be found,
Nor in thy marble vault shall sound
My echoing song; then worms shall try
That long-preserved virginity,
And your quaint honour turn to dust,
And into ashes all my lust.
The grave's a fine and private place,

But none, I think, do there embrace.
   Now, therefore, while the youthful hue
Sits on thy skin like morning dew,
And while thy willing soul transpires
At every pore with instant fires,
Now, let us sport us while we may;
And now, like amorous birds of prey,
Rather at once our time devour,
Than languish in his slow-chapt power!
Let us roll all our strength, and all
Our sweetness up into one ball;
And tear our pleasures with rough strife,
Thorough the iron gates of life!
Thus, though we cannot make our sun
Stand still, yet we will make him run.

Andrew Marvell

The second text is a speech by the then British Prime Minister, Margaret Thatcher, delivered at a rally of Conservative women shortly after the war fought between Britain and Argentina over a group of islands in the South Atlantic, called the Falklands Islands, in 1982. The war was won by Britain, and was a major factor in Margaret Thatcher's victory in the general election the following year.

The Falklands Factor

Today we meet in the aftermath of the Falklands Battle. Our country has won a great victory and we are entitled to be proud. This nation had the resolution to do what it knew had to be done – to do what it knew was right.

We fought to show that aggression does not pay, and that the robber cannot be allowed to get away with his swag. We fought with the support of so many throughout the world: the Security Council, the Commonwealth, the European Community, and the United States. Yet we also fought alone – for we fought for our own people and for our sovereign territory.

Now that it is all over, things cannot be the same again, for we have learnt something about ourselves – a lesson which we desperately needed to learn. When we started out, there were the waverers and the faint-hearts: the people who thought that Britain could no longer seize the initiative for herself; the people who thought we could no longer do the great things which we once did; and those who believed that our decline was irreversible – that we could never again be what we were. There were those who would not admit it – even perhaps some here today – people who have strenuously denied the suggestion but – in their heart of hearts   they too had their secret fears that it was true: that Britain was no longer the nation that had built an Empire and ruled a quarter of the world.

Well, they were wrong. The lesson of the Falklands is that Britain has not changed and that this nation still has those sterling qualities which shine through our history. This generation can match their fathers and grandfathers in ability, in courage, and in resolution. We have not changed. When the demands of war and the dangers to our own people call us to arms – then we British are as we have always been – competent, courageous and resolute.

When called to arms – ah, that's the problem. It took the battle in the South Atlantic for the shipyards to adapt ships way ahead of time; for dockyards to refit merchantmen and cruise liners, to fix helicopter platforms, to convert hospital ships – all faster than was thought possible; it took the demands of war for every stop to be pulled out and every man and woman to do their best.

British people had to be threatened by foreign soldiers and British territory invaded and then – why then – the response was incomparable. Yet why does it need a war to bring out our qualities and reassert our pride? Why do we have to be invaded before we throw aside our selfish aims and begin to work together as only we can work, and achieve as only we can achieve?

That really is the challenge we as a nation face today. We have to see that the spirit of the South Atlantic – the real spirit of Britain – is kindled not only by war but can now be fired by peace.

We have the first prerequisite. We know we can do it – we haven't lost the ability. That is the Falklands Factor. We have proved ourselves to ourselves. It is a lesson we must not now forget. Indeed, it is a lesson which we must apply to peace just as we have learnt in war. The faltering and the self-doubt has given way to achievement and pride. We have the confidence and we must use it.

Just look at the Task Force as an object lesson. Every man had his own task to do and did it superbly. Officers and men, senior NCO and newest recruit – every one realized that his contribution was essential for the success of the whole. All were equally valuable – each was differently qualified. By working together, each was able to do more than his best. As a team they raised the average to the level of the best and by each doing his utmost together they achieved the impossible. That's an accurate picture of Britain at war – not yet of Britain at peace. But the spirit has stirred and the nation has begun to assert itself. Things are not going to be the same again.

Margaret Thatcher, 3 July 1982

Next is an article which appeared in the *Guardian* newspaper in 1985. The writer, Terry Jones, is reacting to developments in the running of the London Underground (tube) system during the second and third Conservative ministries of Margaret Thatcher ('Mrs T').

The final text is an article which appeared in the *Independent* in 1990, on the subject of 'leisurewear', by Jonathan Glancey.

The Tube short-cut to money

INPUT Terry Jones

LAST week, London Regional Transport invited travellers to write and tell them how to improve the tube system. Here's my letter.

Dear LRT.

It's four years now since Mrs T told wicked old London Transport to get stuffed, and put in you boys to slim down the Underground system into a profit-making business that she could sell off. And you've been doing a terrific job.

You've got rid of no less than 1,688 of your staff in the last three years! That's some achievement.

Of course, the Underground is now filthier, less reliable and more dangerous than it's ever been but that isn't really your concern. Your job is to get it to make a profit and I know you'll do it.

You've already cut the budget for lift and escalator maintenance from £11 million to £6 million. And booting-out all those cleaners must have really saved a packet.

At King's Cross, for example, I believe you reduced the cleaning staff from 14 to 2 and a part-timer. And I understand that the escalators are now cleaned only once a week instead of every night. Well done.

You weren't to know that litter could cause fires (even though it happened at Bradford City Football Club and the Fire Brigade warned you it could happen in the tube). Saving lives isn't your business. Your business is saving money, and that's what you did.

What's more I know we can rely on you to keep rebuilding costs (and victim compensation) down to a minimum.

But what to do about the litter? Obviously the last thing you want to do is to go back to employing more cleaners, so I would suggest you stop passengers taking anything that could become litter into the Tube system.

Handbags and pockets should be searched at the ticket barrier, and any droppable articles (such as wrapping paper, tickets, bank notes) should either be confiscated or securely tied to the prospective traveller with lengths of string.

There should also be really tough prison sentences for anyone caught smoking on the Tube and for children who eat sweets or ice-creams whilst travelling. It might also be a good idea to issue every passenger with a brush or duster.

I see no excuse for travellers lolling around in idleness while waiting for trains. It's high time they were put to work cleaning-up the place.

Now I know a lot of wiseacres are saying that it's the cuts in staffing levels that have caused most of the problems since you took over – there are more muggings, less information, dirtier trains and no one to help out in an emergency.

But it's also quite obvious that cutting staff is the only way to make the Underground pay, and I know you've got the ultimate objective of abolishing staff altogether at some stations. My suggestion is: why not go the whole hog and abolish passengers as well?

Without passengers, there would be no need to install expensive automatic barriers and ticket machines. Cleaning staff could probably be cut down to a couple of elderly ladies with mops for the entire system. There would be no need to heat or light the stations, and the frequency of trains could be dramatically reduced down to one or two a day – or even none.

The stations and tunnels could then be sold-off either as nuclear-proof office accommodation or else for growing mushrooms. It's time that people began to understand that the Underground isn't simply there for convenience – it's there to make money. That is the only objective Mrs T has set you, and that's what you must do, regardless of what or who has to suffer in the process.

Terry Jones, the *Guardian*, March 1985

Curse of the day-glo dazzlers

St Thomas Aquinas was fond of saying that the man who was free only in his leisure time was a slave. Aquinas lived a long time ago in Italy, however, and what he said is clearly anathema to the British in 1990. The British believe in leisure. Leisure (along with shopping) is the new religion and its devotees work hard to take it easy.

Among other things, they have caused the building of vast new temples of a type never seen before: the shopping mall, the theme park and the leisure centre. These buildings are the cathedrals, monasteries and hospices of our day.

If you find the leisure creed repugnant, you can escape the theme park and the leisure centre. It is more difficult, however, to avoid the vast shopping mall and its mesmerising air-conditioned nave, aisles, chapels and clerestories with their expensive offerings of luxury goods.

But it is impossible to escape from the habits – the clothes as well as the gum-chewing, burger-stuffing and soft-drink suckling – of the leisure era. In dignified city streets, in country lanes, in shopping arcades up and down the country, in churches, airports and country houses, leisurewear is all intrusive.

A whole nation seems to be dressed, notably at weekends, in man-made fabric representations of the contents of a packet of liquorice allsorts. The strident acid colours of leisurewear dominate every view of every British street, lane and public building.

Architects trying to build even the most sensitive modern building are given a hard time by interfering local planning committees. Anyone, however, can don a garish polyester-nylon tracksuit and waddle shamelessly along a much-loved street lined with beautiful buildings, without fear of censure. Yet leisurewear is visual pollution of the highest order.

It is also damning evidence of a slob culture that seeks to undermine urbane and civilised values. For leisurewear means never having to think about appearances. Leisurewear means never having to straighten a tie or polish a pair of shoes. Leisurewear means never having to step out of your pyjamas. Leisurewear means free advertising for manufacturers: shoes, jeans and T-shirts decked with tags, labels and transfers celebrating company names.

Why do people pay for these clothes? Surely they should be paid for their role as animated billboards? Traditionally, a good English suit hides its label – if it has one – in the lining of an inside pocket.

Today's tracksuits, bomber jackets, trainers and hooded 'mugger' tops are emblazoned with their makers' names, like crests on medieval soldiers' tunics. Many carry crude or insulting messages.

How are you meant to respond to a fat, ill-shaven slob strolling around a National Trust house in the Cotswolds wearing a garish and very sweaty sweatshirt that reads: 'If I wanted to listen to someone talking out of his arse, I would have farted'?

If, however, a Cotswold resident wants to build a very small addition to the back of their house – one that cannot be seen from the road – it will be refused planning permission unless it is designed in a style and materials that ape what went before.

But what is more offensive? A dignified new building that cannot be seen or a T-shirt that will pollute a hundred streets, malls and railway stations?

Leisurewear is meant to be noisy. Its supposedly relaxed nature cannot conceal a strident heart. If you go skiing today, you need dark glasses or goggles, not just to shield your eyes from the sunlight, but to protect them from the kaleidoscopic glare dazzling off polychrome ski outfits. These outfits are designed to draw attention to the individual skier, to say 'Hey! Look at me!'.

Traditional ski outfits were designed in colours that blended with winter mountain scenery. The skier appeared a small part of a much bigger creation. Today the leisure skier has no such modesty.

The joy of traditional clothing – which can range from the most fogeyish city suit to an innovative couture dress – is that it enhances wearer, onlooker and surroundings.

If you stroll along a street in the City of London, you will still find clothes, taxis, buses, police and buildings working together to animate a scene harmoniously. On a country walk, it is still possible to find parts of Britain in which walker, country clothes, dog, horse, farmyard and scenery work together.

As soon as you see someone dressed in day-glo leisurewear in a City street, however, that civic harmony is upset. As soon as you clap eyes on an acolyte of leisure on a country walk, natural harmony is luridly sabotaged. Because it demands very little of people, leisurewear is infectious. Increasingly, people in uniformed jobs adapt their costume to accommodate the dictates of Leisure.

British Rail workers and bus staff have become famous for their scruffy appearance. They have done away with the tie, jettisoned the cap and replaced polished shoes with 'Levis for Feet'.

The point about a uniform is that it identifies public servants. It singles out the person who can be turned to for information or when something goes wrong. When the driver of a train, or the conductor of a bus is dressed Blade Runner-style – a cross between a shopped-out Saturday shopper and a jogger with a beer gut – are you sure you want to turn to him for help? His clothes suggest he doesn't really care about his job.

Perhaps the saddest thing about leisurewear is that it denies great chunks of British society the right to walk with dignity when they lose their youthful looks. Old men confined to leisurewear (through habit or because, at the price most can afford, the market offers little else) look particularly undignified.

Dressed in jacket, tie and hat, the most creaky old man looks good. That can be tested out by ambling through any Italian town. Perhaps old people are accorded greater dignity in Italy than they are in Britain, not because Italians are, on the whole, a more sociable lot than the British, but because they look dignified.

Leisurewear is unlikely to go away just yet. Anything easy is preferable to anything that requires effort, and that goes for dressing as much as it does for most British architecture and design of today.

Grandfather is unlikely ever again to don ironed shirt, tie and cap to prune the rose bushes. His dignity gone, he really doesn't mind looking like a liquorice allsort well past its sell-by date.

Jonathan Glancey, the *Independent*, 1990

Coursework suggestions

- Write a poem in the style and verse form of 'To His Coy Mistress', presenting his 'mistress's' answer to Andrew Marvell.
- Both Andrew Marvell, in 'To His Coy Mistress' (page 280), and John Donne, in 'Song' (page 106), present a fanciful argument in verse on the theme of love. Write about the way each of these poets presents his argument, commenting on the uses of language, imagery and verse form, and the structure of the argument.
- Basing your writing partly on Margaret Thatcher's speech and on the Terry Jones article, and using the last sentence of 'The Falklands Factor' speech as the title, write an article of your own about the current state of Britain.
- Write an article for a newspaper in the ironic style of the Terry Jones piece, pretending to support something which you, in fact, strongly disagree with.
- Write a letter to the *Guardian* or the *Independent* in answer to one of the newspaper articles. You should comment on aspects of the presentation of the argument in the article to which you are responding.
- Compare two of the texts, in terms of their effectiveness in making a case. You should comment on:

  the methods of presenting the case

  the style and language used

  your own response.

SYLLABUS REQUIREMENTS COVERED

The analytical work on media texts in this unit covers a core element (persuasion in media texts) in the examinations of all the syllabuses. The work on poetry is relevant to the poetry questions in the London and NEAB examinations.

The coursework suggestions relate to the coursework requirements of the various syllabuses as follows:

Suggestion 1: London Unit 1, MEG Unit 2, NEAB Original Writing.

Suggestion 2: SEG Unit 4, WJEC Poetry.

Suggestions 3 and 4: London Unit 1, MEG Unit 2, NEAB Original Writing, SEG Unit 2, WJEC Best writing.

Suggestions 5 and 6: NEAB Media.

DRAMA

The study of drama by a major playwright is a requirement for GCSE study. It would obviously be desirable to study and perform a complete full-length play, but with the time-constraints of a one year course, and the fact that written work on drama other than Shakespeare is not required in most syllabuses, it is probably wisest to study a very short work of drama which can be dealt with in a single week.

The work chosen is a one-act play by Alan Ayckbourn, called 'A Talk in the Park'. It is the last of a sequence of five interlinked one-act plays, collectively called *Confusions*, which were first performed in 1974.

Alan Ayckbourn is the most popular British playwright of the second half of the twentieth century. He was born in London in 1939 and pursued a career as an actor and assistant stage manager before writing his first play for the Stephen Joseph Theatre Company in Scarborough, Yorkshire in 1959. He has been artistic director of this theatre since 1971, and his work is always performed there first before moving to London. His plays are comedies of suburban life, often bordering on farce, but with themes frequently closer to tragedy.

The themes that link the five plays making up *Confusions* are loneliness, marital conflict and self-delusion. 'A Talk in the Park' can easily be performed in the classroom with minimal rearrangement. It just needs five pairs of chairs for the performers to move between, representing five park benches.

A Talk in the Park

A park

Four park benches, separated but not too distant from each other. On one sits Beryl, a belligerent young girl at present engrossed in reading a long letter. On another sits Charles who looks what he is, a businessman dressed for the weekend. He is slowly thumbing his way through a thick report. On another sits Doreen, middle-aged, untidily dressed, feeding the birds from a bag of breadcrumbs. On the remaining bench sits Ernest, a younger man. He sits gazing into space. The birds sing. After a moment, Arthur enters. He is a bird-like man in a long mackintosh, obviously on the look-out for company. Eventually, he approaches Beryl's bench.

Arthur Is this seat occupied, by any chance?

Beryl (*shortly*) No. (*She continues to read*)

Arthur Great, great. (*He sits*)

A pause. Arthur takes deep breaths and gives a few furtive glances in Beryl's direction

   Student, I see?

Beryl What?

Arthur Student, I bet. You look like a student. Always tell a student

Beryl No.

Arthur Ah. You look like one. You're young enough to be a student. Quite young enough. That's the life, isn't it? Being a student. Not a care in the world. Sitting in the park on a day like this. In the sunshine. Rare enough we see the sun, eh? Eh? Rare.

Beryl Yes. (*She refuses to be drawn into conversation*)

Arthur Mind you, I shouldn't be here. By rights, I should be at home. That's where I should be. Inside my front door. I've got plenty of things I should be doing. The kitchen shelves to name but three. Only you sit at home on a day like today. Sunday. Nothing to do. On your own – you think to yourself, this is no good, this won't get things done – and there you are talking to yourself. You know what they say about people who talk to themselves? Eh? Eh? Yes. So I thought it's outdoors for you, else they'll come and take you away. Mind you, I'm never at a loss. I'm a very fulfilled person. I have, for example, one of the biggest collections of cigarette cards of anyone alive or dead that I know of. And you don't get that by sitting on your behind all day. But I'll let you into a secret. Do you know what it is that's the most valuable thing there is you can hope to collect? People. I'm a collector of people. I look at them, I observe them, I hear them talk, I listen to their manner of speaking and I think, hallo, here's another one. Different. Different again. Because I'll let you into a secret. They are

like fingerprints. They are never quite the same. And I've met a number in my lifetime. Quite a number. Some good, some bad, all different. But the best of them, and I'm saying this to you quite frankly and
openly, the best of them are women. They are kinder-hearted people.
If I had a choice, I'd be a woman. Now that makes you laugh, I expect, but it's the truth. When I choose to have a conversation, I can
tell you it's with a woman every time. Because a woman is one of
nature's listeners. Most men I wouldn't give the time of day to. Now
I expect that shocks you but it's the truth. Trouble is, I don't get to
meet as many women as I'd like to. My particular line of work does
not bring me into contact with them as much as I would wish. Which
is a pity.

Beryl gets up

Beryl Excuse me. (*She moves off*)
Arthur Are you going?

Beryl moves to Charles's bench

Beryl (*to Charles*) Excuse me, is this seat taken?
Charles (*barely glancing up*) No. (*He moves along his bench*)
Beryl (*sitting*) Thanks. Sorry, only the man over there won't stop talking. I wanted to read this in peace. I couldn't concentrate. He just kept
going on and on about his collections or something. I normally don't
mind too much, only if you get a letter like this, you need all your
concentration. You can't have people talking in your ear – especially
when you're trying to decipher writing like this. He must have been
stoned out of his mind when he wrote it. It wouldn't be unusual. Look
at it. He wants me to come back. Some hopes. To him. He's sorry, he
didn't mean to do what he did, he won't do it again I promise, etc.,
etc. I seem to have heard that before. It's not the first time, I can tell
you. And there's no excuse for it, is there? Violence. I mean, what am
I supposed to do? Keep going back to that? Every time he loses his
temper he . . . I mean, there's no excuse. A fracture, you know. It was
nearly a compound fraction. That's what they told me. (*Indicating her
head*) Right here. You can practically see it to this day. Two X-rays. I
said to him when I got home, I said, 'You bastard, you know what you
did to my head?' He just stands there. The way he does. 'Sorry,' he
says, 'I'm ever so sorry.' I told him. I said, 'You're a bastard, that's what
you are. A right, uncontrolled, violent, bad-tempered bastard.' You
know what he said? He says, 'You call me a bastard again and I'll smash
your stupid face in.' That's what he says. I mean, you can't have a
rational, civilized discussion with a man like that, can you? He's a right
bastard. My friend Jenny, she says, 'You're a looney, leave him for

God's sake. You're a looney.' Who needs that? You tell me one person who needs that? Only where do you go? I mean, there's all my things – my personal things. All my – everything. He's even got my bloody Post Office book. I'll finish up back there, you wait and see. I must be out of my tiny mind. Eh. Sometimes I just want to jump down a deep hole and forget it. Only I know that bastard'll be waiting at the bottom. Waiting to thump the life out of me. Eh?

Charles Yes. Excuse me. (*He gets up*)

Beryl I'm sorry, I didn't mean to embarrass you.

Charles No, no.

Beryl I just had to ...

Charles Quite all right. Quite all right.

Charles moves over to Doreen

(*To Doreen*) Nobody here, is there?

Doreen What?

Charles Nobody here?

Doreen Nobody where? (*She looks around*)

Charles Sitting here.

Doreen No. No.

Charles Sorry. Do you mind if I do? (*He sits*) I won't disturb you. Girl over there's got boy-friend trouble. Comes and pours it all out on me – as if I'm interested. I mean, we've all been through it at one time or another. Why she should think I should be interested. I mean, we've all got troubles no doubt. But we all don't sit on a bench and bore some poor innocent stranger to death. I mean, that in my book spells S for selfishness. And have you noticed that it's invariably the young? They think we haven't been through it. Can't imagine that perhaps we were young, too. Don't know where they think we all came from. I mean, five years ago I had a house in the country, a charming wife, two good children, couldn't imagine a happier family. My wife dies suddenly, my children can't stand the place a moment longer and emigrate to Canada so I sell the house and there I am in a flat I can hardly swing a cat in. But I don't go round boring other people with it. That's life. I've had twenty – no, more like twenty-five, good years. Who am I to complain if I get a few bad ones thrown in as well? Things are going to get worse before they get better. Bound to. And you know an interesting thing about trouble? I always think it's a bit like woodworm. Once you've got a dose, if you're not careful, it starts to spread. Starts in your family and, before you know it, it's into your business. Which explains why I'm sitting here reading a report that's been put together so badly that I've got to read it through on my one day off and condense it into another report before I can even be certain whether I'm bankrupt. I mean, I don't know if you're interested but just take a look at this page here, this is a typical page. Can you make head or tail . . .

Doreen gets up and moves away

(*Muttering*) Oh, I beg your pardon.

Doreen moves to Ernest's bench

Doreen Excuse me.

Ernest Eh?

Doreen Excuse me. May I sit here for a moment? (*She sits*) The man over there has been – you know – I didn't want to make a scene but he – you know. I mean, I suppose I should call the police – but they'd never catch him. I mean, most of the police are men as well, aren't they? Between you and me, I have heard that most of the police women are as well. Men dressed up, you know. Special Duties, so called. So my ex-husband informed me. I mean, it's terrible, you can't sit in a park these days without some man – you know – I mean, I'm on a fixed income – I don't want all that. That comes from my husband. My ex-husband. He runs a pub. In the country. But I had to leave him. We got to the stage when it was either that or – you know. I love dogs, you see, and he would never – he refused, point blank. And the day came when I knew I must have a dog. It became – you know – like an obsession. So I left. I usually have my dog here with me only he's at the vet's. He's only a puppy. They had to keep him in. He's being – you know – poor little thing. He'd have seen that man off. He's a loyal little dog. He understands every word I say to him. Every word. I said to him this morning, Ginger-boy, I said – you're coming down to the vet's with me this morning to be – you know, and his little ears pricked up and his tail wagged. He knew, you see. I think dogs are more intelligent than people. They're much better company and the wonderful thing is that once you've got a little dog, you meet other people with dogs. And what I always say is that people who have dogs they're the nicest sort of people. They're the ones I know I'd get on with.

Ernest gets up

Have you got a dog, by any chance?

Ernest ignores her and creeps behind the trees to Arthur

Ernest (*sitting next to Arthur*) Excuse me. Just taking refuge. Nut case over there. Bloody woman prattling on about her dog. Ought to be locked up. Think's every man's after her. I mean, look. Look at it. After her?

She'd have to pay 'em. You know the sort though, don't you? If you let her talk to you long enough, she'll talk herself into thinking you've assaulted her. Before you know it, she's screaming blue murder, you'll be carried off by the fuzz and that's your lot. Two years if you're lucky. I mean, I came out here to get away from the wife. Don't want another one just like her, do I? I mean. That's why I'm in the park. Get away from the noise. You got kids? Don't have kids. Take my tip, don't get married. Looks all right, but believe me – nothing's your own. You've paid for it all but nothing's your own. Yap, yap, yap. Want, want, want. Never satisfied. I mean, no word of a lie, I look at her some mornings and I think, blimey, I must have won last prize in a raffle. Mind you, I dare say she's thinking the same. In fact, I know she is. Certainly keeps me at a distance. Hallo, dear, put your money on the table and she's off out. Don't see her for dust. Sunday mornings, it's a race to see who can get out first. Loser keeps the baby. Well, this morning I made it first. Here I am in the quiet. Got away from the noise. You know something interesting? Most of our lives are noise, aren't they? Artificial man-made noise. But you sit out here and you can listen – and – well, there's a bit of traffic but apart from that – peace. Like my mother used to say. Shut your eyes in the country and you can hear God breathing. (*He shuts his eyes*)

Arthur (*leaning across to Beryl*) Hey – hey – psst! I've got a right one here. Think's he's listening to God breathing ... (*He laughs*)

Beryl (*leaning across to Charles*) He's talking again. To me. What do you do? (*She smiles*)

Charles (*leaning across to Doreen*) There she goes again. What did I tell you? Chapter Two of the boyfriend saga.

Doreen (*leaning across to Ernest*) He's talking to me. If he does it any more, I'll call the police ...

Ernest (*to Arthur*) Oh, blimey. Why doesn't she go home? Hark at her. Can you hear her? Rabbitting on ...

The following, final section, is played as a Round. Doreen finishes first, then Charles cuts out, followed by Beryl, Arthur, and then Ernest

Arthur (*to Beryl*) Hey – hey.

Beryl continues to ignore him

Oh, suit yourself.

Beryl (*to Charles*) Psst – psst.

Charles ignores her

Oh, be like that.

Charles (*to Doreen*) I say, I say.

Doreen ignores him

Oh, all right, don't then . . .
Doreen (*to Ernest*) Excuse me, excuse me, excuse me.

Ernest ignores her

Oh, really.
Ernest (*nudging Arthur*) Oy – oy.

Arthur ignores him

Oh, all right, then. Don't. Don't then. Might as well talk to yourself.

They all sit sulkily. The Lights fade to a Black-out, and –

the CURTAIN *falls*

Alan Ayckbourn, 'A Talk in the Park'

Discussion and analysis of 'A Talk in the Park'

General

- What are the themes of 'A Talk in the Park'?
- What impression of human life is presented in the play?

Arthur

- Why do you think he picks on Beryl to talk to?
- What impression of his life is Arthur trying to create? Do you think he believes it himself?
- What is *your* impression of Arthur's life?
- Do you think his interest in people is genuine?
- What do you think is the most pitiful thing he says?
- What do you notice about Arthur's style of speech?

Beryl

- Do people like Beryl and her boyfriend really exist, or are they too far-fetched to be true to life?
- Why do you think she wants to talk to Charles?
- Why do you think she hasn't taken her friend's advice and left her violent boyfriend?
- Why do you think Charles moves away from her and sits next to Doris?
- What do you notice about Beryl's style of speech?

Charles

- In what ways is Charles deluding himself?
- Do you think it likely that he really had 'twenty, no, more like twenty-five good years'?
- Do you think there is any hope for him?
- Do you think his 'wormwood' image is an apt one to represent what is happening to him?
- How would you describe Charles's style of speech?

Doreen

- What is Doreen's main problem?
- What do you think the cause of her marriage break-up might have been? Is her explanation of the marriage break-up feasible?
- Why has she taken her puppy to the vet? What do you notice about the way she talks about it?
- Why do you think she considers dogs to be better company than people?
- What is distinctive about her style of speech?

Ernest

- Is Ernest's assessment of Doreen realistic? What does it show about him?
- Reading between the lines, what is he revealing about his marriage?
- What drives Arthur away?
- How would you describe Ernest's style of speech?

The last section

- What is Ayckbourn suggesting about people in the last section of the play?
- Do you think it makes an effective ending to the play?

Conclusions

- Which do you think is the saddest character in the play? Why?
- Do you sympathise with anyone in the play? Why?
- Do you know anyone like any of the people in the play? In what ways are they similar?

Analysing dialogue

Write notes on the distinctive features of the styles of speech in the play. Work out the different ways that Ayckbourn makes their speech seem true to life.

Coursework suggestions

- Write a critical assessment of 'A Talk in the Park', analysing the characters, themes and language of the play.
- Write your own version of 'A Talk in the Park'. Choose one of the characters from Ayckbourn's play and write your own speech for him/her. Then create two other characters to continue the 'talk'.
- Write about the presentation of married life in 'A Talk in the Park' and Thomas Hardy's 'On the Western Circuit' (page 140). You should discuss *how* the impressions are created, as well as what the impressions are.

SYLLABUS REQUIREMENTS COVERED

The coursework suggestions relate to the coursework requirements of the different syllabuses as follows:

Suggestion 1:

MEG: Unit 3

Suggestion 2:

All syllabuses

Suggestion 3:

NEAB IIII: Wide reading

A SHORT STORY FROM ANOTHER CULTURE

T his unit is designed partly for those who need to produce a
coursework piece on a whole work from 'diverse cultures and
traditions' (London and WJEC syllabuses), and partly as practice in prose analysis which features in the examinations of all the
boards. It may also provide stimulus for those who wish to write
another coursework personal writing piece.

The work chosen for analysis is a short story by the South African
writer, Nadine Gordimer, called 'Iπs There Nowhere Else We Can
Meet?'. It comes from her first short story collection *The Soft Voice
of the Serpent*, published in 1953.

Nadine Gordimer has lived all her life in South Africa, where she was
born in 1923. She is a novelist and short story writer, and won the
Nobel Prize for Literature in 1991. She was an outspoken critic of the
apartheid system and of censorship in South Africa, and most of
her work is concerned with the political situation in her native
land. Under the apartheid system, which finally came to an end in
1990, the minority white population controlled the country. Only
whites could vote, and blacks were relegated to 'townships' and
ghettos, well away from the luxurious suburbs which belonged to the
whites.

This story describes a young white woman's first encounter with a
'native' black man.

Is There Nowhere Else Where We Can Meet?

It was a cool grey morning and the air was like smoke. In that reversal of the elements that sometimes takes place, the grey, soft, muffled sky moved like the sea on a silent day.

The coat collar pressed rough against her neck and her cheeks were softly cold as if they had been washed in ice-water. She breathed gently with the air; on the left a strip of veld fire curled silently, flameless. Overhead a dove purred. She went on over the flat straw grass, following the trees, now on, now off the path. Away ahead, over the scribble of twigs, the sloping lines of black and platinum grass – all merging, tones but no colour, like an etching – was the horizon, the shore at which cloud lapped.

Damp burnt grass puffed black, faint dust from beneath her feet. She could hear herself swallow.

A long way off she saw a figure with something red on its head, and she drew from it the sense of balance she had felt at the particular placing of the dot of a figure in a picture. She was here; someone was over there … Then the red dot was gone, lost in the curve of the trees. She changed her bag and parcel from one arm to the other and felt the morning, palpable, deeply cold and clinging against her eyes.

She came to the end of a direct stretch of path and turned with it round a dark-fringed pine and a shrub, now delicately boned, that she remembered hung with bunches of white flowers like crystals in the summer. There was a native in a red woollen cap standing at the next clump of trees, where the path crossed a ditch and was bordered by white-splashed stones. She had pulled a little sheath of pine needles, three in a twist of thin brown tissue, and as she walked she ran them against her thumb. Down; smooth and stiff. Up; catching in gentle resistance as the minute serrations snagged at the skin. He was standing with his back towards her, looking along the way he had come; she pricked the ball of her thumb with the needle-ends. His one trouser leg was torn off above the knee, and the back of the naked leg and half-turned heel showed the peculiarly dead, powdery black of cold. She was nearer to him now, but she knew he did not hear her coming over the damp dust of the path. She was level with him, passing him; and he turned slowly and looked beyond her, without a flicker of interest as a cow sees you go.

The eyes were red, as if he had not slept for a long time, and the strong smell of old sweat burned at her nostrils. Once past, she wanted to cough, but a pang of guilt at the red weary eyes stopped her. And he had only a filthy rag – part of an old shirt? – without sleeves and frayed away into a great gap from underarm to waist. It lifted in the currents of cold as she passed. She had dropped the neat trio of pine needles somewhere, she did not know at what moment, so now, remembering something from childhood, she lifted her hand to her face and sniffed: yes, it was as she remembered, not as chemists pretend it in the bath salts, but a dusty green scent, vegetable rather than flower. It was clean, unhuman. Slightly sticky too; tacky on her fingers. She must wash them as soon as she got there. Unless her hands were quite clean, she could not lose consciousness of them, they obtruded upon her.

She felt a thudding through the ground like the sound of a hare running in fear and she was going to turn around and then he was there in front of her, so startling, so utterly unexpected, panting right into her face. He stood dead still and she stood dead still. Every vestige of control, of sense, of thought, went out of her as a room plunges into dark at the failure of power and she found herself whimpering like an idiot or a child. Animal sounds came out of her throat. She gibbered. For a moment it was Fear itself that had her by the arms, the legs, the throat; not fear of the man, of any single menace he might present, but Fear, absolute, abstract. If the earth had opened up in fire at her feet, if a wild beast had opened its terrible mouth to receive her, she could not have been reduced to less than she was now.

There was a chest heaving through the tear in front of her; a face panting; beneath the red hairy woollen cap the yellowish-red eyes holding her in distrust. One foot, cracked from exposure until it looked like broken wood, moved, only to restore balance in the dizziness that follows running, but any move seemed towards her and she tried to scream and the awfulness of dreams came true and nothing would come out. She wanted to throw the handbag and the parcel at him, and as she fumbled crazily for them she heard him draw a deep, hoarse breath and he grabbed out at her and – ah! It came. His hand clutched her shoulder.

Now she fought with him and she trembled with strength as they struggled. The dust puffed round her shoes and his scuffling toes. The smell of him choked her – It was an old pyjama jacket, not a shirt – His face was sullen and there was a pink place where the skin had been grazed off. He sniffed desperately, out of breath. Her teeth chattered, wildly she battered him with her head, broke away, but he snatched at the skirt of her coat and jerked her back. Her face swung up and she saw the waves of a grey sky and a crane breasting them, beautiful as the figurehead of a ship. She staggered for balance and the handbag and parcel fell. At once he was upon them, and she wheeled about; but as she was about to fall on her knees to get there first, a sudden relief, like a rush of tears, came to her and, instead, she ran. She ran and ran, stumbling wildly off through the stalks of dead grass, turning over her heels against hard winter tussocks, blundering through trees and bushes. The young mimosas closed in, lowering a thicket of twigs right to the ground, but she tore herself through, feeling the dust in her eyes and the scaly twigs hooking at her hair. There was a ditch, knee-high in blackjacks; like pins responding to a magnet they fastened along her legs, but on the other side there was a fence and then the road ... She clawed at the fence – her hands were capable of nothing – and tried to drag herself between the wires, but her coat caught on a barb, and she was imprisoned there, bent in half, while waves of terror swept over her in heat and trembling. At last the wire tore through its hold on the cloth; wobbling, frantic, she climbed over the fence.

And she was out. She was out on the road. A little way on there were houses, with gardens, postboxes, a child's swing. A small dog sat at a gate. She could hear a faint hum, as of life, of talk somewhere, or perhaps telephone wires.

She was trembling so that she could not stand. She had to keep on walking, quickly, down the road. It was quiet and grey, like the morning. And cool. Now she could feel the cold air round her mouth and between her brows, where the skin stood out in sweat. And in the cold wetness that soaked down beneath her armpits and between her buttocks. Her heart thumped slowly and stiffly. Yes, the wind was cold; she was suddenly cold, damp-cold, all through. She raised her hand, still fluttering uncontrollably, and smoothed her hair; it was wet at the hairline. She guided her hand into her pocket and found a handkerchief to blow her nose.

There was the gate of the first house, before her.

She thought of the woman coming to the door, of the explanations, of the woman's face, and the police. Why did I fight, she thought suddenly. What did I fight for? Why didn't I give him the money and let him go? His red eyes, and the smell and those cracks in his feet, fissures, erosion. She shuddered. The cold of the morning flowed into her.

She turned away from the gate and went down the road slowly, like an invalid, beginning to pick the blackjacks from her stockings.

Nadine Gordimer, 'Is There Nowhere Else We Can Meet?'

NADINE GORDIMER

Discussion and analysis

The story can be divided into three sections for the purposes of analysis: before the attack, the attack itself, and after the attack.

Before the attack (up to '... they obtruded upon her')

- How does Gordimer create atmosphere in the first three paragraphs? You might consider the effects of:

  the use of simile and metaphor

  the use of alliteration and assonance

  the choice of adjectives and verbs.

- What is the woman's first impression of the 'native'?
- What impressions have you formed of him by the end of this section?

The attack (from 'She felt a thudding ...' to '... climbed over the fence')

- How is the sense of the woman's fear created in the paragraph beginning 'She felt ...'? You might consider:

  the use of simile

  the use of onomatopoeia

  the effects of the sentence-structure.

- Pick out a phrase in the paragraph beginning 'There was a chest' which you found particularly effective, and say why you chose it.
- The first half of the paragraph beginning 'Now she fought with him' contains a series of sense impressions. Identify them. Say how they add to the dramatic effect of the episode.
- How is her feeling of panic captured in the second half of the paragraph, from 'She ran and ran'? You could look particularly at the choice of verbs.

After the attack (from 'And she was out' to the end)

- How is her feeling of relief created in the first paragraph of the section?
- How do the physical details in the second paragraph of the section add to the impact of the story?
- Why do you think the third paragraph of the section is only one sentence long?
- How does she feel about her experience at the end?
- Why is the story called 'Is There Nowhere Else We Can Meet?'?

Coursework suggestions

- Write a detailed analysis of 'Is There Nowhere Else Where We Can Meet?', showing how Nadine Gordimer creates atmosphere, drama and suspense.
- Compare the ways in which Nadine Gordimer, in 'Is There Nowhere Else Where We Can Meet?', and Daphne du Maurier, in 'The Birds', create a sense of drama and fear.
- Write a story or a descriptive piece in which fear is an important element.

NB: Before writing an analysis of the story or stories, you might like to study Unit 25 (Analysing Short Fiction).

SYLLABUS REQUIREMENTS COVERED

Analysis of twentieth-century prose writing is a feature of all the examinations except NEAB IIII. The coursework suggestions relate to the coursework requirements of the different syllabuses as follows:

Suggestion 1: London: Work reflecting diverse cultures and traditions

WJEC: Other cultures

Suggestion 2: NEAB IIII

Suggestion 3: All syllabuses.

POETRY ANALYSIS

Writing about poetry is a requirement of all the syllabuses. Analysing poems from the pre-release anthology is an examination exercise for London and NEAB, and in the other three boards it features as coursework.

It might, therefore, be worth looking at an illustration of how to write poetry analysis, if you have not already done so. Some further suggestions for coursework pieces on poetry appear at the end of the unit.

Analysing a pair of poems

Two poems by the same poet on a similar theme have been chosen for this sample analysis. The poet is Thomas Hardy, and the poems are 'The Convergence of the Twain' and 'During Wind and Rain'.

Hardy has already been introduced as a short story writer, in Unit 11. As explained on page 139, he devoted the last 30 years of his life to writing poetry, after concentrating on prose for the previous 30 years.

'The Convergence of the Twain' is from a collection of poems called *Satires of Circumstance*, published in 1914. The 'twain' that converged are the *Titanic* and an iceberg. The *Titanic* was the largest ship in the world at the time of her maiden voyage in 1912, and was considered 'unsinkable'. Over 1,500 people perished when the ship hit an iceberg, many of them very wealthy. 'During Wind and Rain' appeared in *Moments of Vision*, published in 1917.

The Convergence of the Twain

(Lines on the loss of the *Titanic*)

I

In a solitude of the sea
Deep from human vanity,
And the Pride of Life that planned her, stilly couches she.

II

Steel chambers, late the pyres
Of her salamandrine fires,
Cold currents thrid, and turn to rhythmic tidal lyres.

III

Over the mirrors meant
To glass the opulent
The sea-worm crawls – grotesque, slimed, dumb, indifferent.

IV

Jewels in joy designed
To ravish the sensuous mind
Lie lightless, all their sparkles bleared and black and blind.

V

Dim moon-eyed fishes near
Gaze at the gilded gear
And query: 'What does this vaingloriousness down here?'

VI

Well: while was fashioning
This creature of cleaving wing,
The Immanent Will that stirs and urges everything

VII

Prepared a sinister mate
For her – so gaily great –
A Shape of Ice, for the time far and dissociate.

VIII

And as the smart ship grew
In stature, grace and hue,
In shadowy silent distance grew the Iceberg too.

IX

Alien they seemed to be:
No mortal eye could see
The intimate welding of their later history,

X

Or sign that they were bent
By paths coincident
On being anon twin halves of one august event.

XI

Till the Spinner of the Years
Said 'Now!' And each one hears,
And consummation comes, and jars two hemispheres.

Thomas Hardy

During Wind and Rain

They sing their dearest songs –
He, she, all of them – yea,
Treble and tenor and bass,
    And one to play;
With the candles mooning each face . . .
    Ah, no; the years O!
How the sick leaves reel down in throngs!

They clear the creeping moss –
Elders and juniors – aye,
Making the pathways neat
    And the garden gay;
And they build a shady seat . . .
    Ah, no; the years, the years;
See, the white storm-birds wing across!

They are blithely breakfasting all –
Men and maidens – yea,
Under the summer tree,
    With a glimpse of the bay,
While pet fowl come to the knee . . .
    Ah, no; the years O!
And the rotten rose is ript from the wall.

They change to a high new house,
He, she, all of them – aye,
Clocks and carpets and chairs
    On the lawn all day,
And brightest things that are theirs . . .
    Ah, no; the years, the years;
Down their carved names the rain-drop ploughs.

Thomas Hardy

Here is the question: In both 'The Convergence of the Twain' and 'During Wind and Rain', Hardy presents a vision of death mocking human contentment. Compare his treatment of the theme in the two poems. You should refer to his language, imagery and symbolism, and the structure of the poems.

A specimen answer

Both poems deal with the vanity of human hopes in the face of death. Though death is not thought about by its victims in either poem, in 'The Convergence of the Twain' it comes suddenly, whereas in 'During Wind and Rain' it creeps up slowly.

'The Convergence of the Twain' begins at the end, with the 'human vanity' and 'Pride of Life' that the *Titanic* and its crew represents lost in the 'solitude of the sea'. As the poem progresses, this vanity is represented by a series of images of wealth: 'mirrors', 'jewels' and 'gilded gear'. The life and luxury they represent is captured by the short, intense lines in which they appear, such as:

> Jewels in joy designed
> To ravish the sensuous mind.

This sense of life is created also by the use of words expressing strong, positive emotions, further enhanced by alliteration, in phrases like 'jewels in joy' and 'gilded gear'. This is, however, undercut by the long, slow final line of each three-line verse, highlighting what has become of them. The jewels, for instance,

> Lie lightless, all their sparkles bleared and black and blind.

Here the language expresses negativity; the use of the hard 'bl' alliteration in this line enhances the sense of deadness rather than life.

In verse six we move from the present, at the bottom of the sea, to the past, as the ship is being built. Hardy now portrays the 'Will' that controls the universe creating a 'sinister mate' for the ship in the form of 'A Shape of Ice'. The contrast between the first two lines and the third is maintained in this section also, as in the verse:

> And as the smart ship grew
> In stature, grace and line,
> In shadowy silent distance grew the iceberg too.

The alliteration of 'smart ship ... stature' and 'grew ... grace' adds to the positive feeling of the words in the first two lines, whereas the 's' alliteration of 'shadowy silent distance' only adds to the ominous feeling of the slow growth of the fatal iceberg in the third line. The mood of grim humour in the poem reaches a climax in the last verse as 'the Spinner of the Years/Said "Now" ' and the great ship is sunk.

'During Wind and Rain' is a poem in four verses of seven lines each. The pattern of the verses is similar to that in 'The Convergence of the Twain'. The first five lines of each verse describe scenes in the life of a family. The lines are again short, creating an impression of vitality, and the sense of domestic harmony is captured in phrases like 'garden gay' and 'blithely breakfasting all', in which alliteration is again used to enhance the impression of life and vigour. This sense is again undercut in the last two lines of each verse. The sixth line of the first verse grimly signals the change:

Ah, no; the years O!

and the line is repeated, with slight variations, like a kind of chorus, in the other three verses. The last line of each verse is again longer and slower, adding to the growing sense of mortality, as the descriptions of the natural scene are used to symbolise human decay and death. The language of these lines is intensely negative and the mood is powerfully ominous, as in the last line of the first verse:

How the sick leaves reel down in throngs.

The personification and assonance of 'sick leaves reel' help to create a dramatic change of mood.

The symbolism reaches a climax of violent intensity in the last line of the third verse, with alliteration vividly enhancing the powerfully expressive language of decay and destruction:

And the rotten rose is ript from the wall.

Meanwhile family life goes on, oblivious to the messages of nature, as:

They change to a high new house,
He, she, all of them, aye,
Clocks and carpets and chairs,
On the lawn all day

The language is gentle, expressing peace and tranquillity, a feeling which is added to by alliteration of 'high new house' and 'clocks and carpets'. The final line of the poem spells out the implications of the final lines of the other verses, as:

Down their carved names the rain-drop ploughs.

Both poems, therefore, convey the same gloomy message through a series of contrasts, although the tone of each poem is different. In 'The Convergence of the Twain' the contrasts are conveyed in a mood of humorous detachment, while in 'During Wind and Rain' the contrasts are more dramatic and, to me, more moving.

Analysis of the answer

Several aspects of poetry analysis should have emerged from this answer; let us try to summarise them.

1 It is written in paragraphs, with a general introduction and conclusion. If you are asked to write an *essay* (see Unit 17) the introduction and conclusion are essential. Even if the form of writing is not specified, it may be a good idea to start with a brief introduction and end with a brief conclusion, as long as they don't take up more than a few minutes.

2 The poems are not summarised. Instead, an overall idea of the subject matter of each poem is given, and comments on details of the poem are linked with analysis of the form, language and literary devices.

3 Quotations are used to illustrate the points made. Many of the quotations are very brief (two or three words) and are just fitted into the sentence in which they appear, rather than being given a line to themselves. If it is necessary to quote at greater length – a complete line or more – it is best to set out the quotations in separate lines of poetry, preceded by a colon.

4 The comments on language are sometimes related to tone or mood. This is a good idea, if you are expected to write about the language of a poem.

5 When literary devices (personification, alliteration, assonance, etc.) are referred to (see Unit 6), the *effects* they produce are always mentioned. You should always try to do this.

6 The analysis of **structure** is related to the development of ideas, which is linked to the verse structure and the variations of line length and verse rhythm. This is what is meant by structure.

Further coursework suggestions on poetry

If you are taking one of the syllabuses which include poetry as a coursework rather than an examination requirement, and you still need to produce a coursework piece on poetry, here are some further suggestions.

Using the specimen answer in this chapter as a guide, write an analysis of two or three of the poems by one of the poets from the list below:

Pre-twentieth century poets

William Blake: 'London' (see Unit 9), 'A Poison Tree', 'The Schoolboy'

William Wordsworth: 'Composed Upon Westminster Bridge' (see Unit 9), 'There was a Boy', 'Nutting'

Twentieth-century poets

Thomas Hardy: 'Neutral Tones', 'The Darkling Thrush'

Grace Nicholls: 'Loveact' (Unit 8), 'Island Man' (Unit 9), 'Two Old Black Men on a Leicester Square Park Bench'

Carol Ann Duffy: 'Translating the English, 1989' (see Unit 9), 'Warming Her Pearls', 'Education For Leisure'

SYLLABUS REQUIREMENTS COVERED

Analysis of specified pre-released poems is an examination requirement for the London and NEAB syllabuses, and poetry analysis features as required coursework in the MEG, SEG and WJEC syllabuses.

The coursework suggestions relate to the syllabus coursework requirements as follows:

MEG: Unit 3.

SEG: Units 4 and 5.

WJEC: Pre-1990.

unit

25

ANALYSING SHORT FICTION

---

nalysing short prose fiction features as an examination or coursework requirement in all the syllabuses. For SEG, stories from 'diverse cultures and traditions' have to be analysed in the examination. MEG includes an analytical response to a pre-released text, also from 'diverse cultures and traditions', as an examination exercise, while NEAB Post-16 includes an examination piece on pre-released pre-1900 stories. Pre-1900 and 'diverse cultures and traditions' prose texts have to be analysed as coursework pieces in the London syllabuses, and NEAB IIII requires a comparison of prose texts. Analysis of prose texts, possibly in the form of comparison, features on the WJEC coursework list.

Two short stories have been chosen for this unit, both from 'diverse cultures and traditions'. A discussion of the stories is suggested, followed by a specimen analysis, and further suggestions for coursework on short prose fiction works are made at the end of the unit.

The first story is by the Mexican writer Octavio Paz. He was born in 1914 in Mexico City. He is a poet, philosopher and short story writer, and won the Nobel Prize for Literature in 1990.

'The Blue Bouquet' is from a collection of stories called *Eagle or Sun*, published in 1951.

The Blue Bouquet

I woke covered with sweat. Hot steam rose from the newly sprayed, red-brick pavement. A gray-winged butterfly, dazzled, circled the yellow light. I jumped from my hammock and crossed the room barefoot, careful not to step on some scorpion leaving his hideout for a bit of fresh air. I went to the little window and inhaled the country air. One could hear the breathing of the night, feminine, enormous. I returned to the center of the room, emptied water from a jar into a pewter basin, and wet my towel. I rubbed my chest and legs with the soaked cloth, dried myself a little, and, making sure that no bugs were hidden in the folds of my clothes, got dressed. I ran down the green stairway. At the door of the boardinghouse I bumped into the owner, a one-eyed taciturn fellow. Sitting on a wicker stool, he smoked, his eye half closed. In a hoarse voice, he asked:

'Where are you going?'

'To take a walk. It's too hot.'

'Hmmm – everything's closed. And no streetlights around here. You'd better stay put.'

I shrugged my shoulders, muttered 'back soon,' and plunged into the darkness. At first I couldn't see anything. I fumbled along the cobblestone street. I lit a cigarette. Suddenly the moon appeared from behind a black cloud, lighting a white wall that was crumbled in places. I stopped, blinded by such whiteness. Wind whistled slightly. I breathed the air of the tamarinds. The night hummed, full of leaves and insects. Crickets bivouacked in the tall grass. I raised my head: up there the stars too had set up camp. I thought that the universe was a vast system of signs, a conversation between giant beings. My actions, the cricket's saw, the star's blink, were nothing but pauses and syllables, scattered phrases from that dialogue. What word could it be, of which I was only a syllable? Who speaks the word? To whom is it spoken? I threw my cigarette down on the sidewalk. Falling, it drew a shining curve, shooting out brief sparks like a tiny comet.

I walked a long time, slowly. I felt free, secure between the lips that were at that moment speaking to me with such happiness. The night was a garden of eyes. As I crossed the street, I heard someone come out of a doorway. I turned around, but could not distinguish anything. I hurried on. A few moments later I heard the dull shuffle of sandals on the hot stone. I didn't want to turn around, although I felt the shadow getting closer with ever step. I tried to run. I couldn't. Suddenly I stopped short. Before I could defend myself, I felt the point of a knife in my back, and a sweet voice:

'Don't move, mister, or I'll stick it in.'

Without turning, I asked:

'What do you want?'

'Your eyes, mister,' answered the soft, almost painful voice.

'My eyes? What do you want with my eyes? Look, I've got some money. Not much, but it's something. I'll give you everything I have if you let me go. Don't kill me.'

'Don't be afraid, mister. I won't kill you. I'm only going to take your eyes.'

'But why do you want my eyes?' I asked again.

'My girlfriend has this whim. She wants a bouquet of blue eyes. And around here they're hard to find.'

'My eyes won't help you. They're brown, not blue.'

'Don't try to fool me, mister. I know very well that yours are blue.'

'Don't take the eyes of a fellow-man. I'll give you something else.'

'Don't play saint with me,' he said harshly. 'Turn around.'

I turned. He was small and fragile. His palm sombrero covered half his face. In his right hand he held a country machete that shone in the moonlight.

'Let me see your face.' I struck a match and put it close to my face. The brightness made me squint. He opened my eyelids with a firm hand. He couldn't see very well. Standing on tiptoe, he stared at me intensely. The flame burned my finger. I dropped it. A silent moment passed.

'Are you convinced now? They're not blue.'

'Pretty clever, aren't you?' he answered. 'Let's see. Light another one.'

I struck another match, and put it near my eyes. Grabbing my sleeve, he ordered:

'Kneel down.' I knelt. With one hand he grabbed me by the hair, pulling my head back. He bent over me, curious and tense, while his machete slowly dropped until it grazed my eyelids. I closed my eyes.

'Keep them open,' he ordered. I opened my eyes. The flame burned my lashes. All of a sudden he let me go.

'All right, they're not blue. Beat it.'

He vanished. I leaned against the wall, my head in my hands. I pulled myself together. Stumbling, falling, trying to get up again. I ran for an hour through the deserted town. When I got to the plaza, I saw the owner of the boardinghouse, still sitting in the front of the door. I went in without saying a word. The next day I left town.

Octavio Paz, 'The Blue Bouquet'

Discussion suggestions

- Do you find this story effective?
- What atmosphere does Paz create in the first part of the story? Pick out quotations to illustrate the atmosphere, and discuss how his uses of language create this atmosphere.
- How would you describe the narrator's mood in the first half of the story? Find quotations to illustrate his mood.
- How would you describe the atmosphere of the second half of the story? Find quotations to illustrate how this atmosphere is created.

- How would you describe the narrator's mood at the end of the story?
- Pick out the two moments in the story which you consider to have the greatest impact, and say why you have chosen them.

The second story is by the black American writer, Alice Walker. She was born in Georgia, in the 'deep South' of the USA, in 1944. She is a novelist, poet, essay writer and critic as well as a writer of short stories, and is probably best known for her novel *The Color Purple*.

The Flowers

It seemed to Myop as she skipped lightly from hen house to pigpen to smokehouse that the days had never been as beautiful as these. The air held a keenness that made her nose twitch. The harvesting of the corn and cotton, peanuts and squash, made each day a golden surprise that caused excited little tremors to run up her jaws.

Myop carried a short, knobby stick. She struck out at random at chickens she liked, and worked out the beat of a song on the fence around the pigpen. She felt light and good in the warm sun. She was ten, and nothing existed for her but her song, the stick clutched in her dark brown hand, and the tat-de-ta-ta-ta of accompaniment.

Turning her back on the rusty boards of her family's sharecropper cabin, Myop walked along the fence till it ran into the stream made by the spring. Around the spring, where the family got drinking water, silver ferns and wild-flowers grew. Along the shallow banks pigs rooted. Myop watched the tiny white bubbles disrupt the thin black scale of soil and the water that silently rose and slid away down the stream.

She had explored the woods behind the house many times. Often, in late autumn, her mother took her to gather nuts among the fallen leaves. Today she made her own path, bouncing this way and that way, vaguely keeping an eye out for snakes. She found, in addition to various common but pretty ferns and leaves, an armful of strange blue flowers with velvety ridges and a sweetsuds bush full of the brown, fragrant buds.

By twelve o'clock, her arms were laden with sprigs of her findings, she was a mile or more from home. She had often been as far before, but the strangeness of the land made it not as pleasant as her usual haunts. It seemed gloomy in the little cove in which she found herself. The air was damp, the silence close and deep.

Myop began to circle back to the house, back to the peacefulness of the morning. It was then she stepped smack into his eyes. Her heel became lodged in the broken ridge between brow and nose, and she reached down quickly, unafraid, to free herself. It was only when she saw his naked grin that she gave a little yelp of surprise.

He had been a tall man. From feet to neck covered a long space. His head lay beside him. When she pushed back the leaves and layers of earth and debris Myop saw that he'd had large white teeth, all of them cracked or broken, long fingers, and very big bones. All his clothes had rotted away except some threads of blue denim from his overalls. The buckles of the overalls had turned green.

Myop gazed around the soft spot with interest. Very near where she'd stepped into the head was a wild pink rose. As she picked it to add to her bundle she noticed a raised mound, a ring, around the rose's root. It was the rotted remains of a noose, a bit of shredding plowline, now blending benignly into the soil. Around an overhanging limb of a great spreading oak clung another piece. Frayed, rotted, bleached, and frazzled – barely there – but spinning restlessly in the breeze. Myop laid down her flowers.

And the summer was over.

Alice Walker, 'The Flowers'

Discussion suggestions

- Do you find this story effective?
- What impressions of the natural setting are created in the first half of the story? Find quotations to illustrate how Walker brings the natural scene to life by her uses of language.
- How is Myop's mood conveyed in the first half of the story?
- What makes the second half of the story horrific? How is the sense of horror created by the uses of language?
- How would you describe Myop's mood at the end of the story?
- Pick out the two moments in the story which you consider to have the greatest impact, and say why you have chosen them.

A specimen analysis

- Read 'The Blue Bouquet' by Octavio Paz and 'Flowers' by Alice Walker. In both of these stories a character sets off on a walk in high spirits, and ends up having a macabre encounter.
  Write about the stories, showing how each writer conveys the setting, atmosphere and mood in the first part of the story, and the sense of horror in the second part. Say which story you find more effective and why.

In 'The Blue Bouquet' the narrator of the story goes for a walk at night. He is in a country town, and he is intoxicated by his closeness to nature, and is in a jubilant mood before his terrifying encounter. This is captured throughout the first half of the story. When he gets up from his hammock, he 'inhaled the country air', as if it gave him new vitality. He feels attuned to the forces of nature, as is shown by the way he personifies the night: 'One could hear the breathing of the night, feminine, enormous'. When he leaves his boardinghouse his feeling of excitement is conveyed in the choice of verb: '*plunged* into the darkness'. Now everything seems intensely alive. A sense impression of the wind is conveyed in a short, punchy sentence, in which alliteration and onomatopoeia are used to add to the feeling of vitality: 'Wind whistled softly'. Further short, intense sentences follow: 'The night hummed, full of leaves and insects. Crickets bivouacked in the tall grass.' The sound of the night is captured in the onomatopoeic word 'hummed', and the use of personification in the word 'bivouacked' again captures the man's feeling of closeness with nature, and delight in it. In another intense short sentence, he uses a metaphor to express his delighted appreciation of nature: 'The night was a garden of eyes'.

Then he hears his assailant closing in on him, and the mood changes suddenly and dramatically. He hears a 'dull shuffle of sandals on the hot stone'. In this sentence, assonance of the long 'u' sound in 'dull shuffle', and the sinister 's' alliteration add to the sense of threat. Short sentences are used now to convey a feeling of panic and terror: 'I tried to run. I couldn't.' When he asks the man: 'What do you want?', the answer, 'Your eyes, mister', is so unexpected and grotesque that it comes as a dramatic shock to the reader. Now the natural setting brings only threat: 'In his right hand he held a country machete that shone in the moonlight'. The man's explanation, that his girlfriend 'wants a bouquet of blue eyes', is absolutely chilling. For a horrifying moment it seems the man is going to remove the narrator's eyes with his machete. This is captured by the words describing the violence of the man's actions: 'he grabbed me by the hair, pulling my head back', and by what he does next: 'his machete slowly dropped until it grazed my eyelids'. The narrator's terror after the man has spared him is captured indirectly by the description of his subsequent actions: 'I ran for an hour through the deserted town', and, in the final sentence: 'The next day I left town'.

In 'The Flowers', the ten-year-old girl's mood is again one of delight in the natural setting of the land round her family's 'sharecropper cabin'. Myop's jubilant mood is captured immediately by physical descriptions. She 'skipped lightly', and she 'worked out the beat of a song on the fence around the pigpen'. Short sentences are again used to capture a sense of the girl's delight in nature: 'Along the shallow banks pigs rooted'. Assonance, in 'shallow banks', and onomatopoeia, in 'rooted', combine to bring the setting to life for the reader. Sense impressions are again captured with great vividness, as in the gentle, almost graceful movement of the 'water that silently rose and slid away down the stream', an effect which is captured partly by the 's' alliteration.

The horror is totally unexpected in this story, and hits the reader like a slap in the face: 'It was then that she stepped smack into his eyes'. Myop's heel gets 'lodged in the broken ridge between brow and nose', which is gruesome in the extreme. A detailed physical description of the corpse is given, every detail, like the 'naked grin' of the decomposing face, and the 'large white teeth, all of them cracked or broken', adding to the sense of horror. The girl's reaction is the opposite of what we might expect. She 'gazed around the spot with interest', and she continues adding to the bouquet of flowers; this adds to the macabre feeling.

A further shock is in store for Myop and the reader, as she notices 'the rotted remains of a noose' near the body, which is 'blending benignly into the soil'. The alliterated phrase 'blending benignly' only adds to the horror of the realisation that the dead man has been lynched, an action which is the extreme opposite of 'benign'. The final two short sentences subtly convey the effect which this discovery has had on the girl, through a symbolic action and statement, the latter being given a paragraph to itself, emphasising the sense of finality that it conveys: 'Myop laid down her flowers. And the summer was over'.

I enjoyed both stories in different ways. On the whole, though, I preferred 'The Flowers', because the double horror of the discovery of the corpse and the noose is so powerfully dramatic and unexpected, and because the profound effect of the second discovery on the girl at the end is conveyed with such subtle symbolism.

Analysis of the answer

Here is a summary of the main features of this analysis:

1 It is written in paragraphs, each dealing with a different part of the question.
2 There is no attempt to summarise the stories. Instead, textual illustrations of the creation of setting, atmosphere and mood and the sense of horror are selected.
3 Each of the textual illustrations is discussed, by:

introducing the textual illustration, by explaining how it relates to the question;

quoting the textual illustration;

discussing *how* the illustration captures the setting, mood, etc.

4 Quotations are short, and are not set out on separate lines.
5 Examples of imagery (metaphor, personification, symbolism, etc.) and figures of sound (onomatopoeia, alliteration, assonance) are referred to, and the effects they produce are explained.
6 Sentence-structure is discussed in terms of how it adds to the atmosphere, etc.
7 The *type* of language is discussed (violent words, gentle words, etc.) to show how atmosphere, horror, etc. are created.

Further coursework suggestion on short prose fiction

- Read *In Love and Trouble* by Alice Walker (a collection of short stories from which 'The Flowers' was taken). Choose two of the stories, and write an analysis of them, discussing how Walker creates atmosphere, setting, character and mood. Say which story you preferred, and why.

SYLLABUS REQUIREMENTS COVERED

Analysis of twentieth-century prose writing is a feature of all the syllabuses.

The coursework suggestion relates to the syllabus coursework requirement as follows:

London: Work reflecting diverse cultures and traditions.
